STUDIES IN
SEMITIC GRAMMATICALIZATION

HARVARD SEMITIC MUSEUM PUBLICATIONS
Lawrence E. Stager, General Editor
Michael D. Coogan, Director of Publications

HARVARD SEMITIC STUDIES
Jo Ann Hackett and John Huehnergard, editors

Syriac Manuscripts: A Catalogue	Moshe H. Goshen-Gottstein
Introduction to Classical Ethiopic	Thomas O. Lambdin
The Songs of the Sabbath Sacrifice	Carol Newsom
Non-Canonical Psalms from Qumran:	
A Pseudepigraphic Collection	Eileen M. Schuller
An Exodus Scroll from Qumran	Judith E. Sanderson
You Shall Have No Other Gods	Jeffrey H. Tigay
Ugaritic Vocabulary in Syllabic Transcription	John Huehnergard
The Scholarship of William Foxwell Albright	Gus Van Beek
Features of the Eschatology of IV Ezra	Michael E. Stone
Studies in Neo-Aramaic	Wolfhart Heinrichs, Editor
Lingering over Words: Studies in Ancient Near Eastern Literature in Honor of William L. Moran	
	Tzvi Abusch, John Huehnergard, Piotr Steinkeller, Editors
A Grammar of the Palestinian Targum Fragments from the Cairo Genizah	Steven E. Fassberg
The Origins and Development of the Waw-Consecutive: Northwest Semitic Evidence from Ugaritic to Qumran	Mark S. Smith
Amurru Akkadian: A Linguistic Study, Volume I	Shlomo Izre'el
Amurru Akkadian: A Linguistic Study, Volume II	Shlomo Izre'el
The Installation of Baal's High Priestess at Emar	Daniel E. Fleming
The Development of the Arabic Scripts	Beatrice Gruendler
The Archaeology of Israelite Samaria: Early Iron Age through the Ninth Century BCE	Ron Tappy
A Grammar of Akkadian	John Huehnergard
Key to A Grammar of Akkadian	John Huehnergard
Akkadian Loanwords in Biblical Hebrew	Paul V. Mankowski
Adam in Myth and History: Ancient Israelite Perspectives on the Primal Human	Dexter E. Callender Jr.
West Semitic Vocabulary in the Akkadian Texts from Emar	Eugen J. Pentiuc
The Archaeology of Israelite Samaria, vol. II: The Eighth Century BCE	Ron E. Tappy
Leaves from an Epigrapher's Notebook: Collected Papers in Hebrew and West Semitic Palaeography and Epigraphy	Frank Moore Cross
Semitic Noun Patterns	Joshua Fox
Eighth-Century Iraqi Grammar: A Critical Exploration of pre-Ḫalīlian Arabic Linguistics	Rafael Talmon
Amarna Studies: Collected Essays	William L. Moran
Narrative Structure and Discourse Constellations: An Analysis of Clause Function in Biblical Hebrew Prose	Roy L. Heller
The Modal System of Old Babylonian	Eran Cohen

STUDIES IN SEMITIC GRAMMATICALIZATION

by

Aaron D. Rubin

EISENBRAUNS
Winona Lake, Indiana
2005

STUDIES IN SEMITIC GRARMMATICALIZATION
by
Aaron D. Rubin

Copyright © 2005
The President and Fellows of Harvard College

Printed in the United States of America

Library of Congress Cataloging-in-Publication Data

Rubin, Aaron D., 1976–
  Studies in Semitic grammaticalization / by Aaron D. Rubin.
    p. cm. — (Harvard Semitic Museum publications) (Harvard Semitic studies ; no. 57)
  Includes bibliographical references and index.
  ISBN 1-57506-923-7 (hardback : alk. paper)
    1. Semitic languages—Grammaticalization. I. Title. II. Series. III. Series: Harvard Semitic studies ; no. 57
  PJ3021.R83 2005
  492'.045—dc22
                                      2005014197

The paper used in this publication meets the minimum requirements of the American National Standard for Information Sciences—Permanence of Paper for Printed Library Materials, ANSI Z39.48-1984.♾™

For my parents

Andrew and Louise Rubin

with love and thanks

Contents

Acknowledgments xi
Abbreviations and Symbols xiii
Transliteration xvii
Text Citation xvii

1 Introduction 1
   1.1 Grammaticalization 1
   1.2 When to Invoke Grammaticalization 6
   1.3 Previous Scholarship on Grammaticalization in Semitic 7
   1.4 Overview of the Present Work 8

2 Classification of Semitic 11
   2.1 Akkadian 12
   2.2 Modern South Arabian 12
   2.3 Ethiopic 13
   2.4 Arabic 13
   2.5 Old South Arabian 14
   2.6 Aramaic 14
   2.7 Hebrew 16
   2.8 Phoenician 16

3 Grammaticalization in Semitic 17
   3.1 Nominal and Pronominal System 18
      3.1.1 Indefinite Articles 18
      3.1.2 Definite Articles 19
      3.1.3 Reflexive Pronouns 19
      3.1.4 Reciprocal Pronouns 22
      3.1.5 Independent Personal Pronouns 23
      3.1.6 Interrogative Pronouns 24
      3.1.7 Gender Markers 25
   3.2 Verbal System 26
      3.2.1 Proto-Afro-Asiatic Tenses 26
      3.2.2 Derived Stems 28
      3.2.3 Auxiliary Verbs and New Tenses 29
         3.2.3.1 'Be' > Auxiliary 29
         3.2.3.2 'Have' > Auxiliary 30
      3.2.4 Verbal Noun or Adjective > New Tense 31
      3.2.5 Past Tense Markers 33

		3.2.6 Present Tense Markers 34
		3.2.7 Future Tense Markers 34
		3.2.7.1 'Go' > Future 35
		3.2.7.2 'Want' > Future 36
		3.2.7.3 Nominal/Adjectival Sources 38
		3.2.7.4 Purpose Clause > Future 39
		3.2.8 Copulae 41
		3.2.8.1 Copulae from Independent Pronouns 41
		3.2.8.2 Copulae from Presentative Particles 42
		3.2.8.3 Copulae from Existential Particles 44
	3.3 Prepositions 46
		3.3.1 PAA, PS 46
		3.3.2 Individual Languages 47
	3.4 Particles 48
		3.4.1 Relatives 48
		3.4.1.1 Demonstrative > Relative 48
		3.4.1.2 Locative > Locative Relative > General Relative 49
		3.4.2 Negative Markers 50
		3.4.3 Genitive Exponents 51
		3.4.3.1 Relative > Genitive Exponent 52
		3.4.3.2 Noun > Genitive Exponent 53
		3.4.3.3 Genitive Exponents as Possessive Pronouns 55
		3.4.3.4 Genitive Exponents > Partitives 57
		3.4.4 Possession 57
		3.4.4.1 Locative > 'Have' 57
		3.4.4.2 Comitative > 'Have' 58
		3.4.4.3 Dative > 'Have' 59
		3.4.4.4 Existence > 'Have' 60
		3.4.5 Existential Particles 61
		3.4.5.1 'Have' > Existential 61
		3.4.5.2 Locative > Existential 61
		3.4.5.3 Copula > Existential 62
	3.5 Conclusions 63

4 Definite Articles 65
   4.1 Introduction 65
       4.1.1 Canaanite 65
       4.1.2 Classical Arabic 66
       4.1.3 Ancient Aramaic 68
       4.1.4 Old South Arabian 68
       4.1.5 Summary 69
   4.2 Origin of Articles in Other Languages 69

Contents

- 4.2.1 Romance 69
- 4.2.2 Slavic 69
- 4.2.3 Germanic 70
- 4.2.4 Conclusions 71
- 4.3 On the Origin of the CS Articles 72
  - 4.3.1 Canaanite and Ancient North Arabian 76
  - 4.3.2 Classical Arabic 77
  - 4.3.3 Aramaic 79
  - 4.3.4 Old South Arabian 80
- 4.4 On the Syntax of the CS Articles 81
  - 4.4.1 The Article and Inherently Definite Nouns 82
  - 4.4.2 The Form of the Noun When Definite 83
  - 4.4.3 The Article on Attributive Adjectives 83
- 4.5 On Grammaticalization 84
- 4.6 Appendix: Articles in Modern Semitic Languages 86
  - 4.6.1 Neo-Aramaic (NENA, Turoyo, NWA) 86
  - 4.6.2 Ethiopic (Tigrinya, Tigré, Amharic) 88
  - 4.6.3 Modern South Arabian 89

5 Direct Object Markers 91
- 5.1 Introduction 91
  - 5.1.1 Canaanite 92
  - 5.1.2 Aramaic 94
  - 5.1.3 Akkadian 105
  - 5.1.4 Arabic 105
  - 5.1.5 Geʻez 107
  - 5.1.6 Tigrinya, Tigré 108
  - 5.1.7 Summary 109
- 5.2 On Prepositional Direct Object Marking in Other Languages 110
  - 5.2.1 Romance 110
  - 5.2.2 Hindi 111
  - 5.2.3 Conclusions 112
- 5.3 On Grammaticalization, DATIVE > ACCUSATIVE 112
- 5.4 On the Origin of Hebrew ʼet / Aramaic ʼyt / yāt 115
  - 5.4.1 Some Older Etymological Proposals 117
  - 5.4.2 Some Recent Etymological Proposals 119
  - 5.4.3 Conclusions on ʼet / yāt 120
- 5.5. On Re-grammaticalization of the *Nota Accusativi* ʼet / yāt 121
  - 5.5.1 Syriac yāt as a Reflexive 121
  - 5.5.2 Accusative > Demonstrative 122
  - 5.5.3 "The Same" 125
- 5.6 Appendix: Other Semitic Direct Object Markers 126

	5.6.1	The Amharic Direct Object Marker	126
	5.6.2	Modern South Arabian Object Pronouns	126

6 Present Tense Markers 129
  6.1 Introduction 129
  6.2 Aramaic *qā*, *k(V)*- 130
      6.2.1 Spanish, Italian, Portuguese (Brazilian), and Swedish 133
      6.2.2 Conclusions 134
  6.3 Arabic *da*-, *qa(d)*-, *gāʿid* 136
      6.3.1 Other Languages 138
      6.3.2 Conclusions 138
  6.4 Arabic *k*- 139
      6.4.1 North African 139
      6.4.2 Anatolian 141
      6.4.3 Conclusions 141
  6.5 Aramaic *b*- 142
      6.5.1 Dutch, German, and English 143
      6.5.2 Portuguese (Continental) and Italian 144
      6.5.3 Conclusions 144
  6.6 Arabic *b*- 145
      6.6.1 Yemeni Arabic *bi*- and its Origin 146
      6.6.2 A Proto-Central-Semitic Parallel to Yemeni? 146
      6.6.3 On the Origin of the Syro-Palestinian and Egyptian *b*- 148
  6.7 Chapter Conclusions 151

7 Summary 153

Bibliography 155
Language Index 175

Acknowledgements

First and foremost, I would like to thank my friend and former advisor, Professor John Huehnergard, whose work was the inspiration for my own, and whose guidance and support has been invaluable. I thank him not only for this, but also for the amount of time he spent reading my drafts, for the many discussions we have had over the years, and for his invitation to participate in the Harvard Semitic Studies series.

This book evolved out of my Harvard University dissertation, for which I owe thanks to many people. Professors Wolfhart Heinrichs and Jay Jasanoff were of great assistance; their feedback and consummate reliability was much appreciated. Professor Irit Aharony provided great moral support and inspiration throughout the writing of my dissertation and beyond. Professors Wheeler Thackston, P. Oktor Skjærvø, Jo Ann Hackett, and Anna Grinfeld were also most helpful on many issues. My colleague and friend Professor Rebecca Hasselbach has also been a great help, coming to my aid many times, helping me to interpret difficult German passages, and discussing various issues with me.

I am also indebted to many scholars from around the world, who were able to share their insights with me via e-mail communications, namely, Professors David Appleyard, Albert Borg, Gideon Goldenberg, Bernd Heine, Otto Jastrow, Geoffrey Khan, Michael Macdonald, Josef Tropper, and Janet Watson.

During the publication process, Michael Coogan gave most generously of his time, and I am extremely grateful to have had him as an editor. This book has been substantially improved thanks to his careful reading and indispensable feedback.

I thank also my dear friend Kimberly De Wall, who served an outstanding editor for the early drafts of the work, and who provided much needed moral support and encouragement during all stages of the writing process.

Financial support for the publication of this book was made available by Ray Lombra of the Penn State Liberal Arts Research Office; additional funds were generously provided by the Penn State Department of Classics and Ancient Mediterranean Studies (Chair: Gary Knoppers) and by the Jewish Studies Program (Director: Brian Hesse). I am very grateful for this support.

Finally, I cannot thank enough my parents Andrew and Louise Rubin, my sister Jill Rubin, and my grandparents Sidney and Evelyn Chairman for their steadfast support and love.

Abbreviations and Symbols

1	first person
2	second person
3	third person
1 Cor.	1 Corinthians
1 Sam.	1 Samuel
1 Thess.	1 Thessalonians
2 Cor.	2 Corinthians
2 Pet.	2 Peter
AA	Afro-Asiatic
acc.	accusative
Akk.	Akkadian
Aram.	Aramaic
Ass.	Assyrian
BDB	Brown, Driver, and Briggs (1906)
Bib. Aram.	Biblical Aramaic
BTA	Babylonian Talmudic Aramaic
c.pl.	common plural
CA	Classical Arabic
CAD	Chicago Assyrian Dictionary
com.	common (gender)
CPA	Christian Palestinian Aramaic
cs	common singular
CS	Central Semitic
Dan.	Daniel
Deut.	Deuteronomy
D.O.	Direct Object
Eccles.	Ecclesiastes
Eg.	Egyptian
Eph.	Ephesians
Eth.	Ethiopic
Exod.	Exodus
Ezek.	Ezekiel
f., fem.	feminine
fp, f.pl.	feminine plural
fs, f.sg.	feminine singular
Gal.	Galatians
Gen.	Genesis

Gesenius	Kautzsch (1910)
Heb.	Hebrew
IE	Indo-European
I.O.	Indirect Object
Judg.	Judges
JPA	Jewish Palestinian Aramaic
KAI #	text number in Donner and Röllig (2002)
KTU #	text number in Dietrich, Loretz, and Sanmartín (1995)
LBH	Late Biblical Hebrew
Lihy.	Liḥyanite
lit.	literally
m., masc.	masculine
mp, m.pl.	masculine plural
ms, m.sg.	masculine singular
Matt.	Matthew
MH	Mishnaic Hebrew
MSA	Modern South Arabian
MT	Masoretic Text (of the Hebrew Bible)
NENA	North-Eastern Neo-Aramaic
neut.	neuter
nom.	nominative
Num.	Numbers
NWA	Neo-West Aramaic
obj.	object
OB	Old Babylonian
OCS	Old Church Slavic/Slavonic
OHG	Old High German
OIc	Old Icelandic
Old Akk.	Old Akkadian
Old Ass.	Old Assyrian
OSA	Old South Arabian
PAA	Proto-Afro-Asiatic
Pal. Targ.	Palestinian Fragment Targum
PCS	Proto-Central Semitic
Phoen.	Phoenician
PIE	Proto-Indo-European
pl.	plural
PN	Personal Name
PWS	Proto-West Semitic
Phoen.	Phoenician
Prov.	Proverbs
PS	Proto-Semitic

rel. pron.	relative pronoun
Rom.	Romans
Sem.	Semitic
Targ. Nf.	Targum Neofiti
Targ. Onq.	Targum Onqelos
Tham.	Thamudic
WS	West Semitic
X > Y	X develops into Y.
X < Y	X derives from Y.
X → Y	X is replaced by Y; this symbol is also used to indicate semantic, as opposed to phonological, development.
*	An asterisk marks a reconstructed form.
**	A double asterisk indicates a non-existent form.
/x/	Forms within slashes indicate a phonemic transcription; here, this is usually done for languages which are attested only in a consonantal script.
<x>	Forms in angled brackets indicate actual consonantal spelling of a word.

Transliteration

In most cases, the standard transliteration systems are employed for each of the Semitic languages. Ge'ez vowels are written *a, u, i, ā, e, ə, o* as in Leslau (1987), while for modern Ethiopic the *a*-vowels are transcribed with *ä* and *a*. Biblical Hebrew is as in Lambdin (1971b). When transcribing Hebrew and older Aramaic dialects, I have not marked spirantization of the *bgdkpt* letters, unless there is some specific reason to highlight the lenition. For Modern Arabic and Aramaic dialects there is no standard, and in fact almost every author has produced his or her own system. On the whole, when transcribing Modern Arabic and Aramaic languages, I have followed the transcription as I found it in the reference. In cases where I had more than one reference book for a single dialect, I occasionally harmonized the transcription of a word. The one consistent harmonizing change is my use of macrons to denote a long vowel, i.e., *ā*, as opposed to *â, aa,* or *a:*. For Maltese, I use the standard spelling system, rather than transcription.

Text Citation

I do not normally indicate texts from which examples are taken (though I do indicate the grammar or dictionary where an example was found); the exceptions are Biblical and Quranic passages, and inscriptional passages which highlight a particularly noteworthy, rare, or unique form.

Chapter 1

Introduction

This book will investigate the process of grammaticalization within the Semitic language family, with two goals in mind. First, it is my intention to help bridge the gap between linguistics and Comparative Semitics, by looking at a range of historical developments within Semitic, old and new, from the perspective of a particular linguistic process. Second, I hope to use this perspective to help shed light on some well-known developments that have hitherto not been satisfactorily explained.

Is this study meant for Semitists or for linguists? It is meant for Semitists, in that I examine some long-standing problems in Semitic from a new perspective, as well as offer a multitude of examples of grammaticalization in order to present these data to Semitists in a new way. At the same time, however, while there is nothing groundbreaking in the way of linguistic theory, linguists interested in grammaticalization will find an abundance of examples that may be worthy of their attention. The field of linguistics is too often foreign to the modern Semitist, and it is hoped that this study will help to rectify that situation in some small way. At the same time, comparative Semitic work, while abundant, is not often accessible to the linguist, or more often does not attract their attention in the first place. Again, it is hoped that this study will be of help, by making more data available for their use. Too often in Semitics, we talk about developments, but neglect to explain what has happened linguistically. To put it rather simply: we discuss the 'what' but not the 'how' or 'why'.

1.1 Grammaticalization

Grammaticalization has been defined in many ways. One of the most widely accepted definitions is that of Kuryłowicz:

> Grammaticalization consists of the increase of the range of a morpheme advancing from a lexical to a grammatical or from a less

grammatical to a more grammatical status, e.g., from a derivative formant to an inflectional one.[1]

Somewhat more transparent is the more recent definition of Hopper and Traugott:

> Grammaticalization [is] the process whereby lexical items and constructions come in certain linguistic contexts to serve grammatical functions, and, once grammaticalized, continue to develop new grammatical functions.[2]

Hopper and Traugott have recently revised this definition, now referring to grammaticalization as a *change*, rather than a *process*, as 'process' implies that grammaticalization is a force with an impetus of its own.[3] My own definition is very similar to their latest, with one important addition:

> Grammaticalization is the change whereby lexical items and constructions come in certain linguistic contexts to *lose their lexical meaning* and serve grammatical functions, or, the change whereby a grammatical item develops a new grammatical function.

The loss of lexical meaning, also called *semantic bleaching* or *desemanticization*, is a defining trait of grammaticalization. For example, the English suffixes '–hood' and '–ly' can be traced back to the Old English nouns *hād* 'condition, state' and *līc* 'appearance, body', respectively. These nouns have long ago lost their original meaning and are now simply derivational suffixes; the Modern English speaker has no notion of the origin of these suffixes. The French negative marker *pas* once had the meaning 'step' (as it still does outside of negative constructions), as in *je ne vais pas* 'I am not going (a) step'. In such negated phrases, *pas* eventually lost its inherent meaning, began to function simply as a negative particle, and was extended to all negative constructions, as in *je ne sais pas*. In spoken French, where one hears *j'sais pas*, *pas* has undergone further grammaticalization, as it has in fact become the sole marker of negation. An example of a grammatical item developing a new grammatical function is the use of French perfect (*passé composé*) as a preterite tense. The *passé composé*—itself a product of grammaticalization, as the lexical verb *avoir* 'to have' has developed into a perfect tense marker—has almost totally replaced the inherited preterite tense (*passé simple*). That is to say, a grammatical item (the perfect

---

[1] Kuryłowicz ([1965] 1975: 52), cited in Heine, Claudi, and Hünnemeyer (1991: 3).
[2] Hopper and Traugott (1993: xv).
[3] Hopper and Traugott (2003: xv). Though I fully agree with Hopper and Traugott, I may still refer to grammaticalization as a process on occasion. I do so with none of the implications Hopper and Traugott warn of.

tense) has developed a new grammatical function (a preterite). Examples of the phenomenon of grammaticalization abound in every language of the world.[4]

The change of grammaticalization goes hand in hand with another important process: *analogy*. Often these two work together in a cyclical process. In the example of French *pas*, given above, there is a cycle of grammaticalization and analogy which can be divided into stages:[5]

Stage 1: a negated verb of motion can be optionally extended by *pas*.
Je ne vais (pas) 'I don't go (a step)'

Stage 2: *pas* underwent semantic bleaching and was reanalyzed as having a grammatical function (grammaticalization).
Je ne vais pas 'I don't go'

Stage 3: *pas* was extended to non-motion verbs (analogy).
Je ne sais pas 'I don't know'

Stage 4: *pas* was reanalyzed as being the primary marker of negation (grammaticalization).
J'sais pas 'I don't know' (Cf. also: *pas encore* 'not yet')

There are some further basic characteristics of grammaticalization which must be addressed:

(1) Grammaticalization proceeds along a 'cline of grammaticality'.

The term 'cline' is used metaphorically to represent the notion that grammaticalization is often not a single change, but rather a series of changes which progress along a universally defined course. One representation of this course (after Hopper and Traugott 2003: 7) is:

CONTENT ITEM > GRAMMATICAL WORD > CLITIC > INFLECTIONAL AFFIX

Only this first change, CONTENT ITEM > GRAMMATICAL WORD, need take place for a form to be called grammaticalized. Like any change in language, there is no one moment when grammaticalization takes place. Rather, the change is gradual. There was no one moment where French *pas* was reinterpreted as a grammatical marker of negativity, but rather there must have been a long period of reanalysis. The example of French *pas*, while convenient, only exemplifies the change CONTENT ITEM > GRAMMATICAL WORD. Let us examine another

---

[4] See Hopper and Traugott (2003), Heine and Kuteva (2002).
[5] French *pas* is one of the most oft-cited examples of grammaticalization. An excellent presentation with discussion can be found in McMahon (1994: 161-64).

grammaticalized form which shows a more advanced development along this cline.

The French future tense paradigm is another oft-cited example of grammaticalization, and one which exemplifies the complete cline as represented above. In Late Vulgar Latin, a periphrastic construction consisting of an infinitive + *habere* 'to have' came to indicate future tense. For example, Latin *cantare habeo*, originally something like 'I have to sing', came to mean simply 'I will sing'. In Modern French, the reflex of this is simply *chanterai*. In this case, the grammaticalization itself took place in Late Latin; the inflected forms of the verb *habere*, in this construction, lost their lexical meaning and acquired a grammatical function. But the change continued along the cline of grammaticality. The auxiliary verb became cliticized to (i.e., inseparable from) the infinitival form, and eventually affixed. The modern future tense inflectional affixes, in the first and second persons plural at least, are not identifiable as forms of the verb *avoir* (for example, *nous chanterons* 'we sing', *nous avons* 'we have'). The fact that the 1pl. and 2pl. future tense markers are not immediately identifiable with their source leads us to the second important characteristic of grammaticalization:

(2) Grammaticalization is often accompanied by irregular phonological reduction (*erosion*).

Linguists operate under the assumption that sound change is regular, yet very often we find that grammaticalized forms violate this maxim. It is not the grammaticalization itself which underlies this tendency, but rather the resulting cliticization of the grammaticalized form.[6] An additional factor is probably the semantic bleaching that accompanies grammaticalization. That is to say, once the lexical meaning of a word has been lost, the pressure to preserve its integrity must be weakened. Interestingly, if the source of a grammaticalized item remains present, the source form and the grammaticalized form will often undergo distinct phonological developments. For example, the English phrase *going to* has two functions, its lexical one and its grammaticalized one, which marks future tense. Both of these functions are illustrated in the following sentences:

Lexical *go*: *I am going to the store.*
Grammaticalized *go*: *I am going to sit here all day.*

In the second example, this form of *go* has entirely lost its lexical use as a verb of motion. Instead, it merely conveys an imminent future action. Now examine this pair of sentences:

---

[6]Hopper and Traugott (2003: 154-59).

Lexical *go*: ***I'm gonna the store.*
Grammaticalized *go*: *I'm gonna sit here all day.*

In the second sentence we find the form *gonna*, an historically irregular development of *going to* that is quite pervasive in colloquial English. Yet the first sentence sounds impossible to a native speaker. The reason is simple: such an irregular reduction only affected the grammaticalized form of *go*. We saw another example above with the English derivational suffix *–ly*. Old English *līc* has its expected modern reflex *like* in the tonic (non-cliticized) form, but we find the reduced *–ly* for the grammaticalized suffix. The English indefinite article *a(n)* derives from the numeral *one*. Yet only with the grammaticalized form do we find the loss of the final *n* before a following consonant. Many of these examples illustrate the third tendency of grammaticalization:

(3) Grammaticalized forms may coexist with their source lexemes.

Often concomitant with this, we find a fourth tendency of grammaticalization:

(4) Grammaticalized forms often exhibit loss of inflection (*decategorialization*).

That is to say, while a lexeme may be inflected for gender, number, case, tense, aspect, and the like, a grammaticalized form often neutralizes these distinctions. Often this is most noticeable when the source lexeme has survived. For example, the English definite article *the* derives from the demonstrative pronoun which has its modern reflex in *that*. Yet *that* still inflects for number (i.e., *that ~ those*), while the grammaticalized article *the* does not. In German, the demonstrative series *der*, *die*, *das* has been grammaticalized as a complementizer (*daß*). In its demonstrative and relative functions, this series inflects for number, gender, and case; yet in its function complementizer, it has but a single uninflected form.

In summary, we must keep in mind the following characteristics of grammaticalization:

(1) A grammaticalized form has been subject to loss of lexical content (*semantic bleaching*).
(2) Grammaticalization proceeds along a 'cline of grammaticality'.
(3) Grammaticalization is often accompanied by irregular phonological reduction (*erosion*).
(4) Grammaticalized forms may coexist with their source lexemes.
(5) Grammaticalized forms often exhibit loss of inflection (*decategorialization*).

These characteristics will be repeatedly demonstrated in chapters 3–6, in the examples of grammaticalization from the Semitic languages. It is important to keep in mind that while these traits are typical of grammaticalization, they do not *define* grammaticalization. Trait 1 is present when we are dealing with the stage CONTENT ITEM > GRAMMATICAL WORD, but not when an already grammatical item develops a new grammatical function. Trait 2 is a property of grammaticalization, but by no means do all grammaticalized forms have to proceed through the entire 'cline'. Finally, traits 3, 4, and 5 do not always accompany grammaticalization, but are merely common tendencies. Though obvious, it should also be pointed out that traits 1, 3, and 5 are linguistic processes that exist outside of the realm of grammaticalization.[7]

1.2 When to Invoke Grammaticalization

Those of us who subscribe to the Neogrammarian principles of historical linguistics take it for granted that sound change is overwhelmingly regular. Yet we have just seen that grammaticalization is often accompanied by irregular sound changes, or *erosion*. And though the irregularity of forms like 'gonna' and numerous others that have arisen via grammaticalization give one pause, we must not abandon the Neogrammarian approach to language change. We may simply say that there is something about the change of grammaticalization that allows a grammaticalized word to be excepted from the normal behavior of words. Perhaps the fact that the word has been disassociated from its original category (e.g., 'going to' is no longer identified as VERB + PREPOSITION) allows this exception. The question of why this tendency for irregular phonetic change exists is not the concern here. I bring this up only as the preface to a caveat for work on grammaticalization.

Since the pursuit of regularity is the goal of the historical linguist, one can suggest that invoking grammaticalization is sometimes an easy solution. That is to say, one might believe that the ability to label something as grammaticalized is an automatic license to claim irregularity. One must beware of this temptation, however, and recognize that grammaticalization is not a fallback category into which one can place any development that cannot be otherwise explained. We must exhaust every attempt to derive attested forms by regular sound change; only then can irregularity of sound change be comfortably excused.

As an example, we can look at the Hebrew relative pronoun *'ăšer*, that was recently the subject of an article by J. Huehnergard (forthcoming). There exists another relative pronoun in Hebrew, clitic *še-*, and there has been a debate for over a century as to whether these two relative pronouns are independent or

---

[7] See L. Campbell (2001) on the importance of this statement.

whether the latter is an irregular reduction of the former. We know that *'ăšer* is grammaticalized (see below, 3.4.1.2), and so we might simply claim erosion for *še-* and be satisfied. Yet many have seen an obvious connection between Hebrew *še-* and the Akkadian relative *ša*. Only after convincing arguments that the Hebrew and Akkadian forms cannot be cognate, based on the principles of regular sound correspondences, can we dismiss this (or any other) theory and accept that *še-* is a reduced form of *'ăšer*.

Much general work has been done on grammaticalization and general categories of grammaticalization (such as the development of verbal systems, pronominal systems, etc.), and so linguists have a very good idea as to the types of changes that fall into this category. When claiming grammaticalization has taken place in a specific language or language family, we can look to this cross-linguistic typological evidence for support. Of course, typology can never prove that a grammaticalization has taken place in, say, Semitic, but such evidence provides a suggested starting point. Cross-linguistic evidence of grammaticalization will be used in this treatment for the purpose of suggesting possible schemes of development.

1.3 Previous Scholarship on Grammaticalization in Semitic

Early allusions to the general process of grammaticalization can be found in the works of von Humboldt (1825) and Gabelentz (1891), but the term "grammaticalization" was coined by the linguist Antoine Meillet in a 1912 article entitled "L'évolution des formes grammaticales," also the first work specifically devoted to the topic.[8]

Meillet (p. 131; translation mine) claims: "These two processes, analogical innovation and the attribution of a grammatical character to a formerly autonomous word [i.e., grammaticalization], are the only ones by which new grammatical forms are fashioned." But he notes soon after that analogy can only apply to forms already in existence. Therefore, he says, "... the only process left [to create a new grammatical form] is the progressive attribution of a grammatical role to autonomous words or to ways of grouping words."

Grammaticalization is, therefore, an obviously important area of study. In the last two decades, there has been a surge of interest in the topic. One may point to such essential works as Heine, Claudi, and Hünnemeyer (1991), Lehmann (1995), Hopper and Traugott (2003), Heine and Kuteva (2003), and important collections of articles such as Traugott and Heine (1991). Yet in the field of Semitics, and for long time in other linguistic fields, this topic was largely

---

[8] On the history of the study of grammaticalization, see Heine, Claudi, and Hünnemeyer (1991: 5-11), or the more comprehensive discussions of Hopper and Traugott (2003: 19-38) and Campbell and Janda (2001).

ignored. In fact, the word 'grammaticalization' does not even appear in the index of one of the most recent and comprehensive handbooks of comparative Semitics (Lipiński 1997). Surprisingly few scholars have directly discussed grammaticalization within Semitic; of notable mention are Givón (1991) on the Hebrew complementizer, Rubba (1994) on Neo-Aramaic prepositions, Simeone-Senelle and Vanhove (1997) on Modern South Arabian and Maltese verbal auxiliaries, Contini (1997) on various aspects of Turoyo, Kouwenberg (1997) on gemination in the Akkadian verb, Voigt (1999) on prepositions, J. Cook (2001) on the Hebrew verb, and Huehnergard (forthcoming) on the Hebrew relative pronoun.[9] Even some of these works are lacking in the linguistic details on how the grammaticalization process works. Of course, actual examples of grammaticalization are present in every grammar of Semitic, whether or not such examples are explicitly labeled as grammaticalization. For example, Leslau (1995: 154) notes that in Amharic, the number 'one' can sometimes function as an indefinite article. This is a clear and extremely common example of grammaticalization, though Leslau does not make any reference to the process. One of the goals of the present work (in particular, chapter 3) is to bring together examples like this one under the heading of grammaticalization.

1.4 Overview of the Present Work

As already noted, cases which exemplify grammaticalization in Semitic are widely known, but are for the most part not adequately described in linguistic terms. I intend to show how a large number of phonological, morphological, and lexical developments in the history of the Semitic languages are the result of grammaticalization. By recognizing these changes as examples of grammaticalization, we can better explain how and why they took place. I will show that by recognizing the characteristic traits of grammaticalization—in particular the phonetic erosion which has a strong tendency to violate regular rules of sound change—we are able to shed light on some long-standing problems of Semitic historical grammar.

Following this introduction, Chapter 2 will briefly outline the classification of the Semitic languages. The specifics of classification will play a role when we discuss the changes that occur in various languages in later chapters. For example, in Chapter 4 (The Definite Article), it is essential that Old South Arabian is considered to be a part of the Central Semitic sub-family. It is particularly important not only to my argument, but also in light of the fact that most other comparative Semitic works classify OSA differently. The section on classification will also be of use to those who are less familiar with Semitic, or some

---

[9]This last item, Huehnergard (forthcoming), can be considered the inspiration for the present work.

branches of Semitic, as this work makes many references to more obscure languages and dialects that will be unknown to some readers.

In Chapter 3 we will examine a wide variety of examples of grammaticalization from every branch of Semitic, both ancient and modern. This chapter will hopefully be of particular interest to linguists for the data it provides. It should also provide Semitists with a good idea of the kinds of issues which may be addressed in the future from this perspective of grammaticalization.

After this data-intensive overview chapter, covering a wide range of changes, I will turn to the main body of this treatment, in which three specific types of grammaticalization will be examined in three respective chapters. In these three chapters, some well-known developments will be re-examined, with the hope that they can be satisfactorily explained. Chapter 4, perhaps the most controversial, will take up the problem of the origin of the definite article in the Central Semitic languages. This has been the focus of a great many previous works, yet there is still no agreed-upon solution. It is by no means assumed that this chapter will provide a solution which will satisfy all, but it is hoped that this chapter will provide new direction. Chapter 5 will look at direct object markers in several Semitic languages. In this case, we will be dealing less with a disputed origin, and focusing more on attempting to provide a reasonable explanation regarding the development of direct object markers. After this, we will look at how some of these direct object markers have undergone grammaticalization themselves, and acquired new grammatical functions. Chapter 6 will examine present tense markers, specifically cliticized prefixes, in modern Aramaic and modern Arabic dialects. Once again, we will attempt to provide satisfactory etymologies, as well as trace their development.

In Chapters 4–6, we will not only deal with Semitic, but also bring in data from a variety of other language families. By studying language change in other languages, we can achieve better perspective on language typology, and look for parallels to help explain changes in Semitic.

While the principal aim of the project is to examine Semitic historical grammar from a new perspective, it will also provide abundant examples for those interested in general studies in grammaticalization. As alluded to above, grammaticalization is a cyclical process. Several Semitic languages are among the longest continually attested languages available for study, and therefore provide a wealth of examples of this cyclicality.

Chapter 2

Classification of Semitic

As there is still no general consensus on the classification of the Semitic languages, it seems worthwhile to outline the classification scheme which will be adhered to in this treatment. The nature of the genetic relationship between the various languages is certainly relevant when discussing problems of a historical nature, as will be done in chapters three to six. I also present this outline of the languages below for the non-specialist who may not be familiar with the lesser known languages or dialects. This chapter is, therefore, mainly intended as a reference.

In the following chapters, some reference will be made to the parent family of Semitic, Afro-Asiatic (also known as Hamito-Semitic). The study of Afro-Asiatic is still in its infancy, despite the claims of many works on the subject. We can divide Afro-Asiatic into the following branches; none of the branches are demonstrably more closely related than the others:[1]

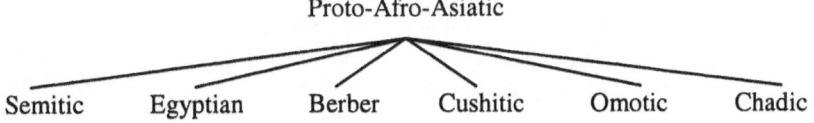

Proto-Afro-Asiatic

Semitic   Egyptian   Berber   Cushitic   Omotic   Chadic

Within the Semitic family, I accept the following classification, essentially following Huehnergard (2004); numbers in parentheses refer to the section below in which the language (group) is discussed:

---

[1] See Hayward (2000), Huehnergard (2004) for an overview of Afro-Asiatic. Some branches do, in fact, appear to share greater similarities (Semitic and Egyptian, or Semitic and Berber, for example), but as yet cannot be proven to form unique sub-families.

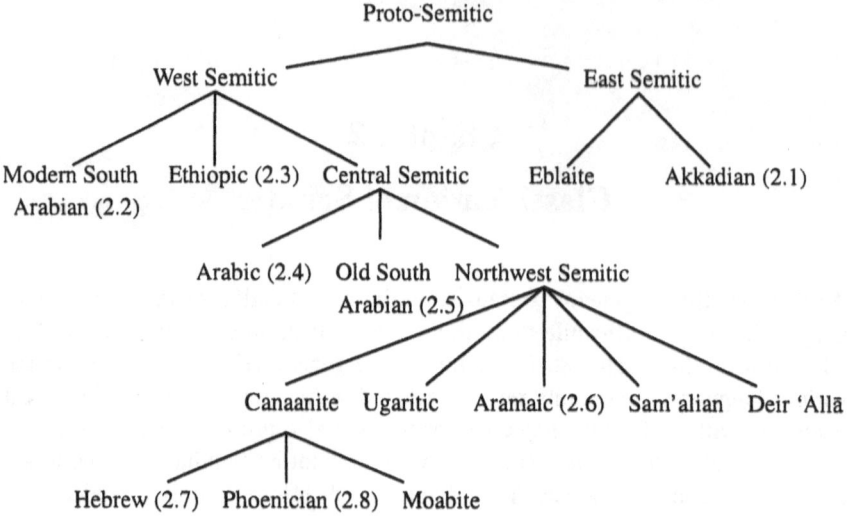

2.1 Akkadian

The oldest Akkadian dialects are known as Old Akkadian, after which period two main dialects are distinguished: Assyrian and Babylonian. The various dialects and periods can be sketched as follows:

                    Old Akkadian
        Old Babylonian   Old Assyrian
        Middle Babylonian Middle Assyrian
        Neo-Babylonian   Neo-Assyrian
        Late Babylonian

All Akkadian forms cited in this work are of the Old Babylonian dialect, unless otherwise noted. The Mari dialect of Akkadian is referred to in Chapter 3; this is a peripheral dialect contemporary with Old Babylonian.

2.2 Modern South Arabian

The Modern South Arabian language family is the least well understood branch of Semitic. Many details of the languages remain unknown, in particular with regard to their historical development; nevertheless, I have made an effort to incorporate data from these languages into this work. The MSA languages discussed herein are Mehri (spoken in Yemen and Oman), Ḥarsūsi (Oman), Jibbali (Oman), and Soqoṭri (on the island of Soqoṭra).[2]

---

[2]See Simeone-Senelle in Hetzron (1997) for an overview of these languages.

2.3 Ethiopic

The following is a classification, based on Hetzron (1972: 119), of the many Ethiopic Semitic languages discussed in this work; omitted are several languages which are not relevant here. Note that Ge'ez, the classical and liturgical language, is no longer spoken. Gafat, and probably Argobba, have also recently become extinct. See Hetzron (1972) for a detailed treatment of the classification of Ethiopian Semitic.

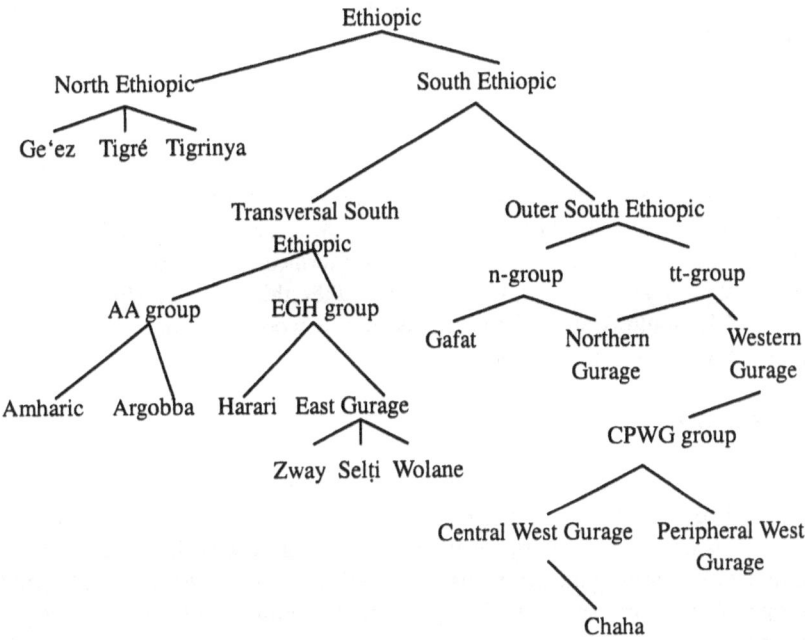

2.4 Arabic

In addition to Classical Arabic, other ancient dialects, known as Ancient (or Old) North Arabian, are attested in inscriptional form.[3] In Chapter 4, we will see that two of these dialects—Liḥyanite and Thamudic—exhibit important evidence regarding the definite article. Modern Arabic dialects are extremely numerous, spreading from Morocco to Iraq, north into Anatolia, and south into African countries like Chad and Sudan. A good number of the modern dialects will be mentioned throughout this work. I refer to them by geographical location, with

---

[3] See Versteegh (1997) for an overview of the history of Arabic and its various ancient and modern dialects. See also M. Macdonald (2004) for a treatment of the ancient inscriptional dialects, and Fischer and Jastrow (1980) on modern dialects.

no concern for genetic classification. It is important to realize that these Arabic dialects are more accurately described as languages, if we use mutual intelligibility as a distinguishing criterion. The modern forms of Arabic are most often designated dialects because they share a literary standard form (Modern Standard Arabic) as the written language, and because of political reasons. Maltese, on the other hand, is normally treated as a separate language, as Malta is ethnically and politically unaffiliated with modern Arab countries and it has its own written standard, using a version of the Roman alphabet; however, the language descends from Arabic like any other modern dialect. It is included here under the heading of Arabic.

2.5 Old South Arabian

The term Old South Arabian, also known as Epigraphic South Arabian and Sayhadic, refers to a group of several inscriptional dialects, namely, Sabaic (also Sabean), Minaic (also Minean), Qatabanic (also Qatabanian), and Hadramitic.[4] As in Arabic, the dialects are perhaps better termed languages, though the limits of attestation and lack of vocalization makes this unclear. Unless otherwise noted, Old South Arabian forms quoted in this work are Sabaic, by far the best-attested member of these dialects.

2.6 Aramaic

Aramaic is quite fragmented dialectally, in both geographic and chronological terms. There is no general consensus on how to divide the dialects, and so various terms can refer to different things depending on who is using them. To go into detail regarding the problems of classification within Aramaic is beyond the scope of this work, so I will simply define the terms used for the dialects which appear herein.[5]

Old Aramaic. This term refers to the Aramaic inscriptions from within the realm of the Assyrian empire, from the ninth and eighth centuries BCE.

Early Imperial Aramaic. There is sparse attestation of Aramaic from the seventh and sixth centuries BCE in both Egypt and Mesopotamia.[6] What is attested is a different dialect than Old Aramaic, but still not the language of the Imperial dialect. Most scholars classify these texts as part of either Old Aramaic or Imperial

---

[4]See Beeston (1984), Nebes and Stein (2004).
[5]See the comprehensive discussion of the classification of Aramaic in Fitzmyer (1979: 57-84). See also Brock (2001) for a very thorough treatment of the history of Aramaic and its many dialects.
[6]See the introduction in Hug (1993).

Aramaic. For example, the sixth century texts from Hermopolis that Hug (1993) treats as Old Aramaic are grouped with the rest of Egyptian (i.e., Imperial) Aramaic by Muraoka and Porten (2003). Here I differentiate these texts from this period, on the basis of chronology, with the term Early Imperial Aramaic.

Imperial Aramaic. Also known as Classical, Official, or Standard Aramaic, Imperial Aramaic denotes the language which spread across the Near East, in standardized form, as the language of successive empires from the sixth to third centuries BCE. Two main witnesses to this dialect are included in this work: Egyptian Aramaic, which is the form of the language used by various communities in Egypt, and the Aramaic of Biblical book of Ezra (4:8–6:18; 7:12–26). The Aramaic of Ezra is not the same dialect of that of Daniel; however, occasionally I use the cover term Biblical Aramaic when the distinction between the dialects of Ezra and Daniel is irrelevant.

Middle Aramaic. By the time the Middle Aramaic dialects are attested, from roughly the third century BCE to the second century CE, geographic dialect variation is quite conspicuous. From this period are attested the Aramaic of the Biblical book of Daniel (2.4b–7:28), inscriptions by the Palmyrene and Nabatean communities, documents from Qumran and the Bar-Kosiba period, and Targums Onqelos and Jonathan, among other sources.[7]

Late Aramaic. Following the second century CE, several very important Aramaic literary traditions developed, and the dialect differences became even more apparent. Syriac, originally the dialect of Edessa, became the main liturgical language of Christianity in the Fertile Crescent, and, as such, is by far the best-attested Aramaic dialect. To the west we find Jewish Palestinian Aramaic (the language of the Palestinian Talmud and Targums), Christian Palestinian Aramaic, and Samaritan Aramaic. To the east of the Syriac territory are found the closely related Jewish Babylonian Aramaic (the language of the Babylonian Talmud) and Mandaic.

Modern Aramaic (Neo-Aramaic). Following the rise of Islam, the use of Aramaic declined dramatically. Today only small pockets of Aramaic-speaking peoples survive in the Near East. While the number of speakers is small, a large number of Aramaic dialects do survive, many of which are really best classified as separate languages. Descendants of the western Late Aramaic dialects are found only in three Syrian villages (Maʻlula, Baxʻa, and Ǧubbʻadin) which speak three closely related dialects. These are collectively referred to as Neo-West-Aramaic (NWA). In the region of Northern Iraq, Southeastern Turkey, and

---

[7] See Boyarin (1981) for an excellent discussion on the classification of Middle Aramaic dialects. Boyarin shows that by this point in the history of Aramaic, a wave-type model is more representative than the tree-model.

Northwestern Iran are (or were) spoken a large number of dialects collectively referred to as North-East(ern) Neo-Aramaic (NENA). Many of these NENA dialects will be cited here, always with specification of the dialect cited. Turoyo is an important Neo-Aramaic dialect, more closely related to NENA than to NWA. Finally, Neo-Mandaic, descended from the Classical Mandaic language and spoken by a small community in Southwestern Iran, forms an eastern branch of Neo-Aramaic.

2.7 Hebrew

In the present study, three main periods of Hebrew are distinguished: Biblical Hebrew, which includes the Hebrew found in the Hebrew Bible and contemporary inscriptions; Mishnaic Hebrew, the Hebrew of the Rabbinic texts; Modern Hebrew, the language of the modern State of Israel. Mishnaic and Modern are occasionally referred to together as Post-Biblical Hebrew. Reference is also made to Late Biblical Hebrew, which includes the Hebrew of the post-Exilic period.[8] Qumran Hebrew, the Hebrew of the Dead Sea Scrolls and contemporary documents, is akin to Late Biblical Hebrew, though is kept separate where appropriate.[9] See Kutscher (1982) or Sáenz-Badillos (1993) for a more detailed discussion of the history of the language and its stages.

2.8 Phoenician

Phoenician inscriptions, attested throughout the first millennium BCE, exhibit diachronic and geographical variation. The dialect of the Phoenician inscriptions found in Carthage and the Carthaginian empire is referred to as Punic. See Hackett (2004) for a more detailed overview.

---

[8]See Polzin (1976).
[9]See Qimron (1986).

Chapter 3

Grammaticalization in Semitic

In this chapter, I will present examples of grammaticalization from within the family of Semitic languages. It goes without saying that such a list cannot be complete, for such material could indeed fill volumes. I do aim to be comprehensive, by which I mean that I will highlight a large variety of types of grammaticalization—including examples from the nominal and verbal systems, prepositions, particles, and more—and give examples from most of the ancient and modern languages. Some of the examples will be obvious and uncontroversial, while others will be original and subject to debate. In addition, some topics will receive a fuller treatment than others, as I have thought worthwhile.

This chapter is intended to serve several purposes. The first is to illustrate how pervasive grammaticalization is, and how much of language change actually falls under this rubric. Second, this chapter allows me to touch on a variety of issues which are interesting, but because of space and time constraints, I am unable to examine in greater detail. Third, it is hoped that this chapter will serve to point out some of the areas that might benefit from further study. Finally, this chapter should be of interest to the general linguist who is more interested in examples of grammaticalization than in the finer points of Semitic historical grammar.

The data presented in this chapter are, for the most part, not new. That is to say, with the exception of some of the etymologies and explanations, what is described below has been described elsewhere. However, rarely have these data been gathered together in one place, even in comprehensive works such as Brockelmann (1908-13). For example, nowhere else is there a discussion on genitive exponents in Semitic which includes as many languages. The same holds true for future tense markers, reflexive pronouns, and many other topics covered below. Also new here is the connection of the data with the concept of grammaticalization, and its presentation in such a framework. For these reasons, it is hoped that this chapter will be of interest to the Semitist and non-Semitist alike.

3.1 Nominal and Pronominal System

3.1.1 Indefinite Articles

One of the simplest and most common examples of grammaticalization is the development of the word 'one' into an indefinite article. English *a, an*, French *un, une*, and Hungarian *egy* are just three well-known examples of this. Many Semitic languages exhibit the same development:

> Biblical Hebrew: *ḥōr 'eḥād* 'a hole' (*'eḥād* 'one') (Ezek. 8:7)[1]
> Biblical Aramaic: *'ében ḥădā* 'a stone' (*ḥădā* 'one (f.)') (Dan. 6:18)
> Geʻez: *'aḥadu bə'si* 'a man' (Job 1:1)[2]

> Amharic: *and ləğ* 'a child' (*and* 'one')[3]
> Turoyo: *ḥa-bayto* 'a house' (*ḥa* 'one')[4]
> NENA (Arbel dialect): *xa nāša* 'a man' (*xa* 'one')[5]

In at least one case, the number 'one' is found in conjunction with the definite article:

> Moroccan Arabic: *waḥed əl-bent* 'a girl' (*waḥed* 'one')[6]

Occasionally we find a different, yet semantically very similar, source for the indefinite article:

> Iraqi (Muslim Baghdadi) Arabic: *'endi fad-bēt* 'I have a house' (*fad* < Classical Arabic *fard* 'single')[7]

It should be noted that while the languages each behave slightly differently in their employment of the indefinite article, in none of the Semitic languages is the indefinite article obligatory (as, for example, the definite article can be) or as commonly employed as the English indefinite article. This can sometimes make it difficult to determine whether the respective words for 'one' should be translated as an indefinite article or something like 'a certain'. See the grammars ref-

---

[1] There are many places in the Bible where *'eḥād* could be construed as an indefinite article, but where a translation 'a certain' or 'one' is just as feasible. See Rendsburg (2002: 30-32) for a nice discussion of this problem and a compilation of BH examples.
[2] Tropper (2002a: §52.22).
[3] Leslau (1995: 154).
[4] Jastrow (1992: 20).
[5] Khan (1999: 195-203; 2001).
[6] Harrel (1962: 147).
[7] Blanc (1964: 118-19). Also see Abu-Haidar (1991: 111-12).

erenced for details on usage.

3.1.2 Definite Articles

These will be discussed in chapter four.

3.1.3 Reflexive Pronouns

Proto-Semitic had no (reconstructable) reflexive pronouns. In the Semitic languages, reflexivity can be expressed by the verbal pattern (e.g., Arabic *xaba'a* 'to hide', *taxabba'a* 'to hide oneself') or may have no unambiguous expression (e.g., Syriac *nqep leh* 'he joined himself' (Luke 15:15); cf. *sged leh* 'he worshipped him' (Matt. 8:2)). Also extremely common in Semitic and across the world's languages is the shift of a noun referring to the body or part of the body into a reflexive pronoun 'self'.[8] This development prevents ambiguity (as found in the Syriac examples above) and provides a more explicit or emphatic form of expression. Following are examples from across Semitic, grouped by source type:[9]

'soul': Classical Arabic – *nafs*-[10]
Arabic dialects (e.g., Iraqi, Syrian, Egyptian) – *nafs*-[11]
Syriac – *napš*-[12]
CPA, JPA, Targumic – *napš*-[13]
NWA – *nəfs*-[14]
NENA (Arbel) – *noš*-[15]
Biblical Hebrew – *napš*-[16]
Ge'ez – *nafs*-[17]
Tigré – *nos*-[18]

---

[8] For example, in a list of reflexives in 148 languages by Schladt (2000: 120-24), the vast majority are from a word 'body' or a part of the body. Schladt (2000) provides a very nice discussion of the grammaticalization of reflexives, as do König and Siemund (2000).
[9] For a general discussion, see Wright (1890: 128-30), Lipiński (1997: 311).
[10] W. Fischer (2002: 175), Wright (1967 II: §135).
[11] Erwin (1963: 298), Cowell (1964: 467).
[12] Nöldeke (1904a: §223).
[13] Rarer than *garm*- (Müller-Kessler 1991: 72; Sokoloff 2002: 136; Dalman 1905: 115-16).
[14] Arnold (1990: 47-48).
[15] Khan (1999: 87-88).
[16] BDB (659-60), Segal (1927: 208).
[17] Rarer and more limited then *rə's* (Tropper 2002a: 160; Dillmann 1907: §150).
[18] Raz (1983: 41), Leslau (1945b: 185).

              Tigrinya – *näbs-*[19]
              MSA (Ḥarsūsi) – *(ḥe)-nōf-*[20]

              NENA (Qaraqosh) – *rox-*[21]
              Turoyo, NENA (Hertevin) – *rūḥ-*[22]
              Tunisian Arabic – *rūḥ-*[23]
              Algerian Arabic – *rōḥ-*[24]

              NENA (Aradhin, Jilu) – *gyān-*[25]

'bone':   Post-Biblical Hebrew – *ʿaṣm-*[26]
              CPA, JPA, Targumic – *garm-*[27]

'head':   Geʿez – *rəʾs-*[28]
              Amharic – *ras-*[29]
              Tigré – *raʾas-*[30]
              Tigrinya – *rəʾs-*[31]
              Moroccan Arabic – *raṣ-*[32]

              Gafat – *dəma-*[33]

              Akkadian (mainly Mari) – *qaqqad-*[34]

---

[19] Leslau (1941: 46-47).
[20] Johnstone (1977: 94). The other MSA languages possess a similar lexeme.
[21] Khan (2002: 84).
[22] Turoyo: Jastrow (1985: 35-36); NENA (Hertevin): Jastrow (1988: 31).
[23] D. Cohen (1975: 218), Singer (1984: 256). Wright (1967 II: §135) includes Classical Arabic *rūḥ-* in his list of reflexives.
[24] M. Cohen (1912: 341), Grand'henry (1972: 134).
[25] Aradhin: Krotkoff (1982: 23); Jilu: S. Fox (1997: 43). This lexeme is a Kurdish loan. Interestingly, in the Arbel dialect of NENA, this borrowing is the noun 'soul', while the original Semitic root is retained only as a reflexive pronoun (Khan 1999: 87). In Aradhin the borrowing has taken over both functions.
[26] Segal (1927: 206-8). Segal believes Aramaic *garm-* to be a calque of Hebrew, though with its attestation in CPA and the general tendency of Aramaisms to appear in LBH and MH, the opposite seems to me more likely.
[27] Müller-Kessler (1991: 72), Sokoloff (2002: 136), Dalman (1905: 115-16).
[28] Tropper (2002a: 160), Dillmann (1907: §150).
[29] Leslau (1995: 57). See also the study by Goldenberg (1991).
[30] Raz (1983: 41), Leslau (1945b: 185).
[31] Leslau (1941: 46-47).
[32] Harrell (1962: 136).
[33] Leslau (1945: 49).
[34] Von Soden (1995: §43).

'eye':   Classical Arabic – *ʿayn*-[35]

'body':   Chaha – *gäg*-[36]
            Zway, Selṭi, Wolane – *gäg*-[37]

            Akkadian (Old Akk., Old Ass., Mari) – *pagr*-[38]

'owner':   Tigrinya – *baʿl*-[39]

'person',
'essence': Syriac – *qnom*-[40]

            Syrian Arabic – *zāt*-[41]

            (Syriac – *yāt*-)[42]

'state':   Syrian Arabic – *ḥāl*-[43]
            NWA – *ḥol*-[44]

(unknown): Akkadian – *ramān*-[45]

            CPA – *q(y)qn*-[46]

Examples of the reflexive pronoun used as an object are:

<u>Arabic</u>: *qatala nafsahu* 'he killed himself'
<u>Algerian Arabic</u>: *qŏtlu ṛōḥum* 'they killed themselves'

---

[35] Wright (1967 II: §135). The usual word is *nafs*-.
[36] Leslau (1950: 18). The word itself is of Cushitic origin.
[37] Leslau (1999: 25).
[38] Von Soden (1995: §43).
[39] Leslau (1941: 46-47).
[40] Nöldeke (1904a: §223). Much rarer than *nafš*-. The etymology of the word is unclear.
[41] Cowell (1964: 467). This form reflects CA *ðāt* 'being, essence', which itself is historically the feminine form of the determinative-relative *ðū*. Wright (1967 II: §135) includes Classical Arabic *ðāt* in his list of reflexive words.
[42] Nöldeke (1904a: §223) takes this from a noun *yātā*- 'essence', and dismisses any connection with the archaic *nota accusativi* (§287 n. 1). I disagree with Nöldeke's etymology, and derive the reflexive instead from the *nota accusativi*. See below (5.4.1) for further discussion.
[43] Cowell (1964: 467). Wright (1967 II: §135) includes Classical Arabic *ḥāl*- in his list of reflexive words.
[44] Arnold (1990: 47). This is probably an Arabic borrowing.
[45] Von Soden (1995: §43). This is the normal Akkadian term.
[46] Müller-Kessler (1991: 72). Schulthess (1924: 33) offers a possible etymology, namely Greek *kaì ekeînos* 'and that one' > **kēkēnos* > **qēqēn*.

Akkadian: *ramāššu ipaṭṭar* 'he will ransom himself'
Amharic: *rasun gäddälä* 'he killed himself'
CPA: *rm' grmh* /rmā garmeh/ 'he threw himself'
Mishnaic Hebrew: *'al ta'aś 'aṣməkā* 'do not make yourself'
Syriac: *ḥnaq nafšeh* 'he strangled himself'
Tigré: *nosa təšannaqat* 'she hanged herself'
Turoyo: *ḥzéli rúḥi* 'I saw myself'

These pronouns are not restricted to objectival use. They may, in some languages, also serve as intensifiers for subjects or other pronominal forms:

Akkadian: *ramāššu illik* 'he himself went'
Chaha: *(əya) gägäna ätänša* 'I myself will come'
Tigré: *ra'asu 'ət 'ad sa'a* 'he himself ran to the village' (lit., 'himself to village he-ran')
MSA (Harsūsi): *(he)-nōfiye xom* 'I myself want'
JPA (Palestinian Talmudic): *bšm grmh* /bšem garmeh/ 'in his own name' (vs. *bšmh* 'in his name')

3.1.4 Reciprocal Pronouns

Semantically and functionally similar to reflexivity is the notion of reciprocity. Like the former, reciprocity can also be expressed by means of a verbal stem, as in Hebrew *rā'ā* 'see', *hitrā'ā* 'see one another' or Akkadian *ṣabātu* 'to seize', *tiṣbutu* 'to seize one another, quarrel'. Many languages also develop a more explicit means of expressing this concept:

Syriac: *ḥad* ('one') + PREPOSITION + *ḥad*, *nesnōn ḥad l-ḥad* 'they will hate each other'; *b-muzzāgā d-ḥad 'am ḥad* 'by mixing with each other' (lit., 'of one with one')[47]

Biblical Hebrew: *'îš* ('man') + PREPOSITION + *'āḥîw* ('his brother'), *way-yippārədû 'îš mē'al 'āḥîw* 'they separated from each other' (lit., 'they separated, a man from-upon his brother') (Gen. 13:11); *'îš* ('man') + PREPOSITION + *rēʿēhû* ('his companion'), *way-yakkû 'îš 'et rēʿēhû* 'they killed each other' (2 Kings 3:23)

Post-Biblical Hebrew: *ze* ('this') + PREPOSITION + *ze*, *šiḥrərû ze et ze* 'they liberated each other'[48]

These are essentially periphrastic constructions; they are transparent and we

---

[47]Nöldeke (1904a: §242).

[48]Segal (1927: 208). Segal also gives other possible constructions for Mishnaic Hebrew. This construction with *ze* is also the norm in Modern Hebrew.

might say that they are in an early stage of grammaticalization. That is to say, these lexemes have begun to acquire a grammatical function, but have undergone very little semantic bleaching, no phonetic erosion, and no decategorialization. In some cases such a construction has become frozen (i.e., the preposition and form of the noun do not vary), and demonstrates a more advanced stage of grammaticalization:

> Amharic: *ərs bärs* (< *bä ərs*) 'each other' (**ərs* 'head')[49]
> Zway, Selti, Wolane: *gäg bä-gäg* 'each other' (*gäg* 'body')[50]

In other cases, an even more advanced grammaticalization has resulted in an actual reciprocal pronoun, whose source is not immediately transparent:

> Akkadian: *aḫāmiš, aḫā'iš* 'each other' (< *aḫu-* 'brother')[51]
>
> Syriac: *ḥdāḏe* 'each other' (< *ḥad* 'one') (also evidenced in Neo-Aramaic, for example Turoyo *ḥdoḏe*, NENA (Qaraqosh) *ġdāḏə*, and possibly NENA (Arbel) *dixle*)[52]

3.1.5 Independent Personal Pronouns

Personal pronouns, at least of the first and second persons, are relatively stable cross-linguistically. Semitic is no exception, though we do find examples of pronouns having been replaced by other grammaticalized words. In Amharic, for example, all third person independent personal pronouns have been replaced by a form of the word for 'head' (Geʿez *rəʾs*) plus possessive suffixes.[53]

> Amharic: *ərsu* 'he' (cf. Geʿez *rəʾsu* 'his head; himself')
> *ərsʷa* 'she' (cf. Geʿez *rəʾsā* 'her head; herself')

The reflexive stage, already extant in Geʿez (see above 3.1.3), provided the source for the independent pronominal one. An original 'his head' became 'himself', then simply 'he', and so forth for the other pronouns involved. The original reflexive construction still exists; the modern Amharic word for 'head', *ras*,

---

[49]Leslau (1995: 61-62). See also the study by Goldenberg (1991).
[50]Leslau (1999: 26).
[51]Von Soden (1995: §43).
[52]Syriac: Nöldeke (1904a: §242); Turoyo: Jastrow (1985: 36); Qaraqosh: (Khan 2002: 84); For the Arbel form, Khan (1999: 88) suggests a possible derivation of *ḥdāḏe* > **dxāḏe* > *dixle*.
[53]In the special set of polite pronouns, second persons are included as well. These polite second person forms derive from third person pronouns (cf. German *Sie*, Spanish *usted*). See Leslau (1995: 46ff.) for a complete list of the independent pronouns and their variants.

plus suffixes can be used as a reflexive pronoun (see above 3.1.3). In its use as an independent pronoun, it has been grammaticalized, or more accurately, re-grammaticalized, and phonetically eroded. Parallels can be found in Tigrinya (for all second and third persons) and Argobba (for third persons), for example:

Tigrinya: *nəssu* 'he', *nəssəka* 'you (m.sg.)' (< **nafs-* 'soul')[54]
Argobba: *kəssu* 'he', *kəssa* 'she', *kəssäm* 'they' (< **karś* 'belly')[55]

It has also been suggested (Praetorius 1871: 155) that the Harari second person independent pronouns (*axāx, axāš, axāxāč*) are based on a word *'akāl* 'body', but this is very uncertain. Modern scholars seem not to have perpetuated this etymology.[56]

In Gafat, the third person plural pronoun *əlämu* 'they' derives, by regular sound change, from the Semitic base **kull-* 'all' with a pronominal suffix.[57] In this case, a word meaning 'all of them' has acquired a simple pronominal function. This is reminiscent of English *y'all* < *you all*.

3.1.6 Interrogative Pronouns

In Modern Standard Arabic, as a general rule, *mā* 'what?' is the interrogative used in nominal sentences (*mā hāðā?* 'what is this?'), while *māðā* 'what?' is used in verbal sentences (*māðā qulta* 'what did you say?').[58] In Classical Arabic, such a restriction on *māðā* is already in place, though *mā* is not restricted in such a way. The word *māðā* derives from interrogative *mā* + a demonstrative pronoun *ðā* (cf. accusative determinative pronoun *ðā*, demonstrative *hāðā* 'this'). Essentially, an original construction 'what is it that you are doing?' has become the standard way of saying 'what are you doing?'. French *qu'est-ce que* provides a nice parallel. The Syriac interrogatives *mān / mānā* 'what?' probably derive, as the Arabic form does, from interrogative *mā* + demonstrative *den / dnā*; the distribution of these with the variant *mā* 'what?' is roughly that of Arabic.[59] A similar construction is found occasionally in Biblical Hebrew (e.g., Gen. 12:18 *mazzō(')t 'āśîtā* 'what have you done?'), but it has not been grammaticalized. Huehnergard (2005) discusses these forms in detail, and shows that the construc-

---

[54]Leslau (1941: 45). The etymology, along with other Ethiopic parallels, was pointed out already by Praetorius (1871: 155).
[55]Hudson in Hetzron (1997: 461), Leslau (1997: 20).
[56]There is no mention of Harari in the entry for *'akāl* in Leslau (1987). Wagner in Hetzron (1997: 489) writes that the origin of this base *ax-* is unclear, as is that of the third person pronouns, *az-*.
[57]Leslau (1945: 49).
[58]Badawi, Carter, and Gully (2004: 693-95).
[59]Nöldeke (1904a: §68, §232).

tion itself is a feature of Central Semitic. Yet only in Arabic and Syriac do we find fully grammaticalized interrogative pronouns (*māðā* and *mānā*, respectively) born out of this construction.

In Modern Arabic dialects we find yet another grammaticalized interrogative pronoun. Classical Arabic *'ayyu šay'in*, literally 'which thing?' came to be used as a substitute for 'what?' early on in the vernacular language.[60] Even in Classical texts one finds occasional colloquial forms like *'ayšin* and *'ayš*.[61] Modern dialects provide a wide variety of forms derived from this source, sometimes with the addition of a third person pronominal morpheme, for example Syrian *šū*, Baghdadi *šənu*, Moroccan *āš* or *šnu*, and Northern Yemeni *eyš* or *weyš*, all meaning 'what?'.[62]

Syrian: *šū 'əməlt* 'what did you do?'
Moroccan: *āš dərti / šnu dərti* 'what did you do?'

Arabic *šay'un* 'thing' has in fact been the source for a large number of interrogatives of various types (e.g., Syrian *lēš* 'why?', Iraqi *šgadd* 'how much?', Anatolian *šwaqt* 'when?', Moroccan *škūn* 'who?'), as well as a number of other types of words and grammatical markers, some of which will be dealt with below.[63]

3.1.7 Gender Markers

A case of grammaticalization not at all widespread in Semitic is the development of gender markers. In Semitic, gender is usually determinable by the form of a noun, as well as by the forms of its modifiers. In Ethiopic—already in Ge'ez in fact—the category of gender is quite unstable. Amharic has developed specific markers of gender for human beings and animals, though as the sources are clearly recognizable, the grammaticalizations are at an early stage. For human beings, the markers are *wänd* 'son; male' (cf. Ge'ez *wald* 'son') and *set* 'woman' (< **säb'ət*, cf. Tigrinya *säbäyti* 'woman', Ge'ez *sab'* 'man').[64] Examples are:

---

[60]Brockelmann (1908-13 I: §111b).
[61]W. Fischer (2002: 150).
[62]Syrian: Cowell (1964: 566); Iraqi: Erwin (1963: 293), Abu-Haidar (1991: 82), Mansour (2001); Moroccan: Caubet (1993 I: 170-71); Yemeni: Behnstedt (1987: 89).
[63]For a very fine study of *šay'un* and its derivatives in the modern dialects, see Obler (1975), especially pp. 44-56 on interrogatives. Singer (1958) is a comprehensive study of interrogatives in Modern Arabic. Caubet (1993 I: 170-72) gives a long list of interrogatives deriving from *šay'un* in Moroccan, and Mansour (2001) quite a few in Jewish Baghdadi.
[64]See Leslau (1979 III: 565), Appleyard (1977: 8). I have given here Leslau's derivation of *set* < **säb'ət*, though given the Tigrinya form, a derivation of *set* < **säb'et* < **säbäyt* seems to me plausible.

Amharic: *wänd ləǧ* 'boy', *set ləǧ* 'girl' (*ləǧ* 'child')
wänd hakim '(male) doctor', *set hakim* '(female) doctor'

There are several markers for animals, but an example of one set is *täbat* 'male' (cf. Ge'ez *tabā't*), *anəst* 'female' (cf. Ge'ez *'anəst*):

Amharic: *täbat ahəyya* 'male donkey', *anəst ahəyya* 'female donkey'[65]

3.2 Verbal System

This category is very broad one, and alone could fill volumes. What follows here can only be a sampling of the changes to the Semitic verbal systems that exemplify grammaticalization. For several of the categories (for example, Auxiliary Verbs), I have chosen just one or two languages, even though parallel developments may be found in other Semitic languages. This is for reasons of space, though also because of the fact that the development of the Semitic verbal systems (their morphology and syntax) are relatively well studied, unlike some other topics discussed in this chapter. One small aspect of the verbal system, namely prefixed present-tense markers, is covered in some detail in Chapter 6.

3.2.1 Proto-Afro-Asiatic Tenses

The Proto-Semitic suffix-conjugation, also known as the stative or predicative form,[66] is reconstructable for Proto-Afro-Asiatic, or at least for the shared ancestor of Egyptian and Semitic. Compare the following forms, from Akkadian and Ancient Egyptian:[67]

	Egyptian	Akkadian
1cs	-kwi (-kw, -ki, -k)	-āku
2ms	-t(i)	-āta
2fs	-t(i)	-āti
3ms	-w or --	--
3fs	-t(i)	-at
1cs	-wyn	-ānu
2mp	-tiwny	-ātunu
2fp	-tiwny	-ātina
3mp	-w	-ū
3fp	-w	-ā

---

[65]See further in Leslau (1995: 164-65).
[66]See Brockelmann (1908-13 I: §264f).
[67]See Huehnergard (1987) for a discussion on the use of this conjugation in Akkadian. For further discussion of the Egypto-Semitic comparison, see Rubin (2004).

More importantly in the present context, the suffixes in this conjugation are clearly related to the independent pronouns. Compare the above suffixes to the Akkadian independent pronouns:

	sing.	plural
1c	anāku	nīnu
2m	atta	attunu
2f	atti	attina
3m	šū	šunu
3f	šī	šina

The connection between the first and second person pronouns and the suffixes of the predicative construction is obvious, while the third person pronouns are not to be connected with the verbal suffixes. Instead, the 3fs form of the verbal suffix, in Semitic and Egyptian, is the same as the nominal and adjectival feminine ending. In Semitic, the 3pl. endings correspond to the endings of other finite verbal tenses. The origin of the 3ms verbal suffix is unclear.

What we find in Akkadian is essentially what we find in Syriac: two sets of personal pronouns, one free and one enclitic.[68] The latter have possibly been grammaticalized and phonetically reduced from the former.[69] This development can be illustrated as follows:

Stage 1. *maruṣ anāku 'I am sick' (subsequently grammaticalized)
Stage 2. *maruṣ āku > marṣāku 'I am sick' (phonetic reduction and affixation)

Note that this construction usually occurs with a verbal adjective in Akkadian, though it is occasionally found with a noun, as in sinnišānu 'we are women', rubâku 'I am a prince'.

This form eventually went through reanalysis, and the predicative construction, which has been limited mainly to verbal adjectives, was grammaticalized

---

[68] See Gai (1984) for a brief note on the parallelism of the Akkadian and Syriac constructions.

[69] The first and second person independent pronouns themselves can be reconstructed with an initial element *ʾan- + person marker (PS *ʾan-āku, Eg. in-k). It is also very possible that the verbal paradigm developed at a stage when these person markers were independently functional. This would mean that Stage 1 above was simply *maruṣ āku. Regardless, the important point here is that there has been grammaticalization: the relegation of a pronoun to a verbal inflectional suffix. If the derivation is correct as it stands in the main text above, this would mean that both Egyptian and Semitic underwent the same phonetic reduction, with loss of the initial *ʾan- element subsequent to grammaticalization.

into a full stative tense.[70] The grammaticalization continues, and in West Semitic, this tense becomes a preterite tense (probably via a perfect),[71] almost completely replacing the inherited Proto-Semitic past tense; this development is in fact the defining characteristic of West Semitic.[72]

Stage 3. Arabic *mariḍtu* 'I got sick'[73]

To summarize an already brief discussion, the independent pronouns were grammaticalized in the predicative construction, probably already in Proto-Afro-Asiatic. As a result of this grammaticalization, the pronouns developed enclitic, reduced forms, which subsequently became affixal. The construction that resulted was itself grammaticalized in Semitic, in particular in West Semitic, where it developed into the normal past tense. In Syriac (and other contemporary Aramaic dialects) we also find a similar grammaticalization of the independent pronouns, as will be described below (3.2.4).

3.2.2 Derived Stems

Proto-Semitic possessed a number of derived verbal stems, characterized by a prefixed or infixed *š*, *n*, or *t*. Not only have these stems survived in the descendant languages, but they also seem to have cognates in other branches of Afro-Asiatic. For example, the Semitic Š-stem (also known as the C-stem, for its primarily causative function), is undoubtedly cognate with the Egyptian causative verbal prefix *s-*.[74] Lieberman (1986) has made a thorough survey of these stems, in particular the N-stem. Following many previous scholars,[75] he attempts to trace the elements *š*, *n*, and *t* back to original demonstrative elements. For example, he links the Š-stem with the anaphoric pronouns (e.g., Akkadian *šū*). However, many of the comparisons Lieberman draws are rather less secure than he suggests. For example, to compare the Semitic N-stem, dating back over five thousand years, with a demonstrative element *n* in languages attested only very recently, such as those of the Omotic or Cushitic families, is methodologically unsound. In fact, any reconstruction of Afro-Asiatic stands on shaky ground, all

---

[70]See Tropper (1995) and Kouwenberg (2000) for recent in-depth studies.

[71]For a parallel to the change of STATIVE > PERFECT, compare Classical Greek, where the "perfect" is a clearly stative tense in Homer's language, but a real perfect tense in Attic Greek (see Sihler 1995: 564-66). For the replacement of a preterite with a perfect, we can point to the French *passé composé*.

[72]See J. Fox (2003: 49-50), Huehnergard (2004: §2.3).

[73]In Arabic, as elsewhere in CS, the 1cs suffix *-ku* has been replaced by *-tu*, on analogy with the *t* of the second person suffixes.

[74]See Rubin (2004).

[75]See the plethora of bibliographical references in Lieberman (1986).

the more so when we are dealing with elements consisting of single consonants. Nevertheless, it does seem possible that there is some connection with demonstratives and these verbal stems, and thus that we are dealing with a very early example of grammaticalization. Or, to state this from another perspective, the nature of grammatical development is such that these forms must have arisen from some form of grammaticalization, and cross-linguistic evidence tells us that demonstrative elements are a likely source. One must only be wary of the certainty with which we can reconstruct the actual sources.

3.2.3 Auxiliary Verbs and New Tenses

3.2.3.1 'Be' > Auxiliary

As in so many of the world's languages, the verb 'to be' has become a grammaticalized auxiliary in many of the Semitic languages. Because this is so prevalent across Semitic, and because in each language this includes multiple tenses, I will just include two relevant examples here.

In Syriac (as in many other Aramaic dialects), the verb hwā 'to be' can be used in conjunction with the basic tenses to express a certain aspect. Most often when this verb is used as an auxiliary, it appears in a reduced (enclitic) form (h)wā; the exception is when the auxiliary precedes the main verb. When used in conjunction with the imperfect or participle, it denotes a past frequentative or habitual action, and with the perfect (= preterite) tense it expresses a pluperfect, or even a true present perfect.[76] For example:

> Syriac: *kad nergaz (h)wā* 'whenever he was angry (would get angry)'; *mqarrbīn (h)waw leh ṭlāye* 'they were bringing children to him' (Mark 10:13); *d-(')emret (h)wêt l-kon* 'that I have told you'

Similar developments can also be found in Ge'ez, Post-Biblical Hebrew, Arabic, and elsewhere in Semitic.

In Amharic, the grammaticalization has in some cases progressed further. The auxiliary verb *allä* 'to be' (< **hälläwä*) has become cliticized, and then affixed to the main imperfect verb. The result can no longer be called a compound tense, but a primary tense; in fact, this new tense has replaced the inherited present (or, imperfect) tense in positive main clauses.

> Amharic: *yəsäbrall* 'he breaks, is breaking, will break' (< *yəsäbr* + *allä*; note the phonetic reduction); *əfälləgallähu* 'I want, will want'[77]

---

[76] For details, see Nöldeke (1904a: §263, §268, §277).
[77] Leslau (1995: 341-47).

Other compound tenses still exist in Amharic, as described in Leslau (1995: 315ff.).

3.2.3.2 'Have' > Auxiliary

This category may seem puzzling, given that Proto-Semitic and the majority of its descendent languages do not possess a verb meaning 'have'. But in fact, a construction equivalent to 'have' has been the cause of a major reorganization of the verbal system of the Eastern Aramaic dialects.

Already in Syriac, it was possible to express a perfect tense by means of a construction which consisted of the passive participle plus the preposition *l-* 'to, for'.[78] For example:

> Syriac: *gbar lā ḥkīm lī* 'I have not known a man' (Luke 1:34); *w-(')āp-lā 'en 'īt rūḥā d-qudšā šmīʿ lan* 'we have not even heard if there is a holy spirit' (Acts 19:2)

In modern Aramaic dialects, with the exception of NWA and Neo-Mandaic, this construction has developed from a perfect into a preterite and has completely replaced the Semitic suffix-conjugation as the regular means of expressing the past tense, as in:

> Turoyo: *grəšli* 'I pulled' (with m.sg. object, or implied 'him'); *grišoli* 'I pulled' (with f.sg. object, or implied 'her'); *grišili* 'I pulled' (with pl. object, or implied 'them') (< *grīš/grīšā/grīšīn lī*)[79]
>
> NENA (Qaraqosh): *ptəxla* 'he opened' (with m.sg. object); *ptixala* 'he opened' (with f.sg. object); *ptixila* 'he opened' (with pl. object) (< *ptīḥ/ptīḥā/ptīḥīn leh*)[80]

Most scholarly works assume that the original construction meant something like 'written by me', thence reinterpreted as 'I wrote'.[81] Jastrow (1992) even refers to this Neo-Aramaic tense as the 'ergativ flektiertes Präteritum'.

Kutscher (1969) has argued that, in fact, this Eastern Aramaic construction is a calque from a Persian perfect tense with auxiliary 'have'. Essentially, the Syriac phrase *šmīʿ lī* is equivalent to English 'I have heard', French *j'ai écouté*,

---

[78] Nöldeke (1904a: §279). Parallel constructions are also found in Mandaic and BTA.
[79] Jastrow (1985: 129-31).
[80] Khan (2002: 91-95).
[81] Cf. Nöldeke (1904a: §279), Brockelmann (1908-13 I: §264e), Lipiński (1997: §42.20).

or any other perfect tense with the auxiliary verb 'have'.[82] The preposition *l-* plus a suffix is the Aramaic equivalent of the verb 'have'. The fact that the participle agrees in number and gender with the object is presumably what leads many to call this an ergative construction, but compare the identical situation French: *la valise, je l'ai prise; je les ai prises*.

The first known occurrence of this construction comes from an Imperial Aramaic document of the fifth century BCE, i.e., during the Persian period. The construction is only found in Eastern dialects, which have been in closer contact with Persian and other Iranian languages.

3.2.4 Verbal Noun or Adjective > New Tense

In many cases a new verb tense or aspect has arisen not from the grammaticalization of an auxiliary, but simply from the reanalysis and grammaticalization of an existing verbal noun or verbal adjective. We saw above (3.2.1) that a verbal adjective developed into a stative tense already in Proto-Afro-Asiatic. Here we will focus only on two other such examples, Neo-Aramaic and Tigrinya, in which, like the Proto-Afro-Asiatic stative, a grammaticalized pronominal form has fused with a verbal noun or adjective to create a fully conjugated tense.

In the attested histories of both Hebrew and Aramaic, we see that the present active participle becomes an actual present tense. Already in Biblical Hebrew, the present active participle is often translatable as a present tense, as in:

> Biblical Hebrew: *kol-ʾăšer rōmēš ʿal-hā-ʾădāmā* 'everything that creeps on the ground' (Gen. 7:8)

But in Post-Biblical Hebrew, the participle becomes the regular mode of expressing the present, while in Biblical Hebrew it is not.[83] It is important to note that even when the participle attains the status of a finite verb, it retains its nominal inflection, marking gender and number only.

In contemporary dialects of Aramaic, usage is as in Biblical Hebrew. For example:

> Biblical Aramaic: *gubrayyā dî-dnā binyānā bānayin* 'the men who are building this building' (Ezra 5:4)

In later dialects we find an important difference in the use of this form. The participle is properly a nominal form, historically inflected for number and gender

---

[82]In addition to Kutscher (1969), see also Benveniste's (1966: 176-86) discussion of this construction in Old Persian. D. Cohen (1984: 513-17) discusses both Kutscher's and the traditional derivations of the Aramaic forms.
[83]See Gordon (1982) on the development of the Hebrew participle.

only; in Syriac and other later dialects, we find inflection for person as well. First, we find that the independent personal pronouns have developed enclitic forms, which often act as the copula in a nominal sentence (see below, 3.2.8.1). For example:

<u>Syriac</u>: *w-'enā 'aprā (')nā* 'I am dust' (Gen. 18:27)

These enclitic pronouns are also often used with a participle, which is still technically a nominal form, even though its use is often verbal:

<u>Syriac</u>: *'āmar (')nā lkōn* 'I say to you' (Matt. 3:9)

Subsequently, in their use with the participles, the enclitic pronouns often coalesce completely:[84]

<u>Syriac</u>: *'āmarnā lkōn* 'I say to you' (Matt. 11:11); *w-'en 'āmrīnan ... 'abdīnan leh daggālā* 'if we say ... we make him a liar' (1 John 1:10) (*'āmrīnan < 'āmrīn nan*)

Eventually, these enclitic pronouns fuse completely with the participial forms, resulting in a present tense which is fully conjugated for person, gender, and number. This tense is found as such in Neo-Aramaic:

<u>Turoyo</u>: *(ko-)domaxno* 'I sleep' (< **dāmeknā*); *(ko-)dəmxina* 'we sleep' (< **dāmkīnan*)[85]

Ethiopic provides another interesting example of this type of grammaticalization. In Ge'ez, the form called the perfective active participle (variously known as the gerund, verbal infinitive, or converb) has the base form *qatil-*.[86] It is marked for person, number, and gender, and is inflected like a noun in the accusative with possessive suffixes. In Lambdin's words, "the perfective active participle is used to express the fact that an act has been completed prior to the time of the main verb."[87] It is always subordinate to another verb, and corresponds to an English temporal clause or participial phrase. For example:

<u>Ge'ez</u>: *wa-nabiro qarbu xabehu 'ardā'ihu* 'after he sat down, his disciples came to him' (Matt. 5:1); *wa-taṭamiqo 'iyasus sobehā waḍ'a 'əm-māy* 'and

---

[84] Nöldeke (1904a: §64).

[85] Jastrow (1985: 145-48; 1992: 28-29). On the prefix *ko-*, which marks present indicative, see below, 6.2.

[86] See J. Fox (2003: 190-91) for a discussion of this noun pattern in Ethiopic and elsewhere in Semitic.

[87] Lambdin (1978: 140-41). See also Dillmann (1905: §§123-24) and Tropper (2002a: 44.32, 55.2) for further discussion.

when Jesus had been baptized, he immediately came up from the water' (Matt. 3:16); *wa-ṣawimo ... 'əm-dəxra-zə rəxba* 'having fasted ... afterwards, he was hungry' (Matt. 4:2)

In Tigrinya, this form has attained full verbal status as a past tense, relegating the inherited past tense (PS suffix-conjugation) to mainly literary usage.[88] For example:

Tigrinya: *säbirä* 'I broke'; *bäliʿka* 'you ate'; *nab färänsa käydu* 'he went to France' (*käydu* < *käyidu*); *rädyo 'ityopya gäliṣa* 'Radio Ethiopia reported'

3.2.5 Past Tense Markers

In Arabic, the particle *qad* is used in conjunction with the perfect to indicate a completed action relative to another; its meaning essentially corresponds to the English perfect tenses:[89]

Classical Arabic: *qad māta* 'he has/had died'; *qad qāmati ṣ-ṣalātu* 'the (time of) prayer has come'

The source of this particle *qad* is presumably the verb *qad(d)ama* 'to precede, go before, do before'.[90] We can assume an original hendiadys of the two verbs, as we find in Geʿez constructions like *la-'əlla qadama 'a'maromu* 'those whom he knew beforehand' (Rom. 8:29) and *'aqdamku wa-nagarkukəmu* 'I told you beforehand' (1 Thess. 3:4).[91]

From the same source, and with a parallel development, we find the particle *qam-* or *kəm-* in some dialects of North-Eastern Neo-Aramaic. In NENA, however, the particle is a more general past tense marker. Looking specifically at the NENA dialect of Qaraqosh, we find that there is already a past tense, *qṭallə* 'he killed', which is historically the passive participle *qṭīl* plus a declined form of the preposition *l-* (see above, 3.2.3.2). In Aramaic, a pronominal direct object is also expressed with a declined form of *l-* (see below, 5.1.2). Therefore, when expressing a past tense verb with a pronominal object, instead of using the past tense *qṭallə* plus object suffix, resulting in an awkward **qṭallələ*, where the morpheme *lə* once marks the subject and once the object, this dialect attaches a prefix *kəm-* to the present tense base.[92] Thus we find:

---

[88] On the function of this tense in Tigrinya, see Leslau (1941: 84-87), Melles (2001: 53-54).
[89] Wright (1967 II: §§2-3). W. Fischer (2002: 106).
[90] See Bloch (1946-49) for a discussion.
[91] See also Tropper (2002a: §54.6).
[92] Khan (2002: 99, 140, 316-17).

NENA (Qaraqosh): *ptəxlə* 'he opened', but *kəm-patəx-lə* 'he opened it'

A similar situation is found in other NENA dialects, including that of Aradhin. For example:[93]

NENA (Aradhin): *ptixle ṭāra* 'he opened a door', but *qam-pātix-le* 'he opened it'

Nöldeke (1868b: 296) was probably the first to suggest the root √*qdm* as the source for this particle. However, his source lexeme *qdām* is problematic, as this word is a preposition 'before', not an adverb as his translation of 'earlier, beforehand' suggests.[94] Much more likely is Maclean's (1895: 82) suggestion of a verbal origin (i.e., hendiadys), though for phonetic reasons I might advocate the peal form *qdam*, rather than pael *qaddem* as he does.[95] Pennacchietti (1997) disagrees and instead suggests that the source of this past tense marker is the participle *qā'im* 'standing'. But in fact, this exact form is unarguably the source for the present-tense marker *k-* found in many Neo-Aramaic dialects (see below, 6.2), and so Pennacchietti's suggestion is highly improbable. Further evidence in favor of *qdam* or *qaddem* as the source lexeme is the form *təm-* (< **dVm-*) found in the Senaya dialect.[96]

3.2.6 Present Tense Markers

These will be discussed in chapter six.

3.2.7 Future Tense Markers

Proto-Semitic had no discrete means of expressing of the future tense, but several languages have developed explicit means via an auxiliary verb or grammaticalized auxiliary particle. The verbs 'go' and 'want' provide most of the

---

[93] Krotkoff (1982: 27-28). See Khan (1999: 118-19) on Arbel, which does not have this particle and solves the problem of pronominal suffixes in a different way.
[94] D. Cohen (1984: 520) also promotes this adverbial source.
[95] Maclean has very good reason to suggest *qaddem*, as this form is well attested in Syriac in a hendiadys construction. In the Syriac New Testament, I found *qaddem* used in such a way twenty-three times (fifteen in the 3ms): Matt. 24:25; Mark 1:35, 13:23; Acts 1:16, 2:31, 3:18, 9:29, 21:29; Rom. 8:30, 9:11, 11:35; 2 Cor. 7:3; Gal. 3:8 (2x); 1 Thess. 3:4; Eph. 1:4 (2x), 1:9, 1:11; Hebrews 11:40; 2 Pet. 3:2; Jude 1:4, 1:17. Only twice, in 1 Cor. 11:21 and 2 Pet. 3:17, did I find the peal form used in hendiadys, and in both cases as a present participle, 3ms and 3mp, respectively. Still, the source of the NENA prefix cannot conclusively be shown to be the pael *qaddem*, as opposed to the peal *qdam*.
[96] See W. Heinrichs (2002: 241).

various future tense markers that have developed in Semitic, a fact which is also true cross-linguistically. Other sources are also attested, as will be shown below.

3.2.7.1 'Go' > Future

One common source for a future tense marker is the verb 'to go', which of course has also been grammaticalized in English (*I'm gonna*; see above, 1.1). In Modern Hebrew we see this with the auxiliary verb *la-lexet* 'to go', the use of which is almost certainly a calque of English. In this case the form is grammaticalized, as it loses its basic meaning of motion, but it retains its full form and inflection.

> Modern Hebrew: *'ani holex la-xanut* 'I am going to the store'; *'ani holex liqro(') 'et ze* 'I'm going to (gonna) read this'; *'anaxnu holxim liqro(') 'et ze* 'we're going to (gonna) read this'

In Arabic dialects, including Syrian, Lebanese, Egyptian, Iraqi, and others, the participle *rāyiḥ* 'going' is used to indicate future tense; this grammaticalization has most often resulted in the complete lack of inflection, and in phonological reduction.[97] Thus we find the forms *raḥ* (Lebanese, Syrian, Iraqi, Kuwaiti), *ḥa* (Egyptian), and *laḥ* (Damascus Syrian), among others, used as future markers:

> Lebanese Arabic: *raḥ-iktub maktūb* 'I am going to write a letter'; *raḥ-niktub maktūb* 'We're going to write a letter'[98]
>
> Iraqi Arabic: *raḥ-yiji* 'He is going to come'[99]
>
> Egyptian Arabic: *huwwa ḥa-yiktib il-gawāb* 'He's going to write the letter'[100]

In Moroccan, the same construction is found with the form *ġadi* 'going', likewise indeclinable, and sometimes shortened to *ġad* or *ġa*:[101]

> Moroccan Arabic: *aš ġadi nelbes* 'What am I going to wear?'

In other Moroccan dialects, as well as in Tunisian Arabic, one finds *māš(i)*, the

---

[97] See Fischer and Jastrow (1980: 75) for an overview of modern dialectal future markers. Brustad (2000: 241-46) presents another comparative overview.
[98] Thackston (1996: 61-62).
[99] Erwin (1963: 138-39).
[100] Mitchell and El-Hassan (1994: 13).
[101] Harrell (1962: 183-84), Caubet (1993 II: 172-77), Brustad (2000: 241). As Caubet notes, this verbal root (Classical Arabic *ġadā* 'to go away') survives only in the active participle, both independently and as an auxiliary.

active participle of another verb 'to go':[102]

> Moroccan Arabic: *māš nžīš dāba* 'I'll come now'
> Tunisian Arabic: *māš imūt bəžžūʿ* 'He's gonna die of hunger'

Similarly, the Maltese future tense markers *se/sa/ser* are reduced forms of the participle *sejjer* [sɛyyɛr] 'going'.[103] For example:

> Maltese: *Se nikteb lil ħija* 'I'm gonna write to my brother'; *Meta sa jiġi Malta ħuk?* 'When will your brother come to Malta?'

It should be noted that Maltese has another future particle *ħa*, cognate with Egyptian *ḥa*, Lebanese *raḥ*, etc., discussed above.[104]

3.2.7.2 'Want' > Future

In other Arabic dialects, the source of the future tense marker is a verb 'to want', which of course is also the source of English *will*. Fischer and Jastrow (1980: 75) assume an imperfect form *yibġa / yibġi* as the source for the attested particles *bā-* and *b(i)-*; this is supported by the use of the full form as a modal verb, and even occasional future-like usage (as in the Egyptian example below):[105]

> Kuwaiti Arabic: *ʿali b-yaktib maktūb* 'Ali will write a letter'[106]
> Northern Yemeni Arabic: *bā-yahabūllanā* 'they will give us'[107]
> Egyptian Arabic: *ʾabʾa ʾadfaʿ kām?* 'How much shall I pay?' (*ʾabʾa* < **abġa*)[108]

---

[102]On Moroccan, see Brustad (2000: 241); see also Fischer and Jastrow (1980: 75, 264). On Tunisian, see D. Cohen (1975: 137). Tunisian also has a variant form *bāš* (Singer 1984: 310-11).

[103]In Maltese, this root exists only as a participle. Its source is Classical Arabic *sāra* 'to set out, travel, go'. Vanhove (1993: 175) seems to take Arabic *ṣāra* 'to become' as the source, but the quality of the Maltese vowels, along with the closer semantic fit of *sāra*, make this unlikely. See Vanhove (1993: 175-84) on the use of this future tense marker, as well as Ambros (1998: 132).

[104]Vanhove (1993: 187-91) discusses the possible semantic differences between Maltese *se* and *ħa*.

[105]These particles *bā-* and *b(i)-* are unrelated to the present tense marker *b-* in Levantine and Egyptian Arabic (see below, 6.6).

[106]Al-Najjar (1984: 82-90).

[107]Behnstedt (1987: 54, 161, 207).

[108]Mitchell and El-Hassan (1994: 28). On the Moroccan use of this root as a modal, see Caubet (1993 II: 136-38).

In Standard (San'ani) Yemeni Arabic, the future tense marker for the first person singular is *šā-*, which derives from *ašti* 'I want' (or another form of this verb).¹⁰⁹ According to J. Watson (p.c.), this prefix was used for all persons until the early twentieth century, but has now been replaced in all but the first person by *ʿa-*. This new prefix also appears with the first person singular (in the form *ʿad-*, a clue to its origin), but with a slightly different nuance than *šā-*. The prefix *ʿad-* indicates a non-specific or probable future, while *šā-* refers to a definite future with regard to a specific point in time.¹¹⁰ The ultimate origin of *ʿa-* / *ʿad-* remains unclear, but it seems likely that the source is the verb *ʿāda* 'to do again, to return', used in hendiadys, or via its derivative particle *ʿād-* 'still' (cf. Heb. *ʿôd*). Examples are:

> Yemeni Arabic: *šā-jī* 'I will come/be coming'; *ʿad-ajī* 'I will probably come'; *šā-tisawwī l-ġadā* 'She will make lunch'

To the Yemeni prefix *ʿa(d)-*, we can compare also the Maltese use of *ʿād* (spelled *għad*) to indicate future. *Għad* is not the general future tense marker (see above, 3.2.7.1), but can indicate a future event that may take place some day.¹¹¹ For example:

> Maltese: *Għad tirnexxi* 'You will succeed'; *Għad issir negozjant kbir* 'You will become a great merchant'

In many NENA dialects, an original Aramaic construction *bʿe d-* 'it is desired that' or *bāʿe d-* 'wants that' has been grammaticalized into a future tense prefix.¹¹² The reflexes, such as Qaraqosh *bəd-* (often realized as *bət-* or even *b-* or *d-*), Urmia *bit-*, Jilu *bt-*, and simply *b-* in other dialects (e.g., Hertevin), make it impossible to determine whether the source form was *bʿe* (passive participle) or *bāʿe* (present active participle). Examples are:

> NENA (Qaraqosh): *bəd-pátəx* 'he will open'; *b-gárəš* 'he will pull'¹¹³
> NENA (Aradhin): *bet-xāzin* 'I will see'¹¹⁴
> NENA (Urmia): *bit-pātix* 'he will open'¹¹⁵
> NENA (Hertevin): *m-napli* 'they will fall' (*m-n-* < **b-n-*)¹¹⁶

---

¹⁰⁹This is Classical Arabic *ʾaštahī* 'I desire, crave'.
¹¹⁰See Watson (1993: 52 n. 5; 1996: 73).
¹¹¹Vanhove (1993: 194-95).
¹¹²Nöldeke (1868b: 295), Khan (2002: 98 n. 6).
¹¹³Khan (2002: 98).
¹¹⁴Krotkoff (1982: 33).
¹¹⁵Tsereteli (1978: 58).
¹¹⁶Jastrow (1988: 54-55).

In fact, the Aramaic source verb *bʿā* 'to want' is cognate with the Arabic verb *baġā*. So, the same PS root *√bġy has independently developed into a future tense marker in dialects of both Arabic and Aramaic.

Modern South Arabian also utilizes the verb 'to want' (*ḥōm* or *xōm*) as a grammaticalized future tense marker, though fully inflected:

<u>Mehri</u>: *hayōm ṯōm təgzā* 'the sun is going to set' (cf. *ḥōm ḳahwēt* 'I want coffee')[117]

<u>Harsūsi</u>: *xōm əxdēm* 'I will work'[118]

3.2.7.3 Nominal/Adjectival Sources

Classical Arabic optionally uses the particle *sawfa*, or its reduced form *sa-*, along with the imperfect—which on its own can be either present or future—to make a future meaning explicit:[119]

<u>Classical Arabic</u>: *sawfa nuṣlīhi nāran* 'We will burn him with fire'; *sa-nubayyinuhu* 'We will explain it'

As evidenced by its Aramaic and Hebrew cognates, the word *sawfa* originally means 'end', or more precisely 'in the end', as it is probably a frozen accusative. In fact, the Hebrew cogener can actually be used to express future tense in Mishnaic Hebrew, though in a different construction. In MH, the word *sôp* 'end' takes a pronominal suffix to express the logical subject, and is followed by an infinitive or (rarely) a participle:[120]

<u>Mishnaic Hebrew</u>: *sôpô lîttēn* 'he will (eventually) give'; *sôpô yôrēš* 'in the end he will inherit'

In some dialects of Middle Aramaic there is a periphrastic future tense, formed with the passive participle *ʿtīd* 'prepared, ready' with either *l-* 'to' + an infinitive, *d-* 'that' + an imperfect, or even a bare participle. For example:

<u>Syriac</u>: *ʿtīd d-nētē* 'he will come'; *da-ʿtīd l-mehwā* 'that will be'[121]

<u>JPA</u>: *malkā mšîḥā d-ʿtîd l-mêqām* 'the King Messiah who will arise' (Targ.

---

[117]Simeone-Senelle and Vanhove (1997: 86-87).
[118]Ibid.; Johnstone (1977: 145).
[119]Wright (1967 I §361b; II §8c), W. Fischer (2002: 105). Rundgren's (1955: 122-23) derivation of *sa-* from a demonstrative element *s-* should be rejected.
[120]Segal (1927: 167).
[121]Payne Smith (1903: 431).

Nf., Gen. 49:11);[122] *d-ʿtyd l-mqwm* 'who will arise' (Pal. Targ., Exod. 17:16); *d-Y ʿtîd ʿābed* 'what the Lord will (or: is about to) do' (Pal. Targ., Gen. 41:25)[123]

The construction is found in Mishnaic Hebrew as well, where it is undoubtedly an Aramaic borrowing.[124] In none of the languages is the construction with *ʿtîd* at all common, except apparently in post-Mishnaic, pre-Modern Hebrew.[125]

3.2.7.4 Purpose Clause > Future

In Tigrinya, the source of the future tense construction is a purpose clause. A purpose clause is formed with the particle *kə-* plus a verb in the imperfect:[126]

Tigrinya: *kəbällaʿ ʾədälli ʾalloku* 'I want to eat' (lit., 'that-I-eat I-want I-am') (*kəbällaʿ < kə + ʾəbälläʿ*)

The form with prefixed *kə-* can, by extension, also be used in conjunction with the copula to express the future tense:

Tigrinya: *kəbällaʿ ʾəyyä* 'I will eat'

The extension of a purpose clause to a future tense construction COPULA + PURPOSE CLAUSE can be compared to an English sentence like 'I am to eat lunch with him tomorrow', where this use of the infinitive probably stems from its use in purpose clauses, e.g., 'I want to eat'.

The Tigrinya particle *kə-* is possibly to be connected with the Semitic subordinating conjunction reflected in Biblical Hebrew *kî*. According to Leslau, however, the ultimate source of this *kə-* is *ʾənka* (in Geʿez, 'so, then, therefore').[127] If Leslau is correct, we are dealing with two stages of grammaticalization in Tigrinya; first a particle has come to mark a subordinate purpose clause, and then via re-grammaticalization, the use of the particle has been extended to express future time.

The expression of the future in Tigré essentially parallels that of Tigrinya. In Tigré the particle *ʾəgəl*, like Tigrinya *kə*, functions as what S. Raz has called a

---

[122]See Sokoloff (2002a: 422).
[123]See Fassberg (1990: §129g). In the example from Gen. 41:25, I transcribe *ʿābed*, even though the text has a *pataḥ* under the *ʿayin*, since this text uses *pataḥ* for long and short *a*.
[124]Segal (1927: 167).
[125]Ibid.
[126]Leslau (1941: 89-90).
[127]Leslau (1941: 91) does not explicitly say so, but his evidence (especially §108d) makes this clear. See Tropper (2002a: §45.81) for Geʿez usage of *ʾənka*. See also M. Cohen (1924: 71) who connects Tigrinya *kə* with Arabic *kay* 'so that'.

quasi-infinitive marker in a construction like:

> Tigré: *səʾlika ʾəgəl ʾənsaʾ ʾəfatte* 'I want to take your picture' (lit., 'your picture that I take I want')

This quasi-infinitive then can be used with the copula *tu* to express the future:[128]

> Tigré: *fagər basaʿ ʾəgəl nigis tu* 'Tomorrow we will go to Massawa (= *basaʾ*)'[129]

The word *ʾəgəl* is also a preposition meaning 'to, for'. It is most likely to be connected with Arabic *li-ʾajli* 'because of, for the sake of' (cf. also *li-ʾajli ʾan* 'so that').[130] In Tigré, we also find the form grammaticalized as the direct object marker (see below, 5.1.6).

A purpose clause also seems to be the source of the future marker *ta-* (variants *tə* or *də-*) in *qəltu* Mesopotamian dialects of Arabic. The source lexeme is *ḥattā*, which followed by the subjunctive means 'so that, in order that' both in literary Arabic and in some colloquial dialects. For example:

> Modern Standard Arabic: *ḥaḍarū ḥattā yaḥṣulū ʿalā š-šahādati* 'they came to get the degree' (lit., 'in order that they get')[131]

> Yemeni Arabic: *maʿāhum filūs ḥattā yištaraw al-ayšā hāðī* 'they have money to buy things' (lit., 'so that they [can] buy things')[132]

Examples of its grammaticalized form as a future marker are:

> *qəltu*-Arabic (Mardin): *taʾašrab* 'I will drink'
>
> *qəltu*-Arabic (Siirt): *təyāxev* 'he will take'[133]
>
> *qəltu*-Arabic (Jewish ʿAqra): *tašrab* 'I will drink', *tətəšrab* 'you (m.sg.) will drink'[134]

In one sub-dialect of *qəltu*-Arabic, that of Tuzlagözü, the future marker is *lē-*. This derives from the conjunction *li-/la-*, which has the same function as *ḥattā*. This example more closely parallels the situation in Tigré, in that the basic function of Arabic *li-/la-*, like Tigré *ʾəgəl*, is as a preposition 'to, for'.

---

[128] Raz (1983: 68-69).

[129] Raz has *ʾnigis*, but this is clearly a misprint.

[130] Leslau (1945b: 184 n. 104), with further references. Leslau also suggests a connection with Hebrew *biglal* 'because of', which is possible.

[131] Abboud and McCarus (1983: 384-85); Badawi, Carter, and Gully (2004: 626-27).

[132] Watson (1993: 358-59).

[133] Jastrow (1978: 302-3). Fischer and Jastrow (1980: 154).

[134] Jastrow (1990: 65).

Modern Standard Arabic: *qaddamū ṭalaban li-yaʿmalū* 'they submitted a request to work' (lit., 'in order that they work')[135]

qəltu-Arabic (Tuzlagözü): *lēṛō* 'he will go'; *lētṛō* 'you will go'; *laṛō* 'I will go'[136]

3.2.8 Copulae

There is no verb 'to be' reconstructable for Proto-Semitic.[137] In the ancient Semitic languages, the present tense of 'be' need not be expressed verbally;[138] the copula is simply understood, as in the following examples:

Akkadian: *Ḫammurapi šarrum ša Bābilim* 'Hammurapi is/was (the) king of Babylon'[139]

Biblical Hebrew: *YHWH malkēnû* 'The Lord is our king' (Isaiah 33:22)[140]

Arabic: *'al-waladu ṣaġīrun* 'The boy is small'[141]

Geʿez: *ziʾana māy* 'The water is ours'[142]

Copulae do, however, develop in some languages via grammaticalization.

3.2.8.1 Copulae from Independent Pronouns

In many languages, a redundant, or appositional, personal pronoun can act as a pseudo-copula.[143] In older Aramaic dialects, these appositional pronouns must be grammaticalized to some degree, as they develop special reduced enclitic forms (see above, 3.2.4):[144]

Syriac: *malka-w* 'He is king' (< *malkā hū*); *ʾenā (ʾ)nā malkā* 'I am the king'

On the use of these enclitic pronouns to mark person for the present tense, see

---

[135] Abboud and McCarus (1983: 385); Badawi, Carter, and Gully (2004: 617).
[136] Jastrow (1978: 303-4).
[137] The root *√hwy is Proto-Semitic, as evidenced by Akkadian *ewûm* 'to become', Hebrew *hāyā* 'to be', and Aramaic *hwā* 'to be'. However, given its meaning in Akkadian, and its restricted use in Hebrew and Aramaic, in PS this probably had the meaning 'to become', and cannot be considered a true copula.
[138] See, for example, Huehnergard (1986) and bibliography therein.
[139] Huehnergard (1986), Huehnergard (1997: §2.5).
[140] Gesenius (§14).
[141] W. Fischer (2002: 189-91).
[142] Dillmann (1907: §194), Tropper (2002a: 213-15).
[143] See Lipiński (1997: §50.9).
[144] Nöldeke (1904a: §64, §312).

above (3.2.4).

Ge'ez also makes use of the personal pronouns to express a copula, though the third person can often be used as a generic form, regardless of the subject:[145]

> Ge'ez: *zəntu wə'ətu walda nəguś* 'This is the son of the king'; *'ana nəguś 'ana* OR *'ana wə'ətu nəguś* 'I am the king'

For the first two of these three Ge'ez examples, we can still legitimately call this an appositional construction. With the latter, however, the third person pronoun has clearly become a grammaticalized copula. This is a nice demonstration of the tendency of grammaticalization to neutralize gender, number, and person distinctions, i.e., decategorialization. The tendency for phonological reduction can be seen in the Tigré, where the third person pronouns have also clearly been grammaticalized as a copula:[146]

> Tigré: *ḥabru qäyəḥ tu* 'His color is red'; *'aman ta* 'It is true' (cf. *hətu* 'he', *həta* 'she')

3.2.8.2 Copulae from Presentative Particles

Amharic and some North African dialects of Arabic provide nice examples of a copula which has been grammaticalized from a presentative particle, a development which is not included in Heine and Kuteva's *World Lexicon of Grammaticalization* (2002).

In Amharic, the present copula has a base *n(ä)-*, which is followed by suffixes that are essentially those of object pronouns.[147] Examples are:

> Amharic: *yäne näw* 'It is mine'; *bäṭam ṭänkarra näññ* 'I am very strong'

For the source of this base *n(ä)-*, we can compare the Ge'ez presentation particle *na-* 'behold, here is, there is', as in:[148]

---

[145]Dillmann (1907: §194), Lambdin (1978: 29-30), Tropper (2002a: 215-17).
[146]Leslau (1945b: 193). Lipiński (1997: §49.19) has a very different view on the origin of the Tigré copula.
[147]Leslau (1995: 271-73).
[148]Leslau (1987: 380) supports this etymology. Lipiński (1997: §§49.18-21) suggests that the *n-* of the Amharic base goes back to an Afro-Asiatic pronominal element. This is quite conjectural, and positing the Amharic copula as deriving directly from an AA particle is far-fetched. There are many stages of development between AA and Amharic, so without Semitic evidence from nodes closer to AA, our derivation from the Proto-Ethiopic node is much more likely.

Ge'ez: *naya 'amata 'əgzi'abḥer* 'Here I am, the servant of God' (Luke 1:38)[149]

In some dialects of Algerian, Tunisian, and Moroccan Arabic, we also find a presentative particle *ṛā-* (+ object suffixes) that has become a grammaticalized copula. The source of this particle is frozen masculine singular imperative of the Classical Arabic verb *ra'ā* 'to see', which itself does not otherwise survive in these dialects. The presumed derivation is 'See me (as/being) X' → 'I am X'. In each dialect, the use of the copula differs slightly. In Algerian, this copula is used if the subject is a pronoun or, with a nominal subject, if the copula has the rough meaning of 'be located, be in a state/condition, exist'. For example:

Algerian Arabic: *ṛāni ṣġēr* 'I am young'; *Moḥammed ṛāh b-ḫēr* 'Mohammed is well'; *ṛāha mṛēḍa* 'she is sick'; *hūwa ṛāh f-əl ḥammām* 'He is at the bath-house'; *ṛāni bīn ət-ṭabla w-əl-kursī* 'I'm between the table and the chair'[150]

In Tunisian, this copula is used to convey a sense of notification or warning (*avertissement*).[151] Note also that the masculine singular form can optionally serve as a generic form for any person:

Tunisian Arabic: *əl-waqt ṛāw qrīb* 'The time is near'; *ṛāni mṛīḍ* '(Know that) I am sick'; *ṛāw mrīḍ* '(Know that) I am/you are/he is sick'

Moroccan seems to have a distribution similar to that of Tunisian, though this particle is also used as in Algerian:[152]

Moroccan Arabic: *əl-mudīra ṛāni āna hīya* 'The director, it's me!' (lit., 'I am she'); *fäyn ṛāk* 'where are you?'; *ṛāni f-əs-sṭaḥ* 'I am on the terrace'; *ṛāni mṛēḍa* 'I am sick'

The presentative particle from which this copula derives is also attested in these and other dialects of Arabic, for example:

Moroccan Arabic: *ṛāni* 'here I am'[153]
Saudi Arabic: *'arni* 'here I am'[154]

---

[149]Tropper (2002a: §45.6; 2002b: 83) compares Ge'ez *na-* (correctly, in my view) to Hebrew *hinnē*, *hēn*, Arabic *'inna* and their cognates in other languages. See below, 4.3, for a discussion of these particles and their possible source.
[150]Tapiéro (2002: 14). See also Grand'henry (1972: 134).
[151]D. Cohen (1975: 138). See also Singer (1984: 258-59).
[152]Caubet (1993 II: 25-27, 35-36, 42).
[153]Harrell (1962: 215).

A parallel use of the presentative particle as a copula is found occasionally with Hebrew *hinnē*, as in:

> Biblical Hebrew: *wa-'ănî hinənî mēbî(') 'et-ham-mabbûl* 'For my part, I am about to bring the flood' (Gen. 6:17)

It is noteworthy that Algerian exhibits a further grammaticalization of the type discussed above (3.2.3.1), namely the use of *ṛā-* as an auxiliary verb to express the present progressive (see also below, 6.4.2). For example:

> Algerian Arabic: *ṛāh ixdem* 'He is working'; *wāš ṛāk ṯhawwəs* 'What are you looking for?'[155]

3.2.8.3 Copulae from Existential Particles

The NWS existential particles, Hebrew *yēš*, Aramaic *'îtay* (later *'ît*), Ugaritic *iṯ*, and their negative counterparts, develop copular functions, most fully in Aramaic. In this capacity, they appear with pronominal suffixes (or, in Ugaritic, with the subject markers of the suffix-conjugation verb) to indicate the logical subject. There are in fact but a handful of examples in Biblical Hebrew and just three known in Ugaritic,[156] though such usage is more common in Mishnaic Hebrew, probably under Aramaic influence. Examples are:

> Biblical Hebrew: *'et-'ăšer yešnô pō 'immānû* 'with those who are here with us' (Deut. 29:14); *'im-yešnô bā-'āreṣ* 'if he is in the land' (1 Sam. 23:23)

> Ugaritic: *'ṯt 'mn mlkt* 'I am with the queen' (KTU 2.13:15); *'mn mlk ... 'ṯt* 'I am with the king' (KTU 2.30:14); *i iṯt aṯrt* 'where is Athirat?' (KTU 1.14: IV: 38)[157]

> Biblical Aramaic: *'im-biśrā' lā' 'îtôhî* '[whose dwelling] is not with the flesh' (Dan. 2:11)

This construction became extremely common in Aramaic, as we find already in

---

[154]Prochazka (1988: 226).

[155]Tapiéro (2002: 97). Algerian also uses the inherited auxiliary *kāna* 'be', as other Arabic dialects do, to express an imperfect, pluperfect, and future perfect..

[156]Hebrew: Joüon (1996: §102k); Ugaritic: Tropper (2000: §75.212.3, note; 2002c: 84 n. 233). The Ugaritic examples were first pointed out by De Moor (1965: 357-58).

[157]This final example may very well be 'as Athirat exists'. This alternative translation is endorsed by De Moor (1965: 357) and Tropper (2002c: 83). For a discussion of this difficult passage, see Caquot et al. (1974: 530 n. w), and further discussion in Caquot et al. (1989: 322-23 n. 9).

Syriac.¹⁵⁸ Examples are:

> Syriac: *ʾītay sabbā* 'I am old' (Luke 1:18); *ʾen ʾa(n)t lā(ʾ) ʾītayk mšīḥā* 'if you are not the Messiah' (John 1:25); *ʾītay ʿabdā d-nāmusā da-ḥṭītā* 'I am a servant of the law of sin' (Rom. 7:25)

The past copula is formed from *ʾīt* plus an inflected form of the verb *hwā* 'to be':

> Syriac: *kad ḥaṭṭāye ʾītayn (h)wayn* 'when we were sinners' (Rom. 5:8)

In fact, many Neo-Aramaic dialects preserve this copular construction, though the system of subject marking has been remodeled. In the third persons, most Neo-Aramaic dialects mark the subject with preposition *l-*; this has probably been remodeled after the verbal system in which subjects are marked with *l-* (e.g., Turoyo *ftəḥ-li* 'I opened', *ftəḥ-lan* 'we opened'; see above, 3.2.3.2). Examples are:

> NENA (Qaraqosh): *bāš-ilə* 'he is good' (*ilə* < *ʾīt leh*); *ʾaxela* 'she is here' (< *hakā ʾīt lāh*); *načar-iwa* 'he was fierce' (*iwa* < *ʾīt hwā*)¹⁵⁹

Finally, we turn to the Akkadian verb *bašûm*. This verb is normally existential in meaning, i.e., 'to exist, be present', but there are a handful of cases where it is used as a simple copula. For example:

> Akkadian: *kīma ilim tabašši* 'you are like a god'; *mišil maṣṣarti mūšum ibašši* 'it was half (way through) the watch, night'¹⁶⁰

The verb is of debatable origin, but it has long been suggested that the source is the preposition **ba-* 'in' + 3ms. *-šu* 'him'. This same construction is the source of Geʿez *bo* 'there is/are', which has long been compared with the Akkadian.¹⁶¹ A parallel can also be drawn with modern Arabic dialectal (e.g., Syrian) *fī* 'there is/are', which ultimately derives from *fīhi* 'in it'. See below (3.4.5.2) for more discussion on these existentials. Clearly, some form of this construction existed in Proto-Semitic, though it is unclear whether we should reconstruct a verb, as in Akkadian, or an uninflected particle, as in Geʿez. A similar dilemma arises with

---

[158] Nöldeke (1904a: §§301-308).

[159] Khan (2002: 125-28). For a discussion of the forms NENA copulae, see Khan (1999: 103-4; 2002: 13-16).

[160] Gilgameš OB Penn ii:11; Atraḥasis i:70. Many thanks to J. Huehnergard for bringing these examples to my attention.

[161] The earliest note on this seems to be Schrader (1872: 304 n. 1). See also Wright (1874: 109), Haupt (1906: 259) and von Soden (1965-81: 112). Note that in Old Akkadian writing of *bašûm*, the signs used for the sibilant in this root alternate between *š-* (= PS **θ*) and *s-*, obscuring the original form (R. Hasselbach, p.c.).

the Akkadian verb *išûm* 'to have' and the NWS existentials represented be Hebrew *yēš*. The relative age of the Akkadian form, along with the very common tendency of copulae to become existentials (cf. below, 3.4.5.3) might lead one to suggest that the Akkadian verb preceded the Ge'ez existential. However, the Arabic form *fī*, and examples like it, would indicate that a direct grammaticalization from 'in it' to 'there is' is more likely, and that the Akkadian verb shows a later change. Finally, the independent creation of Arabic *fī* also might lead one to suggest that the Akkadian and Ge'ez forms could very well be independent innovations.

This leads us to Assyrian dialectal verb *laššu* 'not to be'. This is usually assumed to be formed from the negative particle *lā* + *išû*.[162] However, this derivation is problematic. Akkadian *išûm* 'to have' is most likely to be connected with the NWS existential attested in Hebrew *yēš*, Aramaic *'ītay* (< *'itay*), and Ugaritic *iṯ*, which suggests a root containing PS *θ. Yet Assyrian *laššu* is seemingly to be connected with the Arabic negative copula *laysa*, which requires a PS *s or *^ts. Many scholars have noted this incompatibility.[163] The explanation is actually not that complicated. Consider the Aramaic negative existential *layt*; this is also incompatible with the Arabic form. Yet in this case, it is clear that we simply have an intra-Aramaic development of the negative particle *lā* + the existential *'īt*, i.e., *lā 'īt* > **lāyit* > **lāyt* > *layt*. Might Assyrian *laššu* also be an independent development of *lā* + *išû*? Even better perhaps, since Akkadian *išûm* means 'to have', not 'to be', would be to suggest instead that, while still an independent development, *laššu* is in fact modeled after *bašû*. Thus if *laššu*, like Aramaic *layt*, is an internal development, there need not be any regular correspondence with Arabic *laysa*.

3.3 Prepositions

3.3.1 PAA, PS

Prepositions which are clearly the product of grammaticalized nominal forms can be reconstructed for PS, possibly even PAA. Egyptian *m-q3b* 'in the midst of' (*q3b* 'intestine') is cognate with Hebrew *bə-qéreb* (*qéreb* 'interior, intestine'), Ugaritic (*b-)qrb*, and Akkadian *ina qereb*, all meaning 'in the midst of'. Other such constructions exist as well, though one might argue that they are typologically common and therefore not ascribable to PAA. Examples are:

---

[162]Von Soden (1995: §111a).
[163]Recently, Testen (2000: 86 n. 3), Măcelaru (2003). See Blau (1972) for a review of scholarship and a theory which differs from that offered here.

Egyptian *ḥr ib* 'in the middle of' (*ib* 'heart'), Akkadian *ina libbi* 'idem' (*libbu* 'heart')

Egyptian *m-ʿ* 'in the hand of; together with; from' (*ʿ* 'hand'), Hebrew *bə-yad* 'in(to) the hand of; by (instrumental)' and *miy-yad* 'from (the hand of)' (*yād* 'hand'), Ugaritic *bd* (< **b-yd*) 'in/from the hands of', Akkadian *ina qāti* 'in the possession of' (*qātum* 'hand')[164]

For Proto-Semitic, there are both simple and compound prepositions which developed by grammaticalization from nominal or verbal roots. Examples are:

panū- 'face': Ugaritic *pn* (or *l-pn*), Hebrew *li-pnê*, Akkadian *ina pāni* 'before, in front of'

root √*ʿly* 'to go up': Hebrew *ʿal*, Akkadian *eli*, Arabic *ʿalā*, Aramaic *ʿal* 'on, upon'[165]

3.3.2 Individual Languages

In every Semitic language there are both simple and compound prepositions that have developed via grammaticalization. Below are listed just a small number of examples from a variety of languages. For a more comprehensive treatment of Semitic prepositions, see Brockelmann (1908-13 II: §§259-265), Lipiński (1997: 459-70), or Voigt (1999).[166]

Akkadian: *ina muḫḫi* 'on, over', *ana muḫḫi* 'toward' (< *muḫḫum* 'skull'); *ṣēr* 'on', *ana ṣēr, ṣēriš* 'towards, against' (< *ṣērum* 'back'; cf. MSA below)

Classical Arabic: *ʿinda* 'at, by, *chez*' (probably < root √*ʿmd* 'to support, prop'; cf. Heb. √*ʿmd* 'to stand', *ʿimmādî* 'with me');[167] *janba* 'beside, next to'(< *janb* 'side'); *miṯla* 'like' (< *miṯl* 'image, likeness'); *fawqa* 'above, over' (< root √*fwq* 'to surpass, be superior'); *fī* 'in' (very likely from PS **pV-* 'mouth')

---

[164]While Eg. *ib* and Sem. **libb-* are cognate, Eg. *ʿ* 'hand' and Sem. **yad-* 'hand' are not to be connected. Egyptian /ʿ/ is not the regular correspondent of Sem. /d/, as many today believe (e.g., Rössler 1971, Loprieno 1995). For more on Egypto-Semitic sound correspondences see Rubin (1999), Takács (1999). For more on Egypto-Semitic morphology see Rubin (2004).

[165]It may also be reasonable to suggest that the preposition is primary and the verbal root is secondary.

[166]Voigt includes some discussion of grammaticalization.

[167]Eitan (1928: 49-50) proposes instead an original *ʿan yad* 'from the hand of'.

Hebrew: *lə-pî* 'according to' (< *peh* 'mouth'); *bə-tôk* 'inside' (< *tāwek* 'middle')

Aramaic (Syriac): *ʿal ge(n)b* 'beside, near' (< *ge(n)b* 'side, bank'); *gaw* 'within, inside' (< *gaw* 'interior, innards');[168] *l-ʾappay* 'towards', *ʿal appay* 'upon; in front of; for the sake of' (< *ʾappē* 'face' < PS **ʾanp-* 'nose'); *bātar* 'after' (< **b-ʾatar* 'in the place of' < PS **aθar-* 'place')

NENA (Arbel): *reš* 'upon' (< *reš* 'head');[169] *geb* 'with, chez' (< earlier 'beside, near' < 'side'; cf. Syriac *ge(n)b*, Arabic *janb* above)

Ge'ez: *mā'əkala* 'in the midst of' (< *mā'əkal* 'center, middle'); *wəsta* 'in, into' (< *wəsṭ* 'interior')[170]

Amharic: *bä ... əgər* 'instead of' (< *əgər* 'foot'); *bä ... bet* 'according to, in the opinion of' (< *bet* 'house'); *ğarba* 'behind' (< *ğarba* 'back')

MSA: Jibbali *ʿamq* (variant *ʿaq*) 'in , at', Soqoṭri *b-ʿamq d-* 'between' (< *ʿamq* 'middle'; cf. Hebrew *ʿémeq* 'valley'); Mehri *ṭar / ẓar* 'on' (< 'back', cf. Akkadian *ṣēr* above)

3.4 Particles

3.4.1 Relatives[171]

3.4.1.1 Demonstrative > Relative

We can reconstruct for Proto-Semitic a determinative-relative pronoun **θū* or **ðū*, which was inflected for case, gender, and number. Based on their use in East Semitic, as well as in Arabic, we can safely say that these forms governed genitive nouns or nominalized clauses, either absolutely or in apposition to a preceding noun.[172] The initial consonant is uncertain; Akkadian reflects an initial **θ-*, while the whole of West Semitic reflects an initial **ð-*. In post-Old Akkadian, we find simply a frozen (accusative) form *ša* as the sole relative. Likewise, Ge'ez exhibits a frozen (accusative) form *za-*, and Aramaic exhibits a

---

[168] Rubba (1994) discusses these forms in Aramaic and Neo-Aramaic.

[169] This is really a calque from Kurdish *ser* 'head; on, upon' (Khan 1999: 10, 191). We might then call this "instant" grammaticalization, since it was borrowed and not natively developed; perhaps it is best not called grammaticalization at all.

[170] Akkadian *ištu* 'from, out of' probably shares this etymology (Brockelmann 1908-13 II: §260; Leslau 1987: 620).

[171] See also 3.4.3.1, on the grammaticalization RELATIVE > GENITIVE EXPONENT.

[172] Huehnergard (forthcoming).

frozen (genitive) form *dī* (later *d-*). Reflexes of **ð-* are also found in Ugaritic, early Byblian Phoenician, Biblical Hebrew (rarely), OSA, and MSA.[173]

The relevant issue here is the origin of these determinative-relative pronouns. These forms are connected with the series of near demonstrative pronouns in West Semitic, reflected in Hebrew *ze*, Geʻez *zə-*, Biblical Aramaic (f.sg.) *dā*, Arabic *(hā-)ðā*, etc. This connection between the relative series and the demonstrative series is quite obvious and has long been noted (cf. A. Fischer 1905b). The grammaticalization DEMONSTRATIVE > RELATIVE is extremely common; we can point to English 'that' as a simple parallel.

Some have suggested that this Proto-Semitic root is cognate with Ancient Egyptian *z* 'man' and *zt* 'woman'.[174] Phonologically this works, as Egyptian *z* normally corresponds to PS **ð*, and semantically it works as well. However, we are dealing here with a single consonant and a rough semantic correspondence, so we cannot say with any certainty that these forms should be related. It remains a possibility however, and if correct, would suggest an interesting grammaticalization.

3.4.1.2 Locative > Locative Relative > General Relative

A few Semitic languages exhibit a relative pronoun which derives from a noun **ʾaθar-* 'place' (cf. Akkadian *ašrum*, Aramaic *ʾatrā* 'idem'). This development is best known from Biblical Hebrew, where *ʾăšer* has become the normal relative pronoun (and, later, complementizer), and the lexical form has been lost:

> Biblical Hebrew: *hā-ʾănāšîm ʾăšer bāʾû* 'the men who came' (Gen. 19:5); *ham-māqôm ʾăšer ʿāmad* 'the place where he had stood' (Gen. 19:27)

As J. Huehnergard has shown, the grammaticalization of this word also resulted in its phonetic reduction to *še-* (dialectal *ša-*), already in some early Hebrew dialects (cf. Judges 5:7).[175] In LBH and Mishnaic Hebrew, as well as in Modern Hebrew, this reduced form has replaced the full one. On the Phoenician relative, see the discussion in Huehnergard.

A relative from this same PS lexeme **ʾaθar-* is also found in Akkadian, though mainly limited to its more original (less generalized) locational relative function:[176]

---

[173] For further details, see Huehnergard (forthcoming), Pennacchietti (1968).
[174] See Ember (1917: 84; 1930: 85), M. Cohen (1947: 158). The Egyptian etymological dictionaries of Takács (1999: 177-78) and Vycichl (1983: 181) make no reference to this connection. Takács derives Egyptian *z* from an earlier *z3 < zl*.
[175] Huehnergard (forthcoming). See also Givón (1991).
[176] Von Soden (1995: §116f, §175a).

Akkadian: *imtaši ašar iwwaldu* 'he forgot where he was born'[177]

Akkadian (Old Assyrian): *ašar damqūni lū nīpuš* 'let us do what is proper'[178]

The locative relative use, as found in Akkadian, must have preceded the use of Hebrew *'ăšer* as a general relative pronoun. We can find close parallels to the Hebrew development, in languages such as German (dialectal), Danish, and Modern Greek, where the relative 'where' has become the normal relative.[179]

3.4.2 Negative Markers

In Arabic, the interrogative pronoun *mā* 'what?' has been grammaticalized as a negative particle.[180] Both functions are illustrated in the examples:

Classical Arabic: *mā tilka bi-yamīnika* 'what is that in your right hand?'; *mā ju'tu* 'I am not (have not become) hungry'

Lipiński (1997: §47.15) suggests that the passage from interrogative to negative can already be seen in Hebrew, in a phrase like:

Biblical Hebrew: *ma-bbə-yādî rā'ā* 'what evil is in my hand?' (1 Sam. 26:18)

However, while such a construction is certainly the source of the Arabic negative *mā* (that is to say, 'what evil is in my hand' → 'there is no evil in my hand'), there is no evidence for such a reanalysis in Hebrew. The best translation of the above Hebrew example is simply 'what evil is in my hand?', i.e., 'what am I guilty of?'.

In some Modern Arabic dialects, there is another grammaticalization of a negative marker. We saw in 3.1.6 that Arabic *šay'un* 'thing' gave rise to a host of interrogatives in the modern dialects. The same lexeme is also the source for a negative marker, used in conjunction with an older negative particle. For example:

---

[177] Gilgameš OB Penn ii:5.
[178] *CAD* A/2 415a, cited in Huehnergard (forthcoming: n. 31).
[179] Compare Danish: *Det er en vin der kan drikkes nu.* 'This is a wine that can be drunk now.' (Allan, Holmes, and Lundskær-Nielsen 2000: 65-67); or Modern Greek: O άνθρωπος που είδαμε στην ταβέρνα 'The man whom I saw at the tavern' (Philippaki-Warburton, Holton, and Mackridge 1997: 98-99, 443-45). Joüon (1913: 130 n. 4) noted this Greek parallel, as well as the parallel use of *wo* in dialects of German.
[180] See W. Fischer (2002: 173) for its exact usage. Faber (1991) disagrees with this etymology, and suggests that the negative *mā* derives from a common Afro-Asiatic negative particle. Her evidence is unconvincing.

Egyptian Arabic: *katab* 'he wrote', *ma-katab-š* 'he didn't write'[181]

Yemeni Arabic: *(bi-)yišrabū* 'they drink', *mā yišrabū-š* 'they don't drink'[182]

This change is discussed in detail by Obler (1975: 28-44). As she points out, this is parallel to French *rien* 'nothing' < Latin *rem* (acc. of *rēs* 'thing').

The negative particles *ma* and *-š* are combined into a single particle in various syntactical environments, including non-verbal sentences.[183] For example:

Egyptian Arabic: *miš ana* 'not me' (cf. French *pas moi*)

There is no evidence that this negitival *-š* should be equated with the Ethiopic suffix *–ssa*, as suggested by Lipiński (1997: §54.4).

In (post-Mishnaic) Rabbinic and Medieval Hebrew, we find a different kind of negative particle that has been grammaticalized. The lexeme *šum* 'name', an Aramaized form of Biblical Hebrew *šēm*, seems to have taken on the more general meaning 'something, anything', from which point it was grammaticalized as an indefinite adjective 'any'. With this meaning, it became especially common in negative statements, translatable as '(not) any' (German *kein*). In Modern Hebrew, its use is almost exclusively as a negative, either in an otherwise negated clause, or as a freestanding negative. For example:

Medieval Hebrew: *w-'m tr'h bw šwm ṭ'wt* 'and if you see in it [this book] any mistake'[184]

Modern Hebrew: *'eyn li šum kesef* 'I don't have any money'; *hayu ne'umim, 'ax šum havtaxot* 'There were speeches, but no promises'

In Modern Hebrew, negative *šum* is also found is the very common fixed phrases *šum davar* 'nothing' and *b-šum maqom* 'nowhere'.

3.4.3 Genitive Exponents

In Proto-Semitic, a genitival relationship between nouns was expressed by the construct phrase; there was no special genitive particle like English 'of'. This construction exists and remains widely used in most Semitic languages. In the languages which retain case (Akkadian and Arabic in the following examples), the genitive case marks the governed noun. Examples are:

---

[181] Abdel-Massih et al. (1979: 133-39).

[182] Watson (1993: 260-63).

[183] The form *miš* is actually paralleled nicely by English *not* < Old English *nā wiht* 'not a whit (thing)'.

[184] From the introduction to *Ḥovot ha-Levavot*, Judah ibn Tibbon's twelfth-century translation of an eleventh-century Arabic work by Baḥya ben Joseph ibn Paquda.

Akkadian: *bēl bītim* 'the owner of the house' (lit., owner house)[185]
Hebrew: *bēt ham-melek* 'the house of the king' (lit., house the-king)
Arabic: *kalbu r-rajuli* 'the man's dog' (lit., dog the-man)

In many languages a special genitive exponent developed, often probably as a result of the loss of case-marking. There are two main sources for such words, RELATIVE PRONOUNS and a GRAMMATICALIZED NOUN 'property' or 'thing'.

3.4.3.1 Relative > Genitive Exponent

From the relative pronoun we find:

Akkadian *ša*: *bēlum ša bītim* 'the owner of the house'[186]
Ge'ez *za-*: *wangēl za-'əgzi'əna* 'the gospel of our Lord'[187]
Bib. Aram. *dî*: *nəbiyyayyā dî 'ēlāhā* 'the prophets of God' (Ezra 5:2)[188]
Mehri *ð̣-*: *kīš ð̣-tōmər* 'sack of dates'[189]

In Ge'ez and Mehri, the plural relative pronouns (*'əlla* and *l-*, respectively) can be used after plural nouns, though the singular is commonly used as a generic form. Ge'ez also has a feminine singular relative (*'ənta*) which can be used after feminine nouns. The derivation of this example of grammaticalization (missing from Heine and Kuteva 2002) would have been:

'the house, the one of the king' → 'the house of the king',

after which the determinative/relative pronoun was generalized and, in many cases, its inflection (for gender and number) lost.[190]

On Hebrew *šel* 'of' and Moroccan Arabic *dyāl/d* 'of' see below (3.4.4).

---

[185] One could also say that 'owner-of house' is a literal rendering, since *bēl*, with its lack of case ending, indicates that it is in a construct relationship. The same applies to the Hebrew and Arabic examples.

[186] Von Soden (1995: §137). In Old Akkadian, the particle was declined, making its origin as a determinative pronoun clear.

[187] Tropper (2002a: §52.44).

[188] Old Aramaic has <zy>, reflecting /ðī/ (Degen 1969: 60), while later Aramaic has simply *d-*.

[189] Simeone-Senelle in Hetzron (1995: 412).

[190] See Huehnergard (forthcoming).

3.4.3.2 Noun > Genitive Exponent[191]

Other languages derive their genitive markers from nouns meaning 'property' or 'thing'.[192] For example:

Iraqi, Kuwaiti Arabic *māl* (f. *mālat*, pl. *mālōt*) (< 'property', cf. Classical Arabic *māl*): *il-jāmʿa māl baḡdād* 'the University of Baghdad'[193]

Yemeni Arabic *ḥagg* (f. *ḥaggat*, m.pl. *ḥaggūn*, f.pl. *ḥaggāt*) (< 'property, possession', cf. CA *ḥaqq*): *ḥizwiyih ḥagg walad* 'the story of a boy'; (Northern) *im-farš ḥagg im-dīwān* 'the furniture of the living-room'[194]

Jewish Tunisian Arabic *(n)tāʿ* (< CA *matāʿ* 'property'): *əl-kläm ntäʿ ər-ṛāžəl* 'the words of the man'[195]

Damascus Syrian Arabic *šīt* (pl. *šiyāt*), Palestinian *šēt* (pl. *šayyūt*) (< 'thing', cf. CA *šayʾ*): *l-mōtōr šīt əs-sayyāra* 'the engine of the car'[196]

Chadian Arabic *hanā* (f. *hint*) (< 'thing', cf. CA *hana*): *bēt hanā Mūsa* 'Musa's house'[197]

Tigrinya and Tigré *nāy* (< 'property', cf. Geʿez *nəwāy*): Tigrinya *maṣḥaf*

---

[191] As most of the examples to follow are from Arabic, I will mention here that Harning (1980) is a very fine treatment of the Arabic genitive exponents, though her discussion deals mainly with syntax rather than historical development. She is quite aware of the historical development, however, and mentions (p. 19) that there are two sources for the exponent, as I have done here. None of my data were taken from Harning, whose work I was made aware of after I had compiled my own. Harning remains the definitive work on Arabic genitive exponents. See also Brustad (2000: 70-88) for an excellent discussion of the syntax of the Moroccan, Egyptian, Syrian, and Kuwaiti forms, along with many good examples. Also see Brockelmann (1908-13 II: §161) for an early discussion of many of these forms.

[192] See Heine and Kuteva (2002: 245-46, 296; also 2005: 203) for these words becoming possessives in other languages, such as Haitian Creole and Thai.

[193] Erwin (1963: 375-78).

[194] Watson (1993: 177, 200-24), Behnstedt (1987: 62-63). As Watson notes, the gender and number distinctions are only maintained in northern dialects, for which see Behnstedt. Behnstedt uses the symbol *ś* to respresent a retroflex *š*.

[195] D. Cohen (1977: 252-53). Singer (1984: 441) gives a form *mtāʿ*. For *mtaʿ/ntaʿ* in Jewish Algerian Arabic, see M. Cohen (1912: 364).

[196] Cowell (1964: 490). Obler (1975: 68-70) and Lipiński (1997: §51.19) support this etymology, while Brockelmann (1908-13 II: §161aβ) is unsure. Grotzfeld (1965: 92) notes (already forty years ago) that this lexeme is dying out in Damascene.

[197] Jullien de Pommerol (1999: 100-1).

nāy mamhər 'the teacher's book'; Tigré *nāy 'ətyopya ğewografi* 'geography of Ethiopia'.[198]

As some of the grammars referring to the above (Arabic) cases note, the masculine singular can in many cases be used as a generic form.

In Syrian and Lebanese Arabic, a noun *taba'* (in CA 'follower') has been grammaticalized. This noun most likely acquired the meaning of 'belonging, possession' under the influence of an earlier periphrastic construction *tābi' l-* 'belonging to':[199]

> Syrian Arabic *taba'* (pl. *taba'ūl*, *taba'āt*): *baṭṭāriyye taba' bīl* 'a flashlight battery'.[200]

For the grammaticalization of 'belonging to' into a genitive marker, we can compare the Tok Pisin use of *bilong* (< English *belong*), as in *buk bilong man* 'the man's book'.[201] For a parallel to the use of Syrian/Lebanese *taba'* in idiomatic expressions like *huwwe taba' niswān* 'he is a ladies man' (lit., 'he of women'), we might compare Tok Pisin *man bilong buk* 'a bookish man'.[202]

The Egyptian Arabic genitive exponent *bitā'* (f. *bitā'it*, pl. *bitū'*)[203] is traditionally derived from *matā'* 'property', and this would certainly be feasible given the above examples.[204] The use of *matā'* (or derivation thereof) as a possessive in North African dialects supports this theory. But it seems to me that a metathesis of the *taba'* root attested in the Levantine dialects to the east is perhaps also a legitimate possibility and cannot be ruled out. Either way, we are dealing with an ultimate source lexeme which meant 'property'. It is also important to note that in current Egyptian, *bitā'* is also an independent lexeme meaning 'thing', a fact which highlights the semantic relationship between 'property' and 'thing'.

---

[198] Leslau (1941: 40-2), Raz (1983: 42). This derivation, with which Brockelmann (1908-13 II: §161b) and Leslau (1987: 410) agree, is against that of Rundgren (1955: 213), who sees a demonstrative origin.

[199] The basic meaning of *tābi'* is 'following'.

[200] Cowell (1964: 460, 489), Grotzfeld (1965: 92), Brustad (2000: 70-88). In Lebanese *taba'* is indeclinable (W.M. Thackston, p.c.), and even in Syrian this is often the case (Grotzfeld 1965: 92, Fischer and Jastrow 1980: 91). On the peculiar plural form *taba'ūl*, see Cowell (1964: 489 n. 1).

[201] Verhaar (1995: 194-95).

[202] Brustad (2000: 82). Brustad notes that constructions of this type are also found in Egyptian. On Tok Pisin, see Verhaar (1995: 197).

[203] Abdel-Massih et al. (1979: 15-19), Brustad (2000: 72). Abdel-Massih gives a f.sg. form *bitā'a*, as do Fischer and Jastrow (1980: 220); this is simply the isolated (i.e., non-construct) form of *bitā'it*.

[204] Brockelmann (1908-13 II: §161) and Lipiński (1997: §51.19).

Egyptian Arabic: *il-kitāb bitāʿ il-ʾustāz* 'the professor's book'; *malʿab it-tinis bitāʿ in-nādi* 'the tennis court of the club'

3.4.3.3 Genitive Exponents as Possessive Pronouns

Many of the genitive exponents discussed above can be combined with pronominal suffixes to form possessive adjectives and possessive pronouns. Some examples are:

Syrian Arabic: *iḍ-ḍābit tabaʿu* 'his officer', *hayy tabaʿna* 'this is ours'
Damascus Syrian Arabic: *šyāti hadōl* 'these are mine'
Iraqi Arabic: *ət-talafōn mālak* 'your telephone'
Yemeni Arabic: *is-sayyārit ḥaggī* 'my car'
Egyptian Arabic: *il-mišwār bitaʿha* 'its journey'
Chadian Arabic: *al-kalib da hanāku* 'this dog is yours'
Tigré: *nāye ʾikon* 'it is not mine'

Geʿez does essentially the same thing, though with a morpheme -*iʾa*- (of uncertain origin) attached to the relative, producing the bases *ziʾa*- (< *za* + *iʾa*), f.sg. *ʾəntiʾa*-, and pl. *ʾəlliʾa*-. It should also be noted that in Geʿez these are syntactically possessive pronouns, not adjectives.[205]

Geʿez: *beta ziʾahu* 'his house', *ziʾana māy* 'the water is ours'

Post-Biblical Hebrew and some Aramaic dialects (Biblical, Qumran, Targumic, CPA, Samaritan, Mandaic, Syriac) combine the relative with the preposition *l-* to form possessive pronouns and adjectives, resulting in Hebrew *šel-* and Aramaic *dīl-*.[206] Since the preposition *l-* is used for possession elsewhere (Hebrew *yēš lî*, Syriac *ʾīt lī* 'I have'), this essentially derives from a periphrastic construction: 'the X that is to me' → 'the X that is mine' → 'my X' (not uncommon in Bib. Heb., e.g., 1 Kings 4:2, *haś-śārîm ʾăšer lô* 'his officials'). Aramaic, as noted above, uses the simple relative *dî* (later *d-*) for non-pronominal genitival use, while Hebrew back-forms an independent *šel*, which is used for all genitives:

Modern Hebrew: *ha-bayit šel ha-melex* 'the king's house'; *ha-bayit sheli* 'my house'
Syriac: *ktābā dīl(y)* 'my own book'

---

[205] Lambdin (1978: 224), Tropper (2002a: §51.2).
[206] In Biblical and Qumran Aramaic, the relative *dî* is written separately from *l-*, while in other dialects they combine to form a single word.

Other dialects of Aramaic, including JPA, BTA, Turoyo, NWA (Ma'alula and Ǧubb'adin), and NENA use a form *dīd-* (or reflex thereof) instead of *dīl-*. Some (Sabar 2002: 141) have taken this to be an assimilatory shift of *dīl-* > *dīd-*, while others (Nöldeke 1875: 332 n. 2) derive *dīd-* from *d-* + *yad* 'hand',[207] and still others (T.O. Lambdin, p.c.) see a reduplication of the relative.

<u>JPA (Palestinian Talmudic)</u>: *sb dydk w-hb dydy* 'take yours and give mine'
<u>NENA (Qaraqosh)</u>: *susə didəḥ* 'his horse'

NWA (Bax'a) uses a construction *ći l-*,[208] identical in structure to (and cognate with) the *dīl-* of other Aramaic dialects (*ći < *ti < dī*). Since other NWA dialects use a reflex of *dīd-*, it seems likely that the Bax'a dialect developed this construction independently.

Tigré also exhibits a similar construction, *'əntəl* (often > *'əttəl*), from the feminine relative pronoun (Ge'ez *'ənta*) plus *l-*.[209]

<u>Tigré</u>: *'aḥa 'əntəlna ta* 'the cattle is ours'

Moroccan and at least some dialects of Algerian Arabic have a genitive exponent *dyāl* (variant *d*).[210] Some believe this particle to be a loan from Romance via Andalusian Arabic, but this seems unlikely. It is almost certainly a combination of a relative plus *l-*, thus identical in construction to (though totally independent of) Hebrew *šel* and Aramaic *dīl-*. M. Cohen (1912: 363) notes its demonstrative origin, but does not elaborate. The form of the exponent itself, in particular the *-yā-*, is difficult to explain;[211] but then grammaticalization often causes irregular and bizarre sound changes.

<u>Moroccan Arabic</u>: *l-wəld dyāl t-tažər* 'the son of the merchant'; *z-znaqi d-lə-mdina* 'the streets of the city'; *l-kās dyāli* 'my cup'

Brustad (2000: 85 n. 19) notes that many grammars claim *dyāl* is always, or almost always, used with pronominal suffixes. M. Cohen (1912: 324), in his discussion of Jewish Algerian, claims the same thing. Brustad dismisses these other works as mistaken, but it seems to me that we are simply dealing with a diachronic change. The form *dyāl*, like Aramaic *dīl-*, was indeed once only used with suffixes (strengthening the argument of the connection with the preposition

---

[207] No where else in Semitic does the word 'hand' mark possession, but see Heine and Kuteva (2000: 166) for examples from other language families.
[208] Arnold (1990: 47).
[209] Leslau (1945b: 189, and n. 114).
[210] Moroccan: Harrell (1962: 202-3); Algerian: M. Cohen (1912: 324, 363-64), Grand'henry (1972: 121). See also Harning (1980: 112, 129).
[211] See Harning (1980: 112-13) for a discussion of this etymology.

l-) but has been reanalyzed in exactly the same way as Hebrew *šel*, and can now function independently. This connection is not noted by Harning.

3.4.3.4 Genitive Exponents > Partitives

There are some examples of the genitive exponents being used with a partitive sense. In Moroccan Arabic we find *dyāl* used after the numbers two to ten (also optionally in conjunction with larger numbers) and in certain partitive expressions:[212]

> Moroccan Arabic: *tlāta d-əl-ktūb* 'three books'; *bəzzāf dyāl əš-šqa* 'a lot of work'

Partitive use is not limited to Moroccan. We also find, for example, Chadian Arabic *litīr hanā dihin* 'a liter of oil'.[213]

3.4.4 Possession

It is unclear whether a verb 'to have' should be reconstructed for Proto-Semitic. Akkadian has the verb *išûm* (see below, 3.4.5), but the remaining daughter languages lack such a verb and have grammaticalized various phrasal constructions to express this type of possession.

3.4.4.1 Locative > 'Have'

This change, which is very common typologically, is found in Arabic. The preposition *ʿinda* 'at, *chez*', is used already in Classical Arabic in the sense of 'have'. It remains widespread among the Modern Arabic dialects. For example:

> Classical Arabic: *ʿindaka lahā dawāʾun* 'you possess a remedy for it'[214]
> Moroccan Arabic: *ʿandu al-ktāb* 'he has the book'[215]
> Chadian Arabic: *indi wiléd* 'I have a child'[216]

Note that in Chadian, the prepositional function has been completely lost, and *indi* survives only in this possessive construction.

Another example of how this grammaticalization has been carried to completion can be seen in the way that this construction is treated syntactically in

---

[212] Caubet (1993 I: 150), Brustad (2000: 86).
[213] Jullien de Pommerol (1999: 101).
[214] W. Fischer (2002: 165).
[215] Caubet (1993 II: 51-52).
[216] Jullien de Pommerol (1999: 193).

some dialects. In order to see the verbal quality of this construction, as different from its prepositional origin, compare the following two sets of sentences from Moroccan Arabic:

<u>Moroccan Arabic</u>: *əl-ktāb ma ši ʿandu* 'the book is not at his place'
ma ʿandu-š əl-ktāb 'he doesn't have the book'

In the first example, the negative *ma ši* precedes the predicate of a nominal sentence. The second is negated as a verbal sentence, with *ma* preceding the "verb" and *-š* following. Similar cases can be seen in other dialects, for example in Lebanese, where 'have' is negated by *ma*, as a verbal phrase would be, rather than *muš*, as a non-verbal phrase:[217]

<u>Lebanese Arabic</u>: *ma ʿindi maṣāri* 'I don't have any money'

Geʿez also uses a locative preposition with pronominal suffixes to indicate possession, namely *ba-* 'in'.[218] The form with *ba-* can refer to present or past time, although a verb of existence can be used instead to make a past-tense meaning explicit (see below, 3.4.4.4). The logical object of the *ba-* construction is in the accusative case, showing that the grammaticalization has resulted in a pseudo-verbal construction. Note also that the present tense construction is negated with *ʾal*; this is the only occurrence of this common Semitic negative particle in Geʿez. This suggests that the construction is old. Examples of with *ba-* are:

<u>Geʿez</u>: *bəya beta* 'I have a house'; *bəʾsi botu kəlʾeta daqqa* 'a man had two sons' (Luke 15:11); *wa-ʾal-bomu wəluda* 'but they had no child' (Luke 1:7)

On the use of *bo* (variant *botu*) as an existential particle, see below (3.4.5.2).

3.4.4.2 Comitative > 'Have'

The Arabic preposition *maʿ* 'with' develops a possessive meaning in some modern dialects. For example:

<u>Yemeni Arabic</u>: *maʿī sayyārih* 'I have a car' (lit., 'with-me [is] a car')[219]

In Lebanese Arabic, this is found alongside *ʿinda* (see above) though with a slightly different sense. While *ʿinda* is used for general possession, *maʿ* refers to immediate possession (i.e., 'to have on one's person').[220]

---

[217]Thackston (1996: 40).
[218]Dillmann (1907: §176h), Tropper (2002a: 218).
[219]Watson (1996: 60).
[220]Thackston (1996: 40).

Modern South Arabian languages also use the preposition š- 'with', in a construction parallel to that of Yemeni Arabic.[221] Tense is not expressed. Examples are:

Mehri: *šī ḥmo (lá')* 'I have (no) water'; *šīhəm háwri* 'they had a canoe'

Biblical Hebrew also uses a similar construction, on occasion:

Biblical Hebrew: *mā 'ittānû* 'what have we got?' (lit., 'what [is] with-us') (1 Sam. 9:7)

3.4.4.3 Dative > 'Have'

In Classical and Modern Standard Arabic, another possible means of expressing possession (in addition to the ways outlined in 3.4.4.1 and 3.4.4.2) is with the dative preposition *li-*:

Classical Arabic: *kāna lil-ʿabdi ḥimārun* 'the slave had an ass'[222]

This certainly derives from the possessive use of *li-* in the sense of 'belonging to', common in many Semitic languages, in phrases like:

Classical Arabic: *kitābun lahū* 'a book belonging to him; a book of his'
Biblical Hebrew: *mizmôr lə-dāwīd* 'a Psalm of David' (Psalm 22:1)

A dative preposition, in combination with an existential particle, is used to express possession in Hebrew and Aramaic:

Biblical Hebrew: *wə-kol-yeš-lô* 'and all that he had' (Gen. 39:4); *yeš-lî tiqwā* 'I have hope' (Ruth 1:12); *'ên lāh wālād* 'she had no child' (Gen. 11:30); *melek 'ên lā-'arbe* 'the locusts have no king' (Prov. 30:27)[223]

Syriac: *īt lī baytā* 'I have a house'; *layt lan malkā* 'we have no king' (Hosea 10:3)

---

[221] Johnstone (1987: 200), Simeone-Senelle in Hetzron (1997: 419). This preposition has the allomorph *k-* before nouns. Some dialects of MSA also use locative or dative prepositions. Also note that the parallel constructions of MSA and Yemeni Arabic are probably not coincidental.

[222] W. Fischer (2002: 157).

[223] By my count, the positive construction (*yēš l-*) occurs roughly 20 times in the Bible, 9 of which are in Genesis. The form *yēš* (without pronominal suffixes) occurs 129 times in total (thus, possessives account for about 16%). The form *'ên* without suffixes occurs about 595 times. Having looked only through the 359 where *'ên* appears without a prefixed particle, I found that roughly 80 of these are used in possessive constructions (22%).

In Modern Hebrew, it is clear that the construction is viewed as a verbal one, as the logical subject is normally marked with the *nota accusativi 'et*. That is to say, what is technically the subject of a nominal clause is construed as the object of a verbal one. For example:

Modern Hebrew: *yeš li 'et ha-sefer šelxa* 'I have your book'

This contrasts with the Classical Arabic example 'the slave had an ass' above, where *ḥimārun* 'an ass' is in the nominative case, as the logical subject (or, even, as the predicate of a verbless clause).

A few Arabic dialects also use a construction like that of Hebrew and Aramaic. For example, the dialects of the Jews of 'Aqra and Arbel (Northern Iraq) combine the existential particle *aku* with the dative preposition *l-*:

Jewish Arbel Arabic: *ašqad áku-lǝk* 'how much do you have?'[224]

3.4.4.4 Existence > 'Have'

In the modern Ethiopian languages, the verb 'to have' is expressed with an existential particle (which in each case derives from a copula or verb of existence; see below 3.4.5.3) plus verbal object suffixes. Such a construction already existed as an option in Ge'ez to express 'have' in a non-present tense. Examples are:

Ge'ez: *kono beta* 'he had a house' (lit., 'there-was-to-him a-house')[225]

Chaha: *šǝm närän* 'he has a name' (lit., 'a-name there-is-to-him')[226]

Tigrinya: *'anä bǝ'ray 'alloni* 'I have an ox' (lit., 'I an-ox there-is-to-me')[227]

Amharic: *bet alläññ* 'I have a house' (lit., 'a-house there-is-to-me'); *astämariw lǝǧočč allut* 'the teacher has children' (lit., 'the-teacher children there-are-to-him')[228]

Since these verbal object suffixes can sometimes also indicate indirect objects,[229] this construction is not really much different from that of Hebrew *yēš l-* and Aramaic *'īt l-* (see above, 3.4.4.3).

---

[224]Jastrow (1990: 67).
[225]Note that the object is accusative, as with Ge'ez *bo* 'he has' (3.4.4.1).
[226]Leslau (1950: 23).
[227]Melles (2001: 71).
[228]Leslau (1995: 439-46).
[229]See Leslau (1995: 190).

3.4.5 Existential Particles

3.4.5.1 'Have' > Existential

To the Hebrew existential particle *yēš*, Aramaic *'īṯay* (< **'īṯay*; later *'īṯ*), and Ugaritic *'iṯ*, we can compare Akkadian *išûm* 'to have'.[230] It is quite plausible to assume a grammaticalization of a verb 'have' into an existential (cf. French *il y a*). However, the shift from an existential to a possessive verb is also completely plausible, as we have seen from the many examples of this in Ethiopic languages above (3.4.4.4).[231] Only the earlier attestation of Akkadian suggests the first scenario.

Testen (2000) rejects the connection of Akkadian *išûm* with the NWS existentials, taking it rather as an archaic form of the root √*nṣ'* 'to carry, pick up'. This is an extremely clever suggestion, but the connection with the NWS particles seems too strong to ignore. Testen argues that Old Akkadian spellings with the *sV*-characters (rather than the *šV*-characters normally used to express PS **ṯ*) support his theory, and gives two examples.[232] In fact, one of his examples (*i-su*, *MDP* 14 49) is much better translated as 'take', i.e., from the verb *našûm* rather than *išûm*.[233] In addition, the sibilants (*sV*- and *šV*-characters) are often confused, particularly in the peripheral regions whence these texts originate,[234] and so these very few examples are not good evidence of an original **ś*.

Lipiński (1997: §49.23) suggests that Hebrew *yēš* and its WS cognates are fossilized verbal forms of a root **√yθw* 'to be'. The evidence for this is an Eblaite form *yiθāwu*, glossed in a lexical list as 'to be'. He may be right, but Eblaite evidence must be used with caution.

We should consider the derivation of the WS existentials from a verb 'to have' as likely.

3.4.5.2 Locative > Existential

Several Semitic languages exhibit an existential particle which can be traced to a

---

[230]The connection of Akk. *išûm* with the WS existentials seems to have first been made by Cull (1872), in an article with otherwise questionable proposals concerning the 'Shemitic' (sic) languages.
[231]For a general discussion of both these kinds of grammaticalization, see Heine (1997b: 94-96)
[232]*OAIC* (= Gelb 1955), text 8:15 and *MDP* 14 (= Scheil 1913), text 49. *MAD* 5 (= Gelb 1970), text 21:5, includes another example of *i-su*.
[233]Admittedly, the final *u*-vowel is problematic. *Našûm* is an i-i class verb, so the expected form is *išši*.
[234]R. Hasselbach (p.c.).

locative preposition + pronominal suffix. For example, many modern Arabic dialects use *fī* 'there is' (< *fī-hi* 'in it'):

<u>Syrian Arabic</u>: *hnīk fi bēt* 'over there there is a house' (*fi* < *fī*)[235]
<u>Chadian Arabic</u>: *almi fī?* 'Is there any water?'[236]

Yemeni Arabic *bih* 'there is' is identical in structure, though derives from the preposition *b-*, rather than *fī*:

<u>Yemeni Arabic</u>: *bih bisbās* 'there is chili'[237]

As already seen above (3.4.4.1), Ge'ez uses the preposition *ba-* + suffixes as the equivalent of a verb of possession. Related to this is the use of the third person form *bo* (variant *botu*) as an existential 'there is/are'.[238] The grammatical subject is normally in the nominative, but can also be in the accusative; I would suggest that the use of the accusative arose by analogy with its regular appearance in the possessive construction, in which the accusative is more logical semantically. Again, it should be pointed out that the negative form *'al-bo* shows the archaic negative particle *'al*, and hence the old age of the construction. Examples are:

Ge'ez: *bo-nu rā'əy zəyya* 'Is there a seer here?' (1 Sam. 9:11); *bo xəṣəwāna* 'there are eunuchs' (Matt. 19:12); *wa-'al-bo bet(a) ba-gəbṣ za-'al-bo badn(a) wəstetā* 'and there was no house in Egypt in which there was not a corpse' (lit., 'that there was no corpse in it') (Jubilees 49:5).

We must decide which came first, *bo* 'there is' or *bo* 'he has'. In modern Ethiopic languages, we know that the existential preceded the possessive construction (see above, 3.4.4.4). We do not have such internal evidence to help us with Ge'ez, but there is external evidence that the existential developed first. The Akkadian verb *bašûm* 'to exist, to be' has long been derived from the preposition **ba-* 'in' + 3ms *-šu* 'him', and thus connected with Ge'ez *bo* (see above, 3.2.8.3, especially n. 160). If we assume that these are cognate, then this is good evidence that the existential preceded the use of *bo* as a pseudo-verb 'to have'.

3.4.5.3 Copula > Existential

In North African Arabic dialects, the present participle of the verb *kāna* 'to be' is used to express an existential phrase:

---

[235] Ambros (1977: 93).
[236] Jullien de Pommerol (1999: 201-2).
[237] Watson (1996: 61).
[238] Dillmann (1907: §§192b, 197c), Tropper (2002a: §61.4).

Moroccan Arabic: *mā kāyn-š əl-xobz* 'there is no bread'; *kāyn wāḥed-əl-ktāb fūq əṭ-ṭəbla* 'there is a book on the table'[239]

In Iraqi Arabic, the existential particle is *'aku*. This form may perhaps be explained as a back formation of the negative *māku*, itself a reduced form of *mā yakūn* 'it is not'.[240] Examples are:

Iraqi (Muslim Baghdadi) Arabic: *'aku makātīb 'ili* 'are there any letters for me?'; *māku ḥāja* 'there is no need'

However, C. Müller-Kessler (2003) has recently argued against this derivation, suggesting instead that Iraqi Arabic *'aku* is a borrowing from Babylonian Aramaic (cf. Babylonian Talmudic *'yk'* /īkkā/ 'there is', from an earlier < *'yt + k'*). The modern Mandaic reflex *ekka* (Macuch 1965: 440), for which Müller-Kessler (p. 643) cites a variant *ekko*, provides a form from which the Arabic *'aku* could reasonably derive. Her argument is attractive, but is by no means definitive. The question will probably remain unsettled; we can say that a grammaticalization COPULA > EXISTENTIAL may have occurred in the case of *'aku*, but it is not the only attractive explanation.

Most modern Ethiopian dialects have also developed an existential out of an original copula, as we have seen above (cf. above, 3.4.4.4). Chaha *nära* is particularly interesting, as this derives from the verb *näp^{h}ärä* 'he was' (cf. Ge'ez *nabara*). In other Ethiopic languages, like Amharic, this is the past tense existential, but Chaha has extended this word to include present tense:

Chaha: *at sera nära* 'there is a custom'[241]

3.5 Conclusions

The data in this chapter have, it is hoped, provided the reader with a good sense of the pervasiveness of grammaticalization in Semitic, as well as presented a number of interesting examples of grammaticalization which are both common and uncommon typologically. It is also hoped that this chapter has made clear the importance of recognizing grammaticalization as a an explanation for language change. When one seeks out the origins of a new grammatical form,

---

[239] Caubet (1993 II: 33-35).

[240] For this etymology, see Malaika (1963: 57), Jastrow (1981: 164 n. 1). Diem (1974) derives the particle from a deictic particle *'ak-* + *hū* 'he', citing as evidence Yemeni dialectal *'akuwwa* 'he; he is there'. Diem's theory is unlikely, but cannot be disproven. On the general use of this particle, see Malaika (1963: 57) and Woodhead and Beene (2003: 12). See also Jastrow (1990: 67) on its use in some Northern Iraqi dialects.

[241] Leslau (1950: 23).

grammaticalization should come to mind. At the same time, it should be recalled that individual types of grammaticalization, while unpredictable, tend to repeat themselves throughout the languages of the world. These conclusions will form the basis of our investigations in the following three chapters, when we examine three kinds of grammatical development in much greater detail.

Chapter 4
Definite Articles

4.1 Introduction

My treatment of the definite article will focus mainly on the Central Semitic languages—Canaanite, Arabic, Aramaic, and Old South Arabian—since it is in these languages that the origin of the article has long been debated. Definite articles are attested in other Semitic languages—namely, some of the modern languages of the Ethiopic and Modern South Arabian families—but their origins are less problematic and will be dealt with only briefly. In Central Semitic we find both prefixed articles (Hebrew and Arabic) and suffixed ones (Aramaic and OSA). Scholars disagree greatly as to whether these articles derive from a common source or from multiple sources, as well as over what form the original source or sources had. As there is no definite article in Akkadian or Classical Ethiopic, there was almost certainly no definite article in Proto-Semitic, or Proto-West Semitic. This point is not in question. It follows, therefore, that either the definite article is a Central Semitic development, or a series of independent developments within the different CS languages. Before discussing these problems, a brief sketch of the languages and their respective definite articles is in order.

4.1.1 Canaanite

In Hebrew, the definite article is *ha-*, which is prefixed to its constituent and causes gemination of the following consonant, for example *báyit* 'house', *habbáyit* 'the house'. The form has phonetic variants, which appear when the following consonant is a guttural or *r*. There are various theories regarding the cause of the gemination, though the most obvious would seem to be the result of an assimilated *n*, i.e., supposing an original **han-*. The suggestion of *n* as the source for gemination is certainly logical, since *n* is the *only* phoneme which regularly assimilates to a following consonant in Hebrew.¹ A similar derivation explains the clitic preposition *mi-* 'from', which also causes following gemination, and for which there is a still present an independent form *min* 'from'. Other scholars have suggested an original **hal-* (Wright 1890), **hā-* (Barth 1896), pronominal *hū(')* (Nordheimer 1838-41 I: §648),² and **l-* (Testen 1998). These and other theories will be discussed below. It is noteworthy that the definite article is much less frequent in poetry.³ It does not seem, however, that there is a distinct chronological difference in the use of the article, as the article does appear in some of the oldest poetry, such as the Song of Deborah (Judges 5). In epigraphic Hebrew, the article is regularly used, though occasionally is lacking.⁴

The Phoenician article has the same form as the Hebrew, for example *bt* 'house' *hbt* 'the house'. However, in later Phoenician, and in Punic, the *h* was weakened to ', sometimes even written <'>, reflecting a general trend of confusion of gutturals. Gemination can only be assumed, since the consonantal script does not indicate this (nor vowels for that matter). Our only direct evidence for gemination following the Phoenician article is an inscriptional form *'mmqm* for /'am-maqūm/ 'the place'.⁵

4.1.2 Classical Arabic

The base form of the definite article in Classical Arabic is *'al*, which as in Hebrew, is prefixed to its constituent, e.g., *bayt* 'house', *'al-bayt* 'the house'. The *l* assimilates before coronal consonants, known in Arabic as the "sun letters" (*t, d, ṭ, θ, ð, s, z, ṣ, š, ḍ, ẓ, r, l, n*), and the *'a-* elides when not in sentence initial position.⁶ Thus the article, while always written <'l>,⁷ can appear in four different forms:

---

¹This statement is almost certainly true, but see Testen (1998) for a discussion on the supposed assimilation of *l*. See also n. 38, below.
²The idea of *hū(')* as the source of the article is quite old; it is found, for example, in the popular Hebrew grammars of J. Buxtorf (1620: 29), J. Alting (4th ed., 1686: §104; presumably also in the earlier editions) and A. Schultens (1737: 249). This was not the only theory circulating at such an early date, however. Von Sonnenfels (1757: 658-59), for example, derives the article from the presentative particle *hēn*.
³Gesenius §126h.
⁴Gogel (1998: 173)
⁵KAI 173:5, see Friedrich and Röllig (1999: 70). On the syntax of the article, see Lambdin (1971a) and Firmage (2002).
⁶Therefore, non-elided forms are actually rather rare.
⁷Except after the proclitic preposition *li-* 'to, for', where the *alif* is not written for aesthetic reasons.

1. *'al* – in initial position: *'al-bayt* 'the house'
2. *'aC* (where *C* is identical to the following consonant) – in initial position: *'aš-šams* 'the sun'
3. *l* – in contextual position: *fī l-bayt* 'in the house'
4. *C* (where *C* is identical to the following consonant) – in contextual position: *li-r-rajuli* 'for the man'

In addition to Classical Arabic, we must also take into account the other early Arabian dialects. In Liḥyanite and Thamudic inscriptions, we find an article *h-*, which before gutturals and occasionally elsewhere has the bi-form *hn-*.[8] Beeston believes that the forms of the article provide the main isogloss for dividing ancient Arabian into north-eastern (*'al-*) and north-western (*hn-*) and dialects.[9] Ancient Arabic grammarians also spoke of a Yemenite dialect that used an article *'am-*, as some Yemenite dialects still do today. Still other Yemenite dialects have *'an-*.[10]

Some scholars cite the existence of an article *hl-* as well.[11] This is based mainly on two suggested appearances in inscriptions,[12] and on the variant of a known name in some graffiti.[13] The textual appearances are questionable at best; neither Caskel (1954) nor Beeston (1973) agrees with the reading of *hl-* as the definite article in JSLih 71, while the *hl-* of JSLih 158 has been proven to be the beginning of the Arabian alphabet order.[14] The appearance on a single name is also rather suspect, and names in general provide poor evidence for the phonology of a language.[15] Thus, the existence of an article *hl-* is highly doubtful.

---

[8] W. Fischer (1982: 34), Beeston (1984: 181-82), Sima (1999: 118), and, most recently, M. Macdonald (2000: 41ff. and 2004: §4.3.1). Sima also discusses briefly some of the early scholarship on the North Arabian definite article.
[9] Beeston (1984: 185).
[10] Rabin (1951: 35, 50); Fischer and Jastrow (1980: 121); Behnstedt (1987: 85-86, 215).
[11] See, for example, Wensinck (1931: 53), in which the existence of an article *hl-* plays a crucial role in his argument on the origin of the Arabic article.
[12] JSLih 71 and 158 (= Jaussen-Sauvignac 1914: 423-27, 474-75).
[13] Ryckmans (1956: 11), citing an unpublished text.
[14] For the form in JSLih 71, Caskel (1954: 124) divides the words so that the *h* belongs with the previous word, and reads *-l-* as the Classical Arabic article. Beeston (1973: 69) reads *hā-l-*, with a separate demonstrative *hā* before the Classical Arabic article *-l-*. If Beeston is correct, this would be analogous to Syriac *hāllên* 'these' (< **hā 'illēn*; cf. Bib. Aram. *'illēn*) and, even more so, to modern Syrian Arabic *hal-* 'this/that' (< *hāda l-*; see Cowell 1964: 556-8). On JSLih 158, see Müller in W. Fischer (1982: 22). Also see M. Macdonald (1990: 70 n. 90) for a discussion of these and other possible *hl-* forms.
[15] M. Macdonald (1998).

4.1.3 Ancient Aramaic

As already seen above (2.6), the categoy of ancient Aramaic includes a number of different languages and dialects. In the older epigraphic and literary tongues, we find not a prefixed article, but rather a suffixed article *-a'* (later > *-ā*), always written <'>, e.g., Bib. Aram. *bayit* 'house', *baytā* 'the house'. In Old Aramaic this is most likely a true glottal stop, not just a *mater lectionis*. We assume this because all other examples of final *-ā* at this early stage are indicated in the writing with <-h>.[16] In later dialects, like Syriac, the definite form of the noun (usually called the "emphatic" state) loses its definite meaning and becomes the base lexical form; hence there is no definite article synchronically. So, in Syriac, *baytā* can mean 'house, a house, the house'. This leads to the development of new definite articles in later dialects, as we will see presently (4.6).

4.1.4 Old South Arabian

In OSA the definite article is suffixed.[17] On singular nouns, internal plurals, and external feminine plurals the article is *-n*. For example *hgr-*[18] 'town', *hgr-n* 'the town', *'hgr-n* 'the towns'. On duals and external masculine plurals, the article appears as *-hn*, as in *mhfd-nhn* 'the two towers'; handbooks list this form as *-nhn*, but as the first *n* is really the sign of the dual/masc. plural,[19] we can separate it from the definite article *-hn*. In fact, though we find duals fairly often, external masculine plurals are very rare in OSA. The only sure example of an external masculine plural ending with the definite article is *'rbʿtn m'nhn* 'the four hundred' (*m't* 'hundred').[20]

Discussion of the OSA article is notably absent from most works devoted to the definite articles of CS. This is because, until recently, OSA was not considered a part of CS, but rather has been traditionally grouped with MSA and Ethiopic as South Semitic (for example, Moscati 1964: 13-14).

---

[16]See Degen (1969: 25 n. 4).

[17]The forms here are the Sabaic (Sabean) dialect. See below, 4.3.4, for discussion of Hadramitic forms, and Beeston (1984, appendix) for a review of other dialects.

[18]I have given the form *hgr-* with a hyphen because the indefinite form, when not in a construct (genitival) relationship, would appear as *hgr-m*. The final *-m*, called mimation, is found in Akkadian on non-construct nouns, and in Arabic (where it has become *-n*) as a sign of indefiniteness.

[19]As in Arabic masc. external plurals (*sāriq-* 'thief' ~ *sāriqūna* 'thieves') and Aramaic masc. absolute plurals (*ktāb* 'book' ~ *ktābīn* 'books').

[20]See Beeston (1984: 30, 35) for a discussion of this form.

4.1.5 Summary

The forms of the definite articles in Central Semitic are:

	Prefixed	suffixed
Canaanite	*haC**-	
Arabic	*'al-* ~ *'aC**-	
Tham., Lihy.	*h(n)*	
Aramaic		-*ā(')*
OSA		-*n*, -*hn*

* C is identical to following consonant

4.2 Origin of Articles in Other Languages

Before turning to a comparative discussion of the CS articles and the question of their derivation, it will be valuable to view the history of definite articles in some other language families. We need not look far to find other language families in which both prefixed and suffixed articles are represented.

4.2.1 Romance

The daughter languages of Latin, which had no definite article, have all developed one from a demonstrative:[21]

Latin *ille lupus* 'that wolf' > Spanish *el lobo*, French *le loup*, Italian *il lupo* 'the wolf'

Romanian alone suffixes this inherited demonstrative:

Romanian *lup* 'wolf', *lupul* 'the wolf' (< Latin *lupus ille*)

4.2.2 Slavic

In Slavic, we find a definite article solely in Bulgarian and the closely related Macedonian; the article is suffixed:

Bulgarian, Macedonian *žena* 'woman', *ženata* 'the woman'

---

[21] All languages derive the article from the Latin *ille* series, with the exception of Sardinian—the first language to break from the rest of Romance—and some rural dialects of Catalan, which both have a reflex of the *ipse* series (Posner 1996: 126-30). For example, Sardinian *su lupu* 'the wolf'.

We do not find definite articles elsewhere in Slavic, but we can compare the placement of demonstratives in other languages, where they precede the head noun:

Serbo-Croatian *ta žena*, Polish *ta żona*, Russian *ta žena* 'that woman'

4.2.3 Germanic

In Germanic, we also find preposed and suffixed articles. The situation is slightly different from that of Romance and Slavic, however, in that the articles do not derive from a single source. The basic Proto-Germanic demonstrative, in the singular, had the forms **sa* (masc.), **sō* (fem.), **þat* (neut.) (cf. Greek ὀ, ἡ, το). This set is used as a true demonstrative in Gothic, the oldest attested Germanic language and sole member of the East Germanic branch, as well as in North Germanic, but in West Germanic it doubles as a definite article.

Masc: Gothic *sa wulfs*, Old Icelandic *sá ulfr* 'that wolf'
       Old English *sē wulf*, Old High German *der wolf* 'the wolf, that wolf'[22]

Neut: Gothic *þata barn*, Old Icelandic *þat barn* 'that child'
       Old English *þæt bearn*, OHG *daz barn* 'the child, that child'

Observe that in English, a grammaticalized, reduced form of the demonstrative—namely (Northern) Middle English *þe*, Modern English *the*—became the sole, uninflected form of the definite article, while the neuter forms *that, those* have retained the demonstrative function.

In the North Germanic languages, the definite article, which is suffixed, derives from a different source:

Old Icelandic *ulfr* 'wolf', *ulfrinn* 'the wolf' (< **ulfr inn* < **ulfr hinn*)

The source of the article is likely the demonstrative *hinn* 'this, that', which seems to be a combination of two inherited demonstratives, PIE **k'e-* and **eno-/ono-*. However, it is also possible that the article simply derives from the element **eno-* (i.e., *inn* alone).[23] This combination is also found in (Epic) Greek *keînos* 'that'.[24] We can also see the demonstrative function of the former in Old Church Slavic *sŭ* 'this' and in vestiges elsewhere in Germanic:

---

[22]In OHG, the initial dental of the neuter and oblique forms has spread to the masc. and fem. nominatives. The forms with initial *s-* were subsequently lost in English as well (cf. Middle English *þe*, Modern English *the*).

[23]Prokosch (1938: 273-74).

[24]Attic Greek ἐκεῖνος is formed with an additional deictic element **ε-*; see Sihler (1995: 390).

Gothic *himma daga* 'on this day'; German *heute* < OHG *hiutu* < **hiu tagu* 'today'.[25]

We also find reflexes of PIE **eno-/ono-* in German *jener* 'that', a combination of a pronominal element **j-* + **eno-*. We can see the demonstrative function on its own in OCS *onŭ* 'that, he'.

A reflex of **k'e-* is also seen in the English words 'here', 'hither', etc., and their Germanic cognates, as well as Latin **ce*, in forms such as *cedo* 'give here!' and *ecce* 'look here, here is'. The piling up of pronominal elements, as in the examples here and OIc. *hinn*, German *jener*, and Greek *(e)keînos* above, is not unusual. When this happens, it is natural that the deictic functions of some of the elements to lose their meaning. For example, in the French *ceci, celà, celui-ci*, the specific deictic meaning has been lost (here) in the inherited *ce-* (< Latin *ecce*), its deixis specified by the elements added to it.[26]

4.2.4 Conclusions

What can the examples from these IE languages tell us? We can highlight several points:

1. Both prefixed and suffixed articles may develop in closely related languages, from an earlier ancestor that had no article.
2. Such articles may derive from a single source or not.
3. Demonstrative elements have a tendency to "pile up".
4. There is often a relationship between demonstratives and locative adverbs.
5. The process of grammaticalization can yield a reduced-form article alongside the original demonstratives.

Many more examples of the development DEMONSTRATIVE > ARTICLE could be added here, from languages such as Coptic, Hungarian, Haitian Creole, and scores of others. For some of these, see Heine and Kuteva (2002). It is significant to note that in their comprehensive list of examples of grammaticalization, demonstratives are the *only* source for definite articles. In fact, this is the case in the overwhelming majority of the world's languages which attest definite articles. We can now apply this information to the situation we find in Central Semitic.

---

[25]Prokosch (1938: 273). Note also that the Slavic *sŭ* also survives only in a few vestiges in the modern languages. Interestingly, one in particular parallels the German: Russian *sevodnja* 'today'.
[26]See Sihler (1995: 391).

4.3 On the Origin of the CS Articles

In addition to the treatments of the article in more general works on Semitic or individual languages, such as Brockelmann (1908-13), Bauer-Leander (1922), and Lipiński (1997), there are a relatively large number of works devoted specifically to the definite articles and its origins, including at least four in the past several years.[27] Considering that almost none of these treatments put forth a common theory, and a discussion of each would be somewhat time-consuming, it seems best to present a general overview by type. We can roughly distinguish two main camps:

> 1. The articles can be traced to a demonstrative or deictic particle. In this category fall, among others, the works of Wright (1890), Halévy (1891), Glaser (1897), Barth (1896, 1913), Brockelmann (1908-13), Ungnad (1907, 1908), Bauer-Leander (1922), Blake (1942), Rundgren (1989), Lipiński (1997), Testen (1998), Voigt (1998), Zaborskí (2000), and Tropper (2001). There is, however, no general agreement as to exactly what form this demonstrative had, nor as to whether the CS articles can be traced to a single source. In fact, nearly all these scholars are in disagreement with one another.

> 2. The article developed by a phonological process. Here belong the works of Ullendorff (1965) and Lambdin (1971a).

We could, in fact, further subdivide those in the first camp into subgroups in various ways, such as whether they posit a single origin or not, or whether they posit an original demonstrative or other particle. The situation is further complicated by the fact that few authors treat all four languages in their discussion. In particular, OSA is most often neglected (see above, 4.1.4).

Those in the second camp can be rejected on the following grounds. First, languages do not behave in the way that these scholars propose. Evidence from the world's languages suggests that definite articles *always* develop via grammaticalization, with demonstratives being overwhelmingly the most common source.[28] Second, a very strong case can be made for positing a demonstrative origin in this case, therefore rendering unnecessary the theories that require such complex phonological developments. Finally, they fail to account for the OSA evidence.

Once settled on the idea that the CS articles must stem from a demonstrative, we obviously must ask: which demonstrative? A century ago, when schol-

---

[27]Namely, Voigt (1998), Testen (1998: 135-182), Zaborski (2000), Tropper (2001), all of which present quite different analyses.

[28]See Lyons (1999: 331-34).

ars seemed to be unanimous in positing a demonstrative origin for the CS articles, there were already a number of hypotheses. To cite just a few, Wright (1890: 114) posits a proto-form **hal* (< **hā + l*) for Hebrew and Arabic, *hā* for Aramaic, and derives the OSA article from either a dual or a pronominal suffix. Glaser (1897: 106) suggests the bizarre form **ᵒ/ala-hān* for Hebrew and Arabic. Barth (1913: 77, 133-34) reconstructs **hā* for the proto-Hebrew, but derives the Arabic article from **la*. Ungnad (1907: 211), discussing only Hebrew, suggests an original **han*, citing the Liḥyanite (Ancient North Arabian) article *h(n)* and the Akkadian demonstrative *annû*. This last has a winning advantage, as it references a form which actually *exists* as a demonstrative in Semitic.

The Akkadian demonstrative meaning 'this, these' has the base *anni-*, as found in Old Babylonian m.sg. nom. *annûm*, f.sg. nom. *annītum*, m..pl. nom. *annûtum*, f.pl. nom. *anniātum*. This base could derive from either **hanni-* or **'anni-*, but we can confidently reconstruct **hanni-* based on the Old Akkadian cuneiform writing of this word.[29] This root is also found in the OB adverbs *annânum* 'here', *annīkīam* 'here', *annîš* 'hither'. The far demonstrative 'that, those' has the base *ulli-*, OB m.sg. nom. *ullûm*, etc. The base is also found in the adverbs *ullīkīam* 'there', *ullânum* 'thence', *ullîš(am)* 'thither'.[30]

	near	far
demonstrative	*anni-*	*ulli-*
at	*annīkīam, annânum*	*ullīkīam, ullânum*
to	*annîš*	*ullîš(am)*
from	*annânum*	*ullânum*

In Akkadian, there is a clear relationship between the demonstratives and the locative adverbs. This situation is paralleled in many languages, including English as noted above (4.2.3). Compare the final syllables of Arabic *ðālika* 'that' ~ *hunālika* 'there' (see below and n. 33 for more on Semitic) or the initial consonants of Old Icelandic *hinn* 'this' ~ *hér* 'here', *þat* 'that (neut.)' ~ *þar* 'there'. Also compare Latin *ille* 'that' ~ *illīc* (< *illīce*) 'there', *hic* 'this' ~ *hīc*[31] 'here'; Italian *il* 'the' (< Lat. *ille*) ~ *lì* 'there' (< Lat. *illīc*); or Hindi *yah* 'this' ~ *yahā̃* 'here', *vah* 'that' ~ *vahā̃* 'there'.

The Akkadian demonstratives *anni-* and *ulli-* have cognates in West Semitic,

---

[29]See Hasselbach (2004). The reconstruction of **hanni* is also supported by comparison with assumed WS cognates like Ugaritic *hn-d* 'this', but this argument is rather circular.

[30]In Assyrian, the far demonstrative is formed from a different base, *ammi-* (von Soden 1995: §45g).

[31]Latin *illīc(e)*, *hic*, *hīc* all contain the deictic particle **-ce* mentioned above (4.2.3).

though with altered distribution, and both appearing as near demonstratives.

The WS singular near demonstratives, in most languages, contain a reflex of another PS demonstrative element *ð- (Hebrew ze, Eth. zə, Arabic (hā)ðā, OSA ðn). The root *hanni-, as in Akkadian, is found, however, in combination with the root *ð-, for example Ugaritic hn-d 'this'. It is also found in various locative adverbs, such as Arabic hunā 'here', Ugaritic hn 'here', Hebrew hēnnā 'hither'. We should possibly include here Syriac hārkā (see n. 33), which may be another example of PS *n > r, as discussed in Testen (1985). The root may also appear in the Hebrew particles hinnē, hēn, and their cognates (cf. Latin ecce above).[32] This root is also, in my view, the source of the Canaanite, Aramaic, and OSA articles.

In WS—with the exception of Arabic and MSA—far deixis is normally indicated by the anaphoric pronouns; these are also used in Akkadian where their anaphoric use is distinct from the true deictic ulli- series. For example, Hebrew hay-yeled ha-hû(') 'that child', Akkadian bītu šū 'that (aforementioned) house'. Some languages also have a far demonstrative series which includes a deictic element *-kV, such as Bib. Aram. dēk, Arabic ðāka/ðālika, Ge'ez zəku, all 'that'.[33] The Akkadian far demonstrative ulli- has been restricted to plural use, in most languages (probably PWS) forming a suppletive paradigm with the *ð-series in the singular. Thus, for reflexes of *'ulli-, we find:

	Heb.	Phoen.	Bib. Aram.	Arabic[34]	OSA[35]	Ge'ez	MSA[36]
these (m.pl.)	'ēlle	'l	'ēll(e), 'illēn	(hā)'ulā('i)	'ln	'əllu	lɜ[h]
these (f.pl.)					'lt	'əllā	
those (c.pl.)				'ulā('i)ka		'əlləku	lək
rel.prn. (c.pl)				'ulū[37]		'əlla	l-

---

[32]See Voigt (1995: 525; n. 25), Tropper (2002b).

[33]For locative uses of this element, note Arabic hunā 'here' ~ hunāka 'there'; Bib. Aram. kā 'here', Syriac hārkā 'here', 'aykā 'where', Targ. Onq. hākā 'here', ' ēkā 'where'; Hebrew kō 'here; thus'. Also see Barth (1913: §27).

[34]Arabic has a wide variety of forms. See Wright (1967: 264-74) for a complete treatment.

[35]Here the Sabean forms are given. For other forms, see Kogan and Korotayev in Hetzron (1997) or Beeston (1984).

[36]Given here are the Ḥarsūsi forms. For a full list of forms in the many MSA languages, see Simeone-Senelle in Hetzron: (1997: 394, 412).

[37]This is actually a determinative pronoun, meaning 'the ones of'. The actual relative pronoun (m.pl.) is 'allaðīna. See W. Fischer (2002: 148-49).

This root is, I believe, the source of the Classical Arabic article *'al-*, as I will demonstrate below.

According to the view presented here, the articles of Canaanite, Aramaic, and OSA derive from the same PS source as the Akkadian **hanni-* series, while the Arabic article derives from the same source as the Akkadian **'ulli-* series. To my surprise, this very theory was already posited by the great scholar J. Halévy in a short 1891 article. Let us begin with the Canaanite forms. As noted above (4.1.1), the only reasonable course is to suggest **han-* as the original form of the Hebrew article. Besides the connection with Akkadian **hanni-*, it has the benefit of being phonologically explainable. The phoneme *n* regularly assimilates in Hebrew and Phoenician; therefore the gemination following the article is expected. Other suggestions like **hal* and **hā* cannot be satisfactorily explained.

Halévy's argument, with which I agree wholeheartedly, is the following: To posit a proto-form **hal-* for Hebrew is problematic in that, with the exception of certain forms of the root √*lqḥ* 'take',[38] *l* never assimilates to a following consonant in Hebrew, leaving us without an explanation for the gemination caused by the article. The suggested source *hā* is even more problematic. First, **hā* should have become ***hō* in Canaanite (compare Bib. Aram. *kā* 'here', Hebrew *kō* 'here; thus'). Second, there is no motivation for sequence **hā* + *C* to become *haC-C*.

With a proto-form **han-* established for Canaanite, the suggestion of a change **han-* > **hal-* in Arabic (e.g., Lipiński 1997: §17.4) is problematic, as this requires positing an ad hoc, otherwise unattested and unmotivated sound change. Thus, the theory I present here has the advantage of bypassing this problem (on the *l*-assimilation in Arabic, which must be accounted for in any theory, see below), as well as the fact that the demonstratives from which the articles derive are actually well attested throughout the Semitic languages.

Tropper (2001) presents a theory quite similar to this one, the main difference being his view on Arabic. Tropper believes that the Arabic article derives from **han* as well. Loss of the initial *h* is not problematic, as there are other examples of initial **h* > *'* in Arabic.[39] The *l* which we find in Arabic is, he believes, from an assimilatory change of **han* > **hal* before labial consonants, with the eventual spread of **hal* to other forms. He explains the dialectal Yemenite article *'am-* by a similar assimilation and spread. His main argument is that

---

[38] In fact, forms like *yiqqaḥ* 'he takes' are probably not the result of an assimilation (i.e., < **yilqaḥ*), but rather are likely analogous (by contamination) to the corresponding forms of the root √*ntn* 'to give' (i.e., *yittēn* < **yintin* 'he gives') (Ungnad 1906: 278; Bauer-Leander 1922: §15q).

[39] Such as the C-stem and various particles. See Blake (1915: 375-77), or more recently, Tropper (2003).

the predecessor of the Arabic article cannot have terminated in –*l*, as *l* does not regularly assimilate in Arabic. But this argument is flawed, since *n* does not assimilate in Arabic either! By his reasoning, a proto-form **hal-* should be just as likely as **han-*. In fact, a form terminating in *l* is a more efficient reconstruction, as it does not require the extra steps of dissimilation and subsequent analogical spread. Thus, the reconstruction of an original *'al-*, from the plural demonstrative, as Halévy and I suggest, is more likely. The assimilation of *l-* before certain consonants, which is admittedly irregular, is explainable as the type of irregular sound change that often results from grammaticalization (see below, n. 44). In fact, all of the CS articles exhibit unusual sound changes which are simply the result of grammaticalization (with the exception of Hadramitic, see 4.3.4 below). The changes which led to the attested articles will be discussed in turn, including the Aramaic and OSA data.

4.3.1 Canaanite and Ancient North Arabian

The form reconstructable for PWS is presumably **han*. If we take Akkadian **hanni* to be the PS form, we have assume a reduction from **hanni* to **han* once the form was cliticized. Or, it is also possible to reconstruct a PS **han-*, and suggest a *nisbe* or other suffix for the base of the Akkadian forms.[40] If we assume an original **hanni*, we can explain the loss of the final vowel of the demonstrative, as well as the simplification of the geminate *n*, as results of cliticization; we may simply compare Italian *il* < Latin *ille*. From the **han* stage, the assimilation of *n* is regular before a consonant, and thus the situation in Hebrew and Phoenician is as expected.

Note that there remain some vestigial demonstrative uses of what looks like the definite article in Canaanite, such as Hebrew *hay-yôm* 'today', *hap-paʿam* 'this time', *haš-šānā* 'this year'.[41] This in itself is good evidence that the article developed from an original demonstrative.

Krahmalkov (2001: 87) alleges the appearance of *han* as a demonstrative/article in the Hebrew Bible, citing Genesis 44:8 and Numbers 23:24. In both cases, the Masoretic text has *hēn* 'behold':

> *hēn kesep ’ăšer māṣānû* 'look, the money that we found...' (Gen. 44:8)
> *hen-ʿām kə-lābî(’) yāqûm* 'look, a people rising up like a lion' (Num. 23:24)

Krahmalkov's suggestion, to which it seems no other scholars subscribe, is quite uncertain, but possible. In Num. 23:24 the word *kesep* does seem to be missing

---

[40]So already Brockelmann (1908: §107d); also Tropper (2001: 17).
[41]In addition to German *heute*, mentioned above (4.2.3), compare Syriac *yawmān(ā)* 'today' < **yawmā hānnā* 'this day'.

an article. Targum Onqelos reads as the Masoretes do, translating *hēn* as *hā* 'behold' in both cases. The Septuagint translates the *hēn* of Genesis as 'if' and of Numbers as 'behold'. The Aramaic and Greek evidence is not very helpful, however, as we would not expect the translators to recognize an archaic article *han* at such a late date. Krahmalkov's suggestion can be noted with interest, but not used in any argument regarding the historical form of the article.

Finally for Canaanite, we should note that the *h*- of the article elides following the proclitic prepositions *bə* 'in', *lə* 'to, for', and *kə* 'as'. We find in Hebrew *bə-bayit* 'in a house', *bab-bayit* 'in the house' (< **bə-hab-bayit*). The loss of intervocalic *h* is also found in the imperfect of hiphil (C-stem) verbs, e.g., *yaqṭîl* < **yV-haqṭil*, and elsewhere.[42] In Phoenician, the article was likewise elided after the prepositions *b*-, *l*-, and *k*-, but also—depending on dialect and date—even after some non-clitic prepositions, the direct object marker *'yt*, and the conjunction *w*- 'and'.[43] The elision of the *h* of the article in these environments can be regarded as a product of cliticization. For a parallel in Tigrinya, see below (4.6.2).

The development for the Ancient North Arabian *hn*-dialects is essentially that of Canaanite. The major difference is that, in certain dialects, the *n* does not assimilate before gutturals.

4.3.2 Classical Arabic

Several changes in the phonetic reduction of the article must be accounted for in Arabic. First, the single *l* of the Arabic article, which is to be reconstructed (based on Akkadian, Ethiopic, and NWS evidence) as geminate in its PWS demonstrative source, must be explained. This change, and loss of any final vowel, can be explained as the type of phonetic reduction associated with grammaticalization, as in the example of Italian *il* < Latin *ille* already referenced above. Note, though, that the cognate Arabic demonstratives (see table above) also exhibit a non-geminate *l*, so possibly this gemination was simplified before the grammaticalization of the article. Second, the assimilation of *l* before coronal consonants is explained simply as an irregular by-product of cliticization.[44]

---

[42]Bauer-Leander (1922: §25 II-VI). Their oft-repeated example of the 3ms pronominal suffix, e.g., *lô* 'to him' < **lau* < **lahu* should be ignored. The form *lô* more likely derives from an analogy with this suffix on nominal forms, where *-ô* < **-ōh* < **-uh* < **-uhu*; see Hasselbach 2003.

[43]Lambdin (1971: 326-30), Hackett (2004: §4.4).

[44]Other examples of irregular assimilation of *l*, resulting from cliticization/grammaticalization, can also be found in Ge'ez *'akko* 'not' (< **'al kona*), Amharic *al* > *a(C)* in the negative imperfect (Leslau 1995: 22), and the occasional assimilation of Akkadian (poetic) *el* 'on' > *eC*- (von Soden 1995: §114o).

We must also explain the initial *a*-vowel of the article. What vowel should we reconstruct for the WS plural demonstrative? Akkadian, as we have seen, has *ulli-*. Geʻez *ʾəllu* is of little help, as it can come from either **ʾillū* or **ʾullū*. The Canaanite and Aramaic forms reflect an earlier **ʾilli-*, while the Arabic demonstratives all reflect **ʾulā* or **ʾulu-*. One thing certain is that there is no evidence for an *a*-vowel. The best solution is to assume that the demonstrative was reduced simply to *l-*, the form in which we most often find the article in Classical Arabic. In time, an prothetic syllable *ʾa* was added when the article appeared in initial position, which in fact is very seldom.[45]

It happens that the group of fourteen consonants which trigger assimilation constitute exactly half of the Arabic consonantal inventory. This symmetry prompted Ullendorff (1965) to suggest that this is an artificial situation (i.e., the product of Arabic prescriptive grammarians). This may be the case, and indeed the situation in the modern dialects is not the same as in the Classical language. But it need not be the case, especially since the assimilating letters form a natural class (i.e., coronals).

As for the dialectal Yemenite article, *ʾam-*, I agree with Tropper's analysis that the form is the product of an assimilation. However, whether the source of the form is (Classical Arabic) *ʾal-* or (Ancient North Arabian) *han-* remains unclear. *han-* is a more attractive proposal since in Arabic the nasal *n* regularly assimilates (> *m*) before labials, and since in general a change *n* > *m* is quite common, while a change *l* > *m* is not. The appearance of an article *ʾan-* in neighboring Yemenite dialects (see above, 4.1.2) is also strong evidence in favor of an original *han-*. The article *ʾam-* also brings to mind the Assyrian demonstrative series *ammi-* (see n. 30), but with no other evidence for this base in WS, a connection seems implausible.

As in Canaanite, we find some vestigial demonstrative uses of the article, such as *ʾal-yawma* 'today', *ʾal-ʾāna* 'now'. In addition, a comparison of the Arabic lexeme *hana* 'thing' (and its variant *han*) with demonstrative *han* is tempting.[46]

---

[45] This development is reminiscent of Testen's proposal (1998: 153-55), though he has a completely different source for the article *l-*, namely, an asseverative particle *l*.

[46] W. Heinrichs has kindly made me aware of a cognate Turoyo lexeme *hnō*, used when an intended word escapes one's mind (English 'thingamajig, whatchamacallit'), as well as a lexeme *hnā* which occurs in the Syriac of Bar Hebraeus (Brockelmann 1928: 178). In Turoyo, this has even been turned into a dummy verb, *hnēle* 'he thinged, did this and that', often followed by the intended verb. This Turoyo and Syriac word is another possible remnant of **hanni* in WS, though it may also be a borrowing from Arabic or elsewhere. Sabar (2002: 151), in his dictionary of Jewish (Northeast) Neo-Aramaic, includes a cognate noun *hınnā* (also in Urmian, Maclean 1895: 190) and verb *hnılle*, with similar meaning, though he posits a Kurdish lexeme *hīn* as the source. It should also be men-

4.3.3 Aramaic

It has traditionally been assumed that the Aramaic article *-ā* derives from the presentative particle **-hā*.[47] Other sources have also been suggested, notably an original **-yā* (Aartun 1959) and **-ān* (Voigt 1997). I maintain that the article derives from demonstrative **han*, essentially in agreement with Tropper (2001) who summarizes the following:[48]

Singular: **kalbV-han* 'the dog' > **kalban* > *kalba'* (> *kalbā*).
Dual: **qarnay-han* 'the two horns' > **qarnayyan* > *qarnayya'* (> *qarnayyā*).

In the singular we see a loss of intervocalic *h*, and a subsequent change of word final **-n* > *-'*. The loss of *h* is not problematic,[49] but the change *n* > *-'* warrants some discussion. Tropper presents other evidence for word final **-n* > *-'*, which strengthens his case, namely Aramaic borrowings of Akkadian names, in which an original final *-n* seems to have become *-'*. This gives us the form in Old Aramaic, where we must assume the *aleph* to be consonantal (see n. 16 above). Subsequently, the glottal stop was lost, with compensatory vowel lengthening. The change **-n* > *-'* remains unusual, however, so we must look for an explanation. One attractive possibility is that *kalban* simply became *kalbā*, probably via a stage of nasalization. We can compare the Nabatean Aramaic spellings of Arabic names, where Arabic *-un* simply appears as <w>, *-an* as <'>.[50] This would mean either that the final *aleph* was *never* an actual glottal stop, or that the glottal stop was a secondary development of the kind we see in *lā'* 'no!', as a stressed variant of *lā* Arabic, or *lo'* as a stressed variant of *lo* in Modern Hebrew. If the latter occurred, then we can simply assume the glottal stop was subsequently lost, possibly due to retraction of stress to the penultima. This can be summarized as:

---

tioned that Müller (in W. Fischer 1982: 26) has suggested the Arabic noun *han* as the source for the Ancient North Arabian article.
[47]Brockelmann (1908: §246e) and most subsequent works on Aramaic.
[48]Tropper (2001: 16).
[49]A common change, found also with C-stem verbs. Cf. also Syriac <yhab> /yab/ 'he gave'. On Hebrew, see above (4.3.1) and n. 41.
[50]Cantineau (1930-32 II: 164-68). This spelling convention for *-un* is preserved in the Arabic name *'amr-un* <'mrw>. The accusative *-an* is normally spelled simply <'> in Arabic, even today (except after *tā' marbūṭa*).

Singular: *kalbV-han 'the dog' > *kalban > kalbã > kalbā (? > kalba' > kalbā).

Dual: *qarnay-han 'the two horns' > *qarnayyan > qarnayyā > qarnayyā (? > qarnayya' > qarnayyā).[51]

The base form of the noun in the plural is remarkable, as the article seems to be suffixed to the construct form (see 4.4.2 for further discussion). In Aramaic, as in Hebrew, the dual construct replaces the plural construct, hence Tropper gives the dual forms above. His use of the term "dual" may be anachronistic, since by the time of the appearance of definite article, the replacement of the plural construct by the dual had certainly taken place. Regardless, in the dual/plural forms given, we see an assimilation of *-yh- > yy,[52] and the same subsequent changes as in the singular noun.

Does the Aramaic presentative particle hā also derive from *han? Most likely the answer is yes, thus providing a cognate to Hebrew hinnē, hēn. Some scholars have suggested that this particle hā is the source of the Aramaic article; if so, that would still make the Aramaic article cognate with the rest of CS. However, given that a demonstrative (versus a presentative particle) is a much more likely source of grammaticalization, the derivation presented here seems secure.

4.3.4 Old South Arabian

On singular nouns, internal plurals, and external feminine plurals, we only need to assume a loss of intervocalic h.

hgrn 'the town' (nom.) */hagarān/? < *hgr hn */hagaru han/; 'hgr-n 'the towns' < *'hgr hn

In the form -nhn, really n + hn, found on duals and external masculine plurals, there is no change.

---

[51] Another possibility, suggested to me by E. Bar-Asher, is that han became 'an first. Presuming then a form like accusative *kalba'an, the final -n was simply lost, and, subsequently, so was the final short vowel. This is also more attractive than Tropper's derivation, as the loss of final -n is more common than the change of -n > -'.

[52] The change *Ch > CC (i.e., the progressive assimilation with h; or, possibly, the simple loss of h with concomitant preservation of syllable structure) is found elsewhere in CS, for example Hebrew forms of the type yiqṭəlennû < *yiqṭəlenhu and qəṭālattu < *qaṭalathu (Bauer-Leander 1922: §15b; Hetzron 1969: 105-6 rejects this derivation of yiqṭəlennû). Within Aramaic, a very likely example of the change is found in the Ct-stem 'ittap'al, which derives from *hithap'al (though some may suggest, from *hit'ap'al). Another possible case within Aramaic is yiqṭəlinnun < *yiqṭəlinhun? (J. Huehnergard p.c.).

mḫfd-nhn 'the two towers' (nom.) **/maḫfadānᵃ/ᵢhan/ < *mḫfdn hn*

It is intriguing that the intervocalic *h* would be lost in the first set, but remain in the second. We may suppose that it is due to the long vowel in the dual/external m.pl. suffix or word stress. Or, we may simply assume it to be an irregularity of grammaticalization.

In Hadramitic, the article appears as *-hn* on singular nouns, internal plurals, and external feminine plurals, i.e., in the form underlying the Sabean. The dual (and possibly external m.pl.) form is *-yhn* (occasionally *-yn*).[53] For this, it looks like the article is being attached to the construct form, as in the singular and as we saw on the Aramaic plural above (see 4.4.2 for further discussion). In Sabean, we must assume that—as in Arabic, Aramaic, and Hebrew—the nunation/mimation of the external m.pl. has become a fixed part of the suffix, unlike in the singular. Thus, Hadramitic preserves the more archaic distribution of mimation/nunation.

4.4 On the Syntax of the CS Articles

Some mention should be made of the syntax of the articles. It is noteworthy that in the CS languages we are dealing with, the syntax of the articles is nearly identical. As J. Huehnergard points out:

> [T]he article may appear only on the final member of a construct chain; it may not appear on nouns with suffixes, or on proper nouns; attributive adjectives must agree in definiteness; and predicative adjectives are indicated syntactically, by the lack of an article in conjunction with a definite noun.... When we consider that most of these features are not inevitable, the fact that all of them characterize Canaanite, Aramaic, Arabic, and OSA is very suggestive, I think, of a set of developments in a common ancestor.[54]

Huehnergard then adds that the lack of a definite article in Ugaritic and the Deir 'Allā dialect, the rarity of the article in early Hebrew poetry and the earliest Aramaic inscriptions, and the diversity of the forms across the various languages all indicate that we are more likely dealing with a wave or areal phenomenon rather than a shared innovation.

Huehnergard is certainly correct that the syntax of the CS articles is highly suggestive of a common origin. I think, however, that the lack of an article in the earliest dialects can be explained. The article likely originated, as any new construction does, as a colloquial expression. Thus, the source constructions, with

---

[53] Beeston (1984: 68).
[54] Huehnergard (2005).

the singular and plural demonstrative adjectives *han- or 'al- having a more specialized function, could have been present in PCS. As the languages split and evolved (and the wave model Huehnergard refers to is probably appropriate here), the grammaticalization progressed (i.e., the demonstratives became true articles, in their various forms) and the once vulgar constructions became legitimate ones. Some of the syntactic peculiarities warrant explanation.

4.4.1 The Article and Inherently Definite Nouns

Why does the article not appear on nouns with a possessive suffix or on nouns appearing as the first member of a construct phrase? I believe the answer is simple. In both cases, the noun in question is already semantically definite. Possessed nouns are considered definite in a great many of the world's languages. In English we say 'my son', and not 'the my son' because 'the' is redundant. French *mon fils*, Spanish *mi hijo*, Swedish *min son*, German *mein Sohn* are parallel examples. Further evidence that a possessed noun is considered definite in CS is that in Hebrew and Aramaic a noun with a pronominal suffix requires a definite attributive adjective, and, when acting as the direct object, is usually preceded by a definite direct object marker (Hebrew *'et*, Aramaic *yāt*). A language need not behave this way, as we see in Italian *la mia casa* 'my house'[55] Hungarian *a fiúm* 'my son', and even in Semitic, for example Mehri *a-bət-əh* and Turoyo *u baytayde* 'his house'.[56] As for the nouns acting as the first member of a construct, Brockelmann notes, "Dans toutes les langues sémitiques, sont déterminés par eux-mêmes les noms dont dépend un génitif et qui se trouvent à l'état construit, et par conséquent aussi les noms avec suffixes."[57]

---

[55]Certain nouns denoting close family relations do not take the article, including *mio figlio* 'my son'. See Maiden and Robustelli (2000: §10.6).

[56]For discussion of Mehri, see Sima (2002: 655). In Turoyo, there also exists a set of suffixes which does not require a definite article, but this set is restricted. See Jastrow (1992: §4.2, 7.2).

[57]Brockelmann (1910: §178). We must make a distinction between syntactically definite and definite in translation. I argue that the first member of a construct is syntactically definite by its function in a genitival relationship, just as a noun with a possessive suffix is definite. We might translate the first member as indefinite however, in a phrase like *ben-melek* 'a son of a king', but only the second member of the construct marks this phrase as indefinite. It could also be translated 'the son of a king'. To mark the first member for indefiniteness, one must resort to a periphrastic construction (see Gesenius §127a, §129c).

4.4.2 The Form of the Noun When Definite

A similar phenomenon explains why we find the article attached to the construct form of the Aramaic plural (e.g., Bib. Aram. *malkayyā* 'the kings', construct *malkay*; see 4.3.3), why definite nouns appear without final nunation on Arabic (triptotic) singular, internal triptotic plural, and fem. external plural nouns, and why there is no final mimation on OSA singular, internal plural, and fem. external plural definite nouns. In PS, a noun in construct position did not take final mimation/nunation, while a noun out of construct (i.e., unbound) did. Therefore, a reanalysis must have taken place in PWS or PCS, during which the construct form was reanalyzed as definite based on its syntactic function. The unbound form was thus reanalyzed as indefinite. So in the languages which retained mimation/nunation, namely Arabic and OSA, we find the article on what is historically the construct form.

The above description does not work, however, for the duals or masculine external plurals in Hebrew, Arabic, and OSA, which retain the historical mimation/nunation when the article is added, but not in the construct. There has clearly been some sort of reanalysis of the mimation/nunation as a sign of the plural, rather than as a sign of the unbound state.[58] Hebrew makes this clear, as mimation in Hebrew has been lost as a functioning feature, with the masculine plural suffix *-îm* and dual suffix *-ayim* simply remaining as frozen forms. The exact nature of the reanalysis is unclear.

4.4.3 The Article on Attributive Adjectives

The use of the definite article on attributive adjectives is not problematic. Synchronically in the CS languages, attributive adjectives must agree in gender, number, case (if applicable), and definiteness. Diachronically, the use of the article may simply be a case of agreement, as is seen synchronically. That is to say, speakers interpreted definiteness as a feature of the type gender/number/ case. Or, the use of the article on attributives may originate from appositional use, i.e., Arabic *'al-waladu l-kabīru* 'the big boy' would originally come from 'this boy, this big one'. Of course, the article actually serves an important function here, as it distinguishes an attributive phrase from a predicative one in Canaanite and Aramaic.[59]

Note that while all CS languages adhere to this agreement rule, the situation with demonstrative adjectives is not uniform. In Arabic, demonstrative adjectives precede their head nouns, and so in general do not behave like attributive

---

[58] See Lyons (1999: 93-94) for a short synchronic analysis.

[59] In Arabic, nunation on the predicate adjective provides a further distinction (though it is absent in pause).

adjectives.[60]

More interesting are the Canaanite languages. Hebrew normally uses the article on both the head noun and demonstrative, such as *hay-yeled haz-ze* 'this child'. In contrast, Phoenician usually does not use the article with the demonstrative, as in *hgbr z'* 'this man' (KAI 30:2).[61] Occasionally the Hebrew-type construction is found in Phoenician, and the Phoenician-type construction is found in Hebrew (though very rarely).[62] In both languages a construction without the article on either the noun or the demonstrative is also attested, though very rarely in Biblical Hebrew. It is not surprising that we find the article missing on the demonstrative, or even on the noun; since the original function of the article was a demonstrative as well, there must have been a time when the article would have been redundant. The normal Hebrew construction, with the article on both noun and demonstrative, can be seen as an analogical counterpart to the normal noun–adjective phrase.

4.5 On Grammaticalization

What the majority of the works dedicated to the definite article lack is a discussion of how the change of DEMONSTRATIVE > ARTICLE happened in each of the languages. This is, of course, where grammaticalization enters the picture. Tropper (2001) mentions grammaticalization, but only in passing at the very end of his treatment.

The change DEMONSTRATIVE > ARTICLE is not only one of the most widespread examples of grammaticalization, it is also among the simplest. Heine, Claudi, and Hünnemeyer (1991: 6) call it one of grammaticalization's paradigm examples. This change of DEMONSTRATIVE > ARTICLE has been the subject of a good number of works, usually with the focus on a particular language or language family. Some noteworthy examples are Christophersen (1939), H. Heinrichs (1954), Ultan (1978), Greenberg (1978), Harris (1980), Leiss (1994), Epstein (1995), and Laury (1997). This change is even mentioned in some of the predecessors to the modern study of grammaticalization, for example in von Schlegel (1818: 27-28). Not surprisingly, there is discussion in all general works on grammaticalization as well.

Some examples of grammaticalization involve syntactical restructuring (as seen elsewhere in this work), but this case does not, as the syntactic structure of

---

[60]W. Heinrichs writes (p.c.), "Arab grammarians consider—quite rightly—the head noun to be in apposition to the demonstrative noun."

[61]See Friedrich and Röllig (1999: §299). Moabite behaves the same way; see Garr (1985: 171).

[62]Gesenius §126y.

the determiner-head phrase remains essentially the same.[63] With little, if any, reanalysis, no syntactic change, and only what might be argued as a semantic shift or extension, then why do we even call this grammaticalization? It does not quite fit Meillet's (1912: 131) definition, "le passage d'un mot autonome au rôle d'élément grammatical." That is to say, if we consider the demonstratives as already having a grammatical function, and not simply as autonomous lexemes, we are dealing simply with a shift in grammatical function. But Meillet does not bind himself to this limited definition. He notes, "la grammaticalisation de certain mots crée des formes neuves, introduit des catégories qui n'avait pas d'expression linguistique, transforme l'ensemble du système."[64] That is to say, the emergence of a new grammatical category in the case of DEMONSTRATIVE > ARTICLE is the fundamental reason to call this an example of grammaticalization. We have seen above (1.1) that linguists today speak of a 'cline of grammaticality', along which words or items go not only from lexical to grammatical, but also from less grammatical to more grammatical.[65] Any progress along this cline may be considered grammaticalization.

As noted by Diessel (1999) in his important work on demonstratives, most scholars have assumed that definite articles arise from anaphoric adnominal demonstratives.[66] Anaphoric demonstratives are coreferential with a noun or noun phrase in previous discourse.[67] An example of an anaphoric use of a demonstrative in English is:

We studied grammaticalization. This change is characterized by ...

English of course has no special anaphoric pronoun, though some languages do. Anaphoric demonstrative *pronouns* often develop into third person pronouns, for example Latin *ille* > French *il*. This is the case in Akkadian as well, whose third person pronouns (e.g., *šū* 'he') are identical to the anaphoric demonstratives (e.g., *bītu šū* 'that house').[68] Anaphoric demonstrative *adjectives*, however, have a tendency to develop into definite articles. In many languages which lack a definite article, there exists an anaphoric demonstrative which often translates into English as an article. Indonesian is one example, as are some of the Ethiopian Semitic languages. For example, in Inor, a Peripheral Western Gurage dialect, a postposed third person independent pronoun marks definiteness in this

---

[63]Heine, Claudi, and Hünnemeyer (1991: 219, 276 n. 12).
[64]Meillet (1912: 133).
[65]Hopper and Traugott (2003: 6-7).
[66]Diessel (1999: 128).
[67]Ibid, 95.
[68]Also much of WS, as noted in 4.3 above, for example Hebrew *hû* 'he', *ha-hû* 'that'.

limited sense:[69]

ɔc xuda	gered xida	deegʸa xunoa
boy he	girl she	children they

'the (above-mentioned) boy / girl / children'

One assumes then that an adnominal anaphoric demonstrative which marks definiteness in a limited sense (limited to previous discourse) is extended to mark definiteness in a broader sense (as a definite article).

One can make an even more general statement that spatial deixis is often extended metaphorically to textual (or discourse) deixis.[70] I will not delve into this far-reaching topic here, but we have already seen examples of the relationship between spatial and discourse deixis above in the discussion of the relationship between demonstratives and locative adverbs. Greenberg has discussed this with regard to the definite article, and writes that, "[the definite article] develops from a purely deictic element which has come to identify an element as previously mentioned in discourse."[71]

4.6 Appendix: Articles in Modern Semitic Languages

In addition to the ancient Central Semitic languages, definite articles are also found in other modern Semitic languages. A brief discussion seems appropriate here.

4.6.1 Neo-Aramaic (NENA, Turoyo, NWA)

As noted above (4.1.3), in the history of Aramaic, the article lost its meaning and became lexicalized. In Syriac, *kṯāḇā*, historically the definite ("emphatic") form, can mean 'book', 'a book', or 'the book'. The original indefinite ("absolute") form *kṯāḇ* is rare and restricted to certain syntactical constructions.[72] Thus, Syriac and other dialects of Aramaic were forced to find new ways to express definiteness.[73] In some cases, no definite form has developed, such as in the NENA dialect of Qaraqosh.[74] In other cases, an article was borrowed, as has

---

[69] Chamora and Hetzron (2000: 56).
[70] Heine, Claudi, and Hünnemeyer (1991: 179-82).
[71] Greenberg (1978: 61).
[72] Such as following numbers and the words *kul* 'every' and *dlā* 'without'. See Nöldeke (1904a: §202-204). Note also that adjectives appear in the historically indefinite ("absolute") form when predicative.
[73] See below (5.1.2) for a discussion of marking direct objects as definite by means of *l-* plus a proleptic pronoun.
[74] Khan (2002: 245).

happened in the NENA dialect of the Jews of Arbel.[75] In this dialect, the suffixed article *-ake* (e.g., *yāla* 'boy', *yālake* 'the boy') is borrowed from Kurdish. In yet other dialects, a definite article developed from the native stock, as in Turoyo, where there has been a grammaticalization of the original far demonstrative series.[76] Compare Syriac[77] and Turoyo:

	Syriac	meaning
m.sg.	*haw kalbā*	that dog
f.sg.	*hāy tawrtā*	that cow
m.pl.	*hānnōn kalbē*	those dogs
f.pl.	*hānnēn tawrāṯā*	those cows

	Turoyo[78]	meaning
m.sg.	*u kalbo*	the dog
f.sg.	*i tarto*	the cow
m.pl.	*ak kalbe*	the dogs
f.pl.	*at tawroṯe*	the cows

The Turoyo plural article *aC*, where *C* is identical to the following consonant, derives from **han-*, with a loss of the initial *h-* (as in the singular articles) and assimilation of *n* (which is regular).[79] Before words with an initial vowel, the article appears as either *ann-* or *a''-* (e.g., *ann abne* 'the sons'), and before a word with an initial consonant cluster, the article simply appears as *a-* (*a ktowe* 'the books').[80]

This scenario provides a very nice example of cyclicality:

Stage 1: no definite article
  Proto-Semitic: **bayt-* 'a/the house'

Stage 2: development of a definite article from demonstrative
  Biblical Aramaic: *baytā* 'the house' (< **bayt han*)

---

[75] Khan (1999: 173).
[76] Nöldeke (1881: 226), Brockelmann (1908-13 I: §246eγ); Jastrow (in Hetzron 1997: 357) suggests a derivation from the independent personal pronouns (Syriac *hū, hī*, and *hennōn/hennēn*), a derivation which is certainly simpler phonetically. Tezel (2003: 31) concurs with Jastrow, and provides some discussion of these two theories. Since the personal pronouns in Aramaic can also have a demonstrative function, either etymology for the Turoyo forms will illustrate the same point.
[77] Syriac is not the direct ancestor of Turoyo (nor any modern dialect), but was very closely related to it.
[78] Jastrow (1992: 20). Jastrow writes the article together with the noun (*u=kalbo, ak=kalbe*). In native texts written in Roman script, the article is written as a separate word. In texts written in Syriac script, the singular article is separated from the noun, though the plural is not. Jastrow's method is logical, as the article receives the word stress.
[79] As for the theory outlined in n. 76, we should note that **hen-* > **han-* in Turoyo by regular sound change. Cf. Syriac *'ednā* and Turoyo *'aḏno* 'ear'.
[80] Ibid.

Stage 3: re-analysis of definite marker and loss of definite meaning
Syriac: *baytā* 'a/the house'

Stage 4: development of new definite article from demonstrative
Turoyo: *u bayto* 'the house' (< **haw baytā*)

The Neo-West Aramaic dialects are an interesting case. In these closely related dialects, there is no full-fledged article, but the near demonstrative can be used as an article.[81] So, in the dialect of Maʻlula, *hanna ġabrōna* can mean both 'this man' and 'the man'. To make the demonstrative usage explicitly clear, one may repeat the demonstrative, as in *hanna ġabrōna hanna* 'this man'. This is a nice illustration of grammaticalization in progress.

4.6.2 Ethiopic (Tigrinya, Tigré, Amharic)

Tigrinya presents a situation exactly parallel to that of NWA above (4.6.1), in which the border between demonstrative and definite article remains unclear. The forms *'ətu* (m.sg.), *'əta* (f.sg.), *'ətom* (m.pl.), *'ətän* (f.pl.) are used both as a demonstrative 'that, those' and as a possible definite article.[82] Optionally, the demonstrative adjectives (including the near demonstrative), which precede the noun, may be coupled with a demonstrative pronoun following the noun. For example:

Tigrinya: *mänbär* 'chair', 'a chair', 'the chair';
'ətu mänbär 'that chair', 'the chair';
'ətu mänbär 'ətu 'that chair'

This is another example of grammaticalization in progress. Similar to the situation in Hebrew (see 4.3.1), the article contracts with the proclitic prepositions *bə* 'by, with' and *nə* 'for' (also the accusative marker; see below 5.1.6), as in *bätu* and *nätu* (< **bə-'etu, *nə-'etu*).[83]

In Tigré, the definite article is *lä*, the origin of which is unclear. Leslau (1945b: 183) simply assumes an unspecified demonstrative origin. Many have suggested the PS asseverative particle *lä-*, such as Barth (1913: 78), Hetzron (1972: 20), Testen (1997: 213). J. Huehnergard disagrees, suggesting rather a connection with the relative pronoun *lä* (Geʻez *'ella*). He notes, "The shift from asseverative particle to definite article seems an unlikely transition, although it

---

[81] See Arnold (1990: 43-44, 299) for forms and discussion.

[82] The forms here are those given in Leslau (1941: 38, 58-60), where there are also other variant forms given. Mason (1996: 17), a more recent, though far less rigorous, grammar (actually written in 1968) gives slightly different forms, notably m.sg. *'əti*.

[83] Leslau (1941: 39).

may be argued that both have essentially deictic functions."[84] It might also be possible that the *lä-* results in a reinterpretation of the Ge'ez *qatalo la-neguś* or *betu la-neguś* constructions, which are marked as definite.[85] The problem remains to be solved and will not be examined further here.

In Amharic there is a suffixed article, which has forms for m.sg. (*-u*), f.sg. (*-wa*, *-itu*, or *-it^wa*, used interchangeably), and c.pl. nouns (*-u*, added to the plural suffix).[86] The m.sg. article is identical to the 3ms possessive suffix, so in Amharic "his book" and "the book" are indistinguishable in form. The f.sg. *-wa* is also identical to the 3fs possessive suffix, while the variant *-itu* is composed of a feminine suffix *-it* plus the 3ms possessive, and the variant *-it^wa* is the feminine marker *-it* plus the 3fs possessive suffix. In fact, Ge'ez makes use of an identical construction as an optional marker of definiteness, and the same derivation is assumed.[87] It is normally believed that the definite article in Amharic and this construction in Ge'ez simply derive from the possessive suffixes. In Akkadian there also seem to be traces of a demonstrative use of the possessive suffixes, for example *inūmīšu* 'at that time; then'. If indeed the Amharic article derives from a possessive pronominal suffix, this would be a rare case in which the definite article does not derive from a demonstrative. W. Vycichl had a different interpretation, namely that the Amharic article, as well as the constructions in Ge'ez and Akkadian, derive not from possessives, but rather from demonstrative pronouns.[88] The issue needs to be pursued further, but will not be in this treatment.[89]

There are, of course, many more modern Ethiopic languages, many of which have definite articles. They are normally of the same type as in Amharic, i.e., where the article is identical to the third person possessive suffixes. To go into detail for all of these languages will not contribute anything to the present survey. I therefore refer the reader to the chapters on modern Ethiopic languages in Hetzron (1997) and their bibliographies.

4.6.3 Modern South Arabian

The definite article in the MSA languages was first studied in detail by T. M. Johnstone in a 1970 article, though he offers no etymological discussion. He notes that "the affix *ḥ(a)-/h(a)-* or *a-/ə-* functions as a definite article in Mehri

---

[84]Huehnergard (1983: 579 n. 91).
[85]Tropper (2002a: §52.21d, e).
[86]See Leslau (1995: 155-59) for discussion of forms and syntax.
[87]Tropper (§52.21c); Dillmann (1907: §172).
[88]Vycichl (1957: 169-70).
[89]I hope to return to this problem in a future study.

and Ḥarsūsi," also pointing out comparable affixes in other MSA languages.[90] Sima (2002) discusses these forms further, and suggests an original MSA article *ʾa-, borrowed from local Arabic dialects where ʾal- always assimilates to ʾaC-.[91] It is legitimate to suggest that a definite article has been borrowed; we have seen above (4.6.1) that at least one modern Aramaic dialect has borrowed its definite article from Kurdish. However, the source of the article remains uncertain and will not be examined further in this treatment.

---

[90]Johnstone (1970: 306).
[91]Sima (2002: 666).

Chapter 5
Direct Object Markers

5.1 Introduction

Proto-Semitic possessed a tripartite case system, which included nominative, accusative, and genitive cases. The accusative case ending served, *inter alia*, to mark nominal direct objects. Pronominal direct objects were expressed by a set of suffixes attached to the verb. It is unclear whether we can reconstruct a set of independent object pronouns for Proto-Semitic.[1] Akkadian and Arabic will exemplify the PS system of object marking:

Akkadian: *ibni bītam* 'he built the house'; *ibnī-šu* 'he built it'
Arabic: *yabnī l-bayta* 'he builds the house'; *yabnī-hi* 'he builds it'

A number of languages, however, developed or adapted specific particles to mark direct objects, or at least certain types of direct objects, either because the inherited case system was lost, or for other reasons to be discussed below. This chapter will focus on such direct object markers, also known as *notae accusativi*, in Canaanite, Aramaic, Arabic, Geʻez, Tigrinya, and Akkadian. Direct object markers in other languages will also be included in the broader discussion. After examining the development of these particles, including, of course, their grammaticalization, we will see how some of the Semitic *notae accusativi* have been grammaticalized further and acquired other functions.

In the following sections, the form and distribution of the *notae accusativi* will be outlined for each of the languages or language groups. Aramaic will receive a lengthier treatment, first because its various dialects exhibit quite a bit of variation, and second because this variation over Aramaic's long period of attested development gives us valuable insight pertaining to grammaticalization and its catalysts later in this chapter.

---

[1] See, for example, Lipiński (1997: §36.3) who suggests that there was such a set.

5.1.1 Canaanite

In Biblical and Epigraphic Hebrew, the particle *'et* (variant *'ēt*, when not proclitic)[2] appears before definite direct objects. The category 'definite' includes substantives with the definite article (*hab-bayit* 'the house'), nouns with pronominal possessive suffixes (*bêtî* 'my house'), and proper names. Also included in this category are the words *mî* 'who', *kōl* 'all, everything', the relative pronoun *'ăšer*, and constructions involving numbers.[3] The use of *'et* is noticeably rare in poetry, and in fact never occurs in the oldest poetry (such as Exod. 15:2-18, Deut. 32, Judg. 5).[4] Occasionally *'et* is found before what looks like an indefinite form, but usually where there is clearly a definite meaning and a need to avoid ambiguity. It is also not uncommon to find *'et* before the logical subjects of passive verbs, resulting in a construction that is ergative in appearance. This, however, should be regarded as an internal development.[5]

Hebrew *'et* can also be declined with pronominal suffixes, thus resulting in a set of independent accusative pronouns which serve as an alternative to a pronominal object suffix on the verb. Before suffixes, the base is *'ōt-* (or the orthographic variant *'ôt-*), with the exception of the second persons plural and third feminine plural (and very rarely the third masculine plural) which have the base *'et-*. The shape of the pre-suffixal form will be taken up below (5.4). Examples of the use of *'et* are:

> Biblical Hebrew: *bārā(') 'ĕlōhîm 'ēt haš-šamāyim wə-'ēt hā-'āreṣ* 'God created the heaven and the earth' (Gen. 1:1); *wə-hārəgû 'ōtî wə-'ōtāk yəhayyû* 'they will kill me and keep you alive' (Gen. 12:12); *'ăkalkēl 'etkem* 'I will sustain you' (Gen. 50:21)

> Epigraphic Hebrew: *'rwr h-'dm 'šr yptḥ 't z't* 'cursed be the man who opens this'; *w-šlḥtm 'tm* 'and send them'[6]

In later Hebrew the situation changes somewhat. The use of *'et* with suffixes to indicate pronominal objects is already on the decline in LBH, where we find verbal suffixes or the preposition *lə-* 'to, for' + suffixes used in its stead.[7] The

---

[2]The proclitic (unstressed) form, followed by a *maqqēp* (hyphen) in the Bible, occurs by my count roughly eight times more frequently than the non-clitic (stressed) form.
[3]Gesenius (§117a, b).
[4]Ibid. See also Waltke and O'Connor (1990: 177-85). It is also not uncommon to find *'et* lacking where it is expected in Standard Biblical Hebrew prose.
[5]For recent discussions on the syntax of this particle, see Waltke and O'Connor (1990: 177-85), Garr (1991), and the bibliographies therein.
[6]Silwan 2:2-3 and Arad 24:13, respectively, as they appear in Gogel (1998). See Gogel (1998: 162, 282-84) on this particle in Epigraphic Hebrew.
[7]Polzin (1976: 28-31), Gesenius (§117n).

LBH construction with *lə-* includes nominal objects as well, and its use, or at least its frequency, is most likely due to Aramaic influence.[8] In Qumran and Mishnaic Hebrew, we find pronominal objects almost exclusively indicated by verbal suffixes.[9] C. Cohen (1983) has demonstrated that in Mishnaic Hebrew *'et* indicates a pronominal object only when there is no alternative (i.e., with masculine plural participles or because of syntactic constraints). For more on the situation in Mishnaic Hebrew, see below (5.5.3). Finally, it should be noted that in the Hebrew of the Bar-Kosiba letters (ca. 135 CE), the sequence of the *nota accusativi* plus the definite article (*'et ha-*) is normally reduced to *t-* (= /ta/);[10] this has an exact parallel in Modern Hebrew, where the reduced form /ta/ is often heard, and even written regularly in representations of colloquial speech.

In Phoenician, the direct object marker usually has the form *'yt*, sometimes *'t*, and in late Punic, even simply *t*.[11] We can say with relative certainty that in the form *'yt*, the *y* is consonantal, as *y* is not normally used as a *mater lectionis* in older Phoenician. A probable vocalization of *'yt* is /ʾiyyāt/, based on comparison with Aramaic *yāt* and Arabic *'iyyā-*.[12] Krahmalkov (1992) and Testen (1997) have suggested that *'yt* and *'t* are in fact allomorphs in at least one dialect of Phoenician, though they actually suggest different conditioning factors. Regardless, this is not relevant to the present discussion. Phoenician *'yt* had the same distribution as in Hebrew, which is to say that it appeared before definite objects. However, its use seems to be inconsistent.

Finally, note that, unlike Hebrew, the Phoenician *nota accusativi* is not used with pronominal suffixes. Only twice, in Punic, is *'t* attested with suffixes.[13] Pronominal direct objects are normally indicated by a suffix on the verb, as is also common in Hebrew. Occasionally, the preposition *'lt-* 'on; for' can also be used with suffixes to indicate a pronominal object; it is important to note that the preposition *'lt* is one of the prepositions used to express the dative.[14]

---

[8]Polzin (1976: 64-66).
[9]On Qumran, see Qimron (1986: 75-76); on Mishnaic, see Pérez Fernández (1999: 164), C. Cohen (1983).
[10]See Yadin et al. (2002: 17-18).
[11]Friedrich and Röllig (1999: §255-56). Puech (1982) notes that the earliest Phoenician inscriptions lack the direct object marker (and the definite article). The direct object marker first appears, according to Puech (p. 51), around 900 BCE.
[12]Following Hackett (2004: 355). Friedrich and Röllig (1999: §255) have *'iyat*.
[13]Krahmalkov (2001: 281-85).
[14]Krahmalkov (2001: 74). This preposition has a variety of meanings; see Friedrich and Röllig (1999: §284).

5.1.2 Aramaic

The Aramaic language is, as noted above (2.6), dialectically and chronologically quite diverse. This is also true of the two *notae accusativi*, *'yt* (later *yāt*) and *l-*, whose attestations and distributions vary considerably. For the purposes of this section, we can divide Aramaic into two types: a *yāt* type and a *l-* type, with significant overlap. In the oldest Aramaic inscriptional dialects, known collectively as Old Aramaic, we find a particle *'yt* used before definite direct objects, as well as with pronominal suffixes. This is clearly to be linked with the Hebrew and Phoenician *notae accusativi*. The use of the dative/allative preposition *l-* for the same purposes is found already in Imperial Aramaic. In some dialects, both are in use, sometimes with a distinct preference, sometimes with mutually exclusive functions. Note also that two dialects may have different functions for the same particle. For example, in Nabatean, unlike in Old Aramaic, *yāt* is used with pronominal suffixes, but never alone with nominal objects. The overall picture is immensely complex, but the following investigation of the major dialects, considered in chronological order, will suffice as a general overview. Following the discussion of the individual dialects is a brief summary which makes this wealth of data somewhat easier to consider.

Old Aramaic. The *nota accusativi* *'yt* optionally appears before definite direct objects.[15] The form is also used with pronominal suffixes to indicate pronominal objects, though object suffixes on the verb are more common. For nominal objects there are many examples with no direct object marker. Most scholars claim the attestation of an accusative marker *wt* based on one form <wth> (*wt* with 3ms suffix) in the Zinjirli (Sam'alian) inscriptions.[16] I would hold that this form is not to be connected with the accusative marker *'yt*, but rather belongs with the prepositional base *wt*, attested in the (later) very common compound prepositions *lə-wāt*[17] and *kə-wāt*,[18] and therefore is not relevant to the historical discus-

---

[15] Degen (1969: §37, §47, §71), Fitzmyer (1995: 111). To Degen's examples, we may add the since-discovered Tel Dan inscription (KAI 310), which also attests *'yt*.

[16] KAI 214:28. While most count this dialect as Aramaic (recently: Tropper 1993: 311; Kaufman in Hetzron 1997: 114), some do not (Garr 1985, Huehnergard 1995). I concur with the arguments in Huehnergard 1995, but I include the data under the heading of Old Aramaic here simply for convenience, since all works on the *nota accusativi* do the same. In any case, the exact classification does not affect the discussion.

[17] The earliest attestation I found is in Ezra 4:12, in fact the only attestation in Biblical Aramaic. It does not seem to occur elsewhere in Old or Imperial Aramaic.

[18] Attested first in (pre-Imperial) Egyptian Aramaic in the sixth century BCE. See Hug (1993: 36), text HermB1:7 (= TAD A2.3). Note that in his glossary, Hug lists *kwt* under *'yt*.

sion of the *nota accusativi*. Some hold that all of these forms are related, but that cannot be demonstrated.

Old Aramaic: *'hbd 'yt ktk w-'yt mlkh* 'I shall destroy KTK and its king'; *hn 'y[t]y yqtln* 'if they kill me'[19]

Early Imperial. In the small corpus of material from this period, direct objects are normally unmarked.[20] We do find *'yt* one time, with a pronominal suffix; unfortunately, the context of this form (*'ythm*) has not been preserved. The object marker *l-* is attested twice, once (in a text from Nineveh) before an animate noun and once (in a text from Hermopolis, Egypt) with a pronominal suffix.

Early Imperial Aramaic: *lh šbq 'nh lh ... 'bd 'nh lh* 'I do (will) not leave him ... I am providing (working) for him'[21]

Imperial/Egyptian. Muraoka and Porten (2003: 262-63) describe a situation in which the direct object is normally unmarked, except occasionally by *l-*. Folmer (1995: 340-71) analyzes the situation a bit differently, and notes that *l-* usually marks the direct object, though almost exclusively when animate. Pronominal objects seem to be indicated by verbal suffixes, with the exception of participles, which take *l-* + suffix. Folmer (1995: 108 n. 483; 707) rejects a single possible attestation of *yt* (+ suffix), and interprets it very plausibly as a verbal form instead.

Egyptian Aramaic: *ktšt l-'ntty* 'you struck my wife'; *hškht l-'hyqr* 'I found Ahiqar'; *qtlw l-mrdy'* 'they killed the rebels'[22]

Biblical (Ezra). It must be recalled that Biblical Aramaic is really made up of two dialects. In the Imperial Aramaic dialect of Ezra, there is normally no direct object marker for nouns or pronouns (e.g., 4:23, 5:3, 6:18). There are two good examples of *lə-* being used as a *nota accusativi*, namely, 5:2 (with a pronominal suffix) and 5:12 (with a noun). Also possible examples are 7:25 (twice, with a noun, after a participle) and 5:10 (with a pronominal suffix). In both of these cases, however, the *lə-* can be interpreted as a dative.[23] Thus we have one or two

---

[19]Texts from Sefire, II.C:5 and III:11, respectively, taken from Fitzmyer (1995).
[20]See Hug (1993: 102) for an overall discussion of object marking. On *l-* see Hug, p. 71.
[21]Text HermB 3.5 (Hug 1993: 37-38). This example is also included in Muraoka and Porten (2003, text TAD A.2.4:4). I have not included the example from Nineveh, as there are difficulties in interpretation. See Hug's discussion of text NinU 2 (p. 18).
[22]Muraoka and Porten's (2003) texts TAD B7.2:5, C1.1:76, and C2.1:13, respectively.
[23]See Bauer-Leander (1927: §100w) for a discussion of such ambiguity. A good case is made for 5:10.

examples each of *lə-* with a noun and pronominal suffix. Importantly, all examples are with animate objects, and two (one for sure) are after a participle.

   Biblical Aramaic (Ezra): *hargizû 'ăbāhŏtanā le-'ĕlāh šəmayyā* 'our fathers angered the God of heaven' (5:12); *məsā'ădîn ləhôn* 'helping them' (5:2)

Biblical (Daniel). In the later, Middle Aramaic dialect of Daniel, we find the base *yt* attested once, with a pronominal suffix (*yāthôn*, 3:12). This is significant, as it is the earliest vocalized form of the *yt* particle.[24] Elsewhere throughout Daniel, *lə-* can be used to mark definite direct objects, most often animate.[25]

   Biblical Aramaic (Daniel): *gubrîn yəhûdā'în dî-mannîtā yātəhôn* 'certain Jews whom you appointed (them)' (3:12); *lə-hôbādā lə-ḥakkîmê bābel* 'to destroy the wise men of Babylon' (2:24); *wə-lî ...yəba'ôn* '(they) sought me out' (4:33)

Targumic (Onqelos/Jonathan). In Targums Onqelos and Jonathan, by far the most common accusative marker is *yāt*, essentially used in imitation of the Hebrew *'et*. It is also used to express pronominal objects, though verbal suffixes are quite common as well. The choice of pronominal object marker (i.e., verbal suffix or independent object) is normally dependent on the underlying Hebrew. *l-* is also found as a D.O. marker, though normally where Hebrew lacks *'et*.[26] Occasionally, *l-* is used in conjunction with an anticipatory verbal object suffix.[27] One must be wary when analyzing the Targumic evidence, which by definition exists mainly as a translation of Hebrew texts. The underlying Hebrew text has exerted strong influence on the Aramaic, so the extensive use of *yāt* is undoubtedly due in great part to the Hebrew use of *'et*. This has parallels elsewhere. For example, Ladino (Judeo-Spanish) Bible translations consistently use *a* to translate Hebrew *'et*, as in Genesis 1:1 *alos cielos y ala tierra* 'the heaven and the earth' (Heb. *'ēt haš-šamāyim wə-'ēt hā-'āreṣ*) and Exodus 3:1 *Moše era apacentán a oveğas de*

---

[24] Admittedly, the actual vocalization was not recorded until the late first millennium of the Common Era. In terms of physical attestation, the earliest manuscript with vocalized Aramaic D.O. marker would probably be a Syriac Bible manuscript.

[25] Rosenthal (1963: §182), Bauer-Leander (1927: §100q-x).

[26] See Dalman (1905: 110-11, 226). Dodi (1981: §8.519) simply lists the various forms of *yāt*, without any discussion of syntax.

[27] In this chapter, the terms "anticipatory" and its synonym "proleptic" are used to refer to all redundant verbal suffixes, regardless of whether the independent direct object precedes or follows the verb. Technically, if the object precedes, the verbal suffix is "resumptive". Since anticipatory suffixes are the norm, I use this term to include those cases where the verbal suffix is resumptive.

Yitro 'Moses was tending Jethro's sheep' (Heb. *'et ṣō(')n yitrô*).²⁸ Yet Ladino typically follows Spanish in its use of *a* with only human direct objects (see below, 5.2.1),²⁹ and all Spanish Bible translations I found lacked *a* in these examples, and in many others where it is present in Ladino. Therefore, it seems that the Ladino translation is simply using the direct object marker *a* as a translational device. The translator(s) of Targums Onqelos and Jonathan probably mimicked the Hebrew in the same way. When Targums deviate from the underlying Hebrew, *l-* is the usual D.O. marker.

> Onqelos Aramaic: *wi-y'allǝlûn lanā yāt 'ar'ā wǝ-yātîbûn yātanā pitgāmā* 'they will reconnoiter the land for us and bring us back word' (Deut. 1:22; Heb. *'ēt hā-'āreṣ ... 'ōtānû*); *šabqêh li-lbāšêh* 'he left his garment' (Gen. 39:15, Heb. *way-ya'ăzōb bigdô*); *tabbartānûn li-d-qāmû 'al 'ammāk* 'you broke those who rose against your people' (Exod. 15:7, Heb. *tahărōs qāmękā* 'you break your opponents'); *miṣrā'ê dāḥǝqîn lǝhôn* 'the Egyptians oppress them' (Exod. 3:9, Heb. *lōḥaṣîm 'ōtām*)³⁰

Nabatean. In Nabatean pronominal objects are always expressed by means of *yt-* + suffix, and never with verbal suffixes. The preposition *l-* is not attested at all as a *nota accusativi*. There is no direct object marker before nominal objects.³¹

> Nabatean Aramaic: *mn dy ynpq ythm* 'whoever takes them out...'

Palmyrene. In this dialect there is normally no direct object marker at all. Pronominal objects are expressed exclusively by a verbal suffix, and nominal objects are not marked in any way,³² with the exception of a single occurrence of *yt* before a nominal object:

> Palmyrene Aramaic: *kdy 'ty lk' yt lgyny* 'when he brought the legions here'³³

Qumran. In the Genesis Apocryphon, *l-* is used to mark direct objects, mostly animate.³⁴ Pronominal objects are indicated by means of the verbal suffix, with the exception of participles, which take *l-* + suffix. While *yāt* is not attested in the Genesis Apocryphon, it is attested two, possibly three, times elsewhere: once

---

²⁸Text from Lazar (2000).
²⁹Bunis (1999: 137).
³⁰The text and vocalization is that of Sperber (1992).
³¹Cantineau (1930-32 I: 56-57, 109); Levinson (1974: 61-62).
³²Cantineau (1935: 145).
³³Cantineau (1930 III: 29), text 22:4. More recently published in Hillers and Cussini (1996), text C3932: 4.
³⁴Muraoka (1972: 30-31).

(maybe twice) in 11QtgJob and once in 5Q New Jerusalem.[35]

> Qumran Aramaic (Genesis Apocryphon): *w-mḥw l-rpʾy* 'they destroyed the Rephaim' (21:28); *w-hwʾt ktš' lh w-l-kwl ʾnš byth* 'it kept afflicting him and all the men of his house' (20:17)[36]
>
> Qumran Aramaic (5Q New Jerusalem): *[w-mšḥ 'l kl] ʾspʾ yt d[šʾy lh]* '[and he measured at every] threshold the do[ors on it]' (1.i:17)
>
> Qumran Aramaic (11QtgJob): *w-yplgwn yth* 'and will they divide it' (col. 35:9 = Job 40:30)

Bar-Kosiba. The Aramaic of the Bar-Kosiba (and Wadi Murabbaʿat) documents is kept separate here from Qumran Aramaic, though it is geographically adjacent and attested only a century or two later, because the use of the *notae accusativi* is markedly different. The corpus is small, but there is a rather consistent use of *yt* to mark definite nominal and pronominal objects in the letters.[37] We also find one possible example of *l-* marking a pronominal object (after a participle). In the legal contracts, the use of *yt* is less consistent, and verbal suffixes often indicate pronominal objects. Note also that the Nabatean texts found together with this corpus conform to the pattern described for Nabatean above.

> Bar-Kosiba Aramaic: *l-mḥd yt syph* 'to take the (or: his) sword' (P. Yadin 54: 16); *tšlḥwn ly yt ʾlʿzr* 'you will send me Eleazar' (P. Yadin 50: 4); *w-ʾlm lʾ tšdrwn ythn* 'if you do not send them' (P. Yadin 55: 6); *ʾnḥnh ṣrykyn lh* 'we need him' (P. Yadin 56: 7)[38]

Christian Palestinian. Neither Schulthess (1924) nor Müller-Kessler (1991) makes this clear, but *yt* occurs only with suffixes, indicating pronominal objects. In fact, pronominal suffixes on the verb are relatively rare, thus presenting a situation similar to Nabatean.[39] *l-* with suffixes is used to indicate pronominal objects, though far less often. As for nominal objects, I found that *l-* is used to mark direct objects only when animate. I also found many examples in the CPA Bible translations where the MT has *ʾet* and CPA has nothing (e.g., Exod. 4:15) or *l-* (e.g., 1 Sam. 1:19), as well as where the MT has nothing and CPA has *l-*

---

[35] E. Cook's discussion (1992: 11) of *yāt* mentions two attestations in 11QtgJob, but I found only one in the edition of Fitzmyer and Harrington (1978: 10-46).

[36] The text is that of Fitzmyer (1971) (= Fitzmyer and Harrington 1978: 100-126).

[37] Kutscher (1960-61), Yadin et al. (2002: 25).

[38] The text is that of Yadin et al. (2002). Fitzmyer and Harrington (1978, text pap?ḤevB ar:3), include the example *zbnt lk ... l-bth dyly* 'I have sold to you my house'. I exclude it here in light of its absence from the critical edition of Yadin et al.

[39] Müller-Kessler (1991: 259).

(e.g., Num. 13:28). In addition, there are numerous cases where the MT has a verbal suffix and CPA has *yt*. This demonstrates that CPA was not influenced by Hebrew in this regard, as for example Targum Onqelos probably was.

> CPA: *w-mrʾ ʾlhk ymswr ythwn byn ʾydyk* 'the Lord your God will deliver them to you' (Deut. 7:23, Heb. *û-nətānām*); *w-lʾ mkr lh ʿwd ʾtrh* 'his place does not know him anymore' (Job 7:10, Heb. *yakkîrennû*); *w-ʾkr l-ḥn' ʾtth* 'and he knew Hannah his wife' (1 Sam. 1:19, Heb. *'et ḥannā*); *l-šwrbtʾ d-ʿnq ḥmynh tmn* 'we saw the tribe of Anak there' (Num. 13:28, Heb. *yəlîdê hā-ʿănāq rāʾînû*)[40]

Palestinian Targums. This corpus, which includes the Targum Neofiti and Targum fragments from the Cairo Geniza, usually employs *yāt* to mark a definite direct object, as well as pronominal objects.[41] However, *l-* is also found with nominal direct objects, though less often and almost always when the noun is a proper name. Occasional absences of any direct object marker usually correspond to such a deficiency in the Hebrew text. Verbal suffixes are exceedingly rare; where object suffixes appear in the underlying Hebrew, these texts nearly always employ *yāt-* plus a suffix. Thus the overall situation is the same as that of CPA, a contemporary and co-territorial dialect. As is well known, these Targums are not as literal with regard to the Hebrew original as Targum Onqelos, and there are examples of this with the *nota accusativi*.

> Targum Neofiti: *ṭrwd yt ʾmtʾ hdh w-yt brh* 'expel this handmaid and her son' (Gen. 21:10, Heb. *gārēš hā-ʾāmā haz-zō(ʾ)t wə-ʾet-bənāh*); *w-nšq yth w-ʾyl yth* 'and he kissed him and brought him' (Gen. 29:13, Heb. *wa-ynaššeq-lô wa-ybîʾēhû*); *nsbyt l-hgr w-yhbt yth lk* 'I took Hagar and I gave her to you' (Gen. 16:5, Heb. *nātattî šipḥātî bə-ḥêqekā* 'I gave my handmaid into your bosom')

Samaritan. Samaritan Targumic texts attest *yāt* with and without suffixes, as well as verbal object suffixes, and *l-* with and without suffixes. It is unclear whether there is any pattern, though it does seem that the Samaritan Targum at least was heavily influenced in its choice of *nota accusativi* by the underlying text (cf. the discussion of Targumic above).[42] In the text known as *Memar Marqah*, which unlike the Samaritan Targum, was not a translation, we find a

---

[40] In Müller-Kessler and Sokoloff (1997: 58), this verse is labeled 13:29, following the Vulgate tradition.

[41] Golomb (1985: 65-66, 208-11) discusses Targum Neofiti; Fassberg (1990: 252) discusses the Geniza fragments, with the inclusion of a very nice statistical chart.

[42] I found no special discussion of D.O. markers in Macuch (1982). Tal (2000) provides better information, though as a dictionary its grammatical discussion is very limited.

rather different situation with regard to object marking.⁴³ In this text (not taking into account the abundant Targumic quotes), direct objects are most often unmarked, but we do find *yt* infrequently, though not rarely, marking definite nominal objects. Pronominal objects are often expressed with *yt-* plus a suffix, though verbal object suffixes are also used. I found almost no occurrences of *l-* marking a direct object in this text.

> <u>Samaritan Targumic Aramaic</u>: *w-nsb mš̌h yt 'tth* 'and Moses took his wife' (Exod. 4:20); *w-brkw 'p yty* 'and bless me too'; *w-qbl 'lhym l-ṣlwt l'h* 'God received Leah's prayer' (Gen. 30:17, note Heb. *way-yišmaʿ ...'el lēʾāh*); *w- 'nh mḥbl lwn* 'I will destroy them' (Gen. 6:13, *wə-hinənî mašḥîtām*)⁴⁴
>
> <u>Samaritan Aramaic</u> (*Memar Marqah*): *qṭlt prʿh w-kl ʿmh* 'I slew Pharaoh and all his people' (III, §2); *w-ʿnh ṣbʿtk w-šgrny* 'he answered your cry and sent me' (III, §2); *ʿd 'šmʿk yt qlh* 'so I would make you hear his voice' (III, §2); *w-lʾ šmʿ yt mqrty* 'and he did not hear my call' (IV, §8)

Syriac. The particle *yāt* occurs twelve times in the Syriac translation of the Hebrew Bible (the Peshitta) and a single time in an archaic poem.⁴⁵ Otherwise *yāt* (as an object marker) is absent in Syriac. We must consider the Bible occurrences as influenced by the underlying text, and the poetic example as an archaism or Biblicism. We do, however, in all kinds of Syriac texts, find *l-* used extensively, though not obligatorily, to mark definite direct objects. Its use is noticeably more prevalent when the object precedes the verb. With nominal objects, the verb can optionally have an anticipatory suffix.⁴⁶ So, *bnā baytā* (with no D.O. marker), *bnā l-baytā*, or *bnāy l-baytā* (with anticipatory object suffix) can all mean 'he built the house'.⁴⁷ This final construction, in which the object is essentially repeated, is widely used in later Eastern dialects (BTA and Mandaic), and found occasionally in slightly earlier dialects such as Targumic. It is unknown from the earlier dialects of the Imperial period. Of the three possibilities, the third alone is marked for definiteness; that is to say, it must be translated 'he built the house', while the first two can potentially mean 'he built a house'. This is significant since Syriac—like other later dialects of Aramaic—has lost its definite article (or more precisely, the definite form of the noun has lost its defi-

---

⁴³This text can be found, along with an introduction, in J. Macdonald (1963).
⁴⁴The texts are taken from Tal (1980).
⁴⁵Nöldeke (1904a: §287, n. 1). For an example, see the Peshitta, Genesis 1:1. Also see Littmann (1904: 47-48) for a unique example of *yāt* in a Syriac inscription.
⁴⁶For a discussion of anticipatory (or appositional, or proleptic) pronouns, see Brockelmann (1908-13 II: §152). On the relationship to the parallel Akkadian construction, see Kaufman (1974: 131-32).
⁴⁷See Nöldeke (1904a: §§287-88), for more detail.

nite meaning), so this construction resolves ambiguity and allows for a renewed expression of definiteness.

<u>Syriac</u>: *l-ʿālmā ʾešboq* 'the world I will forsake'; *w-ḥadru(h)y l-bayteh w-(ʾ)aḥdu(h)y leh* 'and they surrounded his house and took him prisoner'

Babylonian Talmudic. BTA attests both *yāt* and *l-* as direct object markers, with and without suffixes.[48] However, *yāt* occurs only in what Margolis (1910: 84) calls the "older" language and what Sokoloff (2002b: 544) calls "archaic and dialectal" texts; Schlesinger (1928: 105), more expressly, identifies *yāt* with texts or sayings of Palestinian origin. With the very close relationship of the Babylonian Talmud to Biblical and Mishnaic Hebrew texts, the latter have undoubtedly influenced the former in many ways, and it would not be surprising to find *yāt* as a Hebraism (i.e., in imitation of Hebrew *ʾet*). Definite nominal objects are usually marked with *l-*, often in conjunction with an anticipatory verbal suffix. BTA patterns with Syriac and Mandaic in this use of an anticipatory verbal suffix (appositional proclitic pronoun). Verbal object suffixes are also extremely common, though *l-* is often used as well to indicate pronominal objects. Margolis notes that with the participle, *l-* dominates as opposed to object suffixes (though not exclusively). In addition, BTA can indicate pronominal objects with an innovative form *l-dyd-*, with an anticipatory verbal object for particular emphasis. The form *dyd-* is actually a possessive pronoun (see above, 3.4.3.3), but is often used in apposition to a pronominal suffix for emphasis.[49] This is an internal development, shared only with Mandaic and Syriac (where it is rare), and has no bearing here on the overall discussion of Aramaic. Examples of the different direct object markers are:

BTA: *w-ʾšqy yt ʾrʿ* 'irrigate the field'; *ʾlbyš ythwn* 'he dressed them'; *w-lʾ šbyq lhy* 'he did not let them'; *w-ksy lyh l-ywmʾ* 'it concealed the sun'; *gbrʾ d-trqyh l-glyh* 'a man who locked his door'; *ḥzy l-dydy* 'look at me'; *šdywh l-dydh* 'they cast *him*'

Mandaic. In Classical Mandaic, definite direct objects are very often marked by *l-* (or *ʿl*, which is interchangeable with *l-* in all its functions), most often with a co-referential verbal suffix. This goes for pronominal objects as well, though these are often accompanied by the additional preposition *dyl-*, a form that is

---

[48] Margolis (1910: 84-86), Schlesinger (1928: 101-6), Sokoloff (2002b: 544-55, 611-12).
[49] This construction seems to be an extension of its possessive use in a phrase like *brʾy dydy* 'my (own) son', where *dydy* is in apposition to the suffix *-y* on the noun. By extension we see prepositional phrases like *mynʾy dydy* 'from me', as well as the direct object usage shown here.

identical in use and etymology to Babylonian Talmudic *l-dyd-*.⁵⁰

Mandaic: *l-ʿwrbʾ lʾṭh w-l-yʾwnʾ byrkh* 'he cursed the raven and blessed the dove'; *lkwn dylkwn mʾlbyšnʾlkwn* 'I clothe you'; *lkwn qʾryn* 'I call you'

The above data can be summarized in the following table:

used	*yāt* w/ suffixes	*yāt* w/ def. nouns	*l-* w/ suffixes	*l-* w/ def. nouns
Old Aramaic	✓	✓		
Early Imperial	1x		1x	1x (animate)
Egyptian			w/ participles	rare/animate
Biblical Ezra			1 or 2x	1 or 2x (animate)
Biblical Dan.	1x		✓	✓
Targums O/J	✓	✓	rare	rare
Nabatean	✓			
Palmyrene		1x		
Qumran	1x	1x	w/ participles	animate (mostly)
Bar-Kosiba	✓	✓		1x (legal text)
CPA	✓		rare	animate
Pal. Targums	✓	✓		animate
Samaritan	✓	✓	(in Targum)	(in Targum)
Syriac		13x	✓	✓
BTA	✓ (archaic)		✓	✓
Mandaic			✓	✓

I have grouped the above table roughly by dialect group. Now, if we analyze the data together, we can observe a diachronic situation that can be sketched as follows:

---

⁵⁰Nöldeke (1875: §270), Macuch (1965: 420).

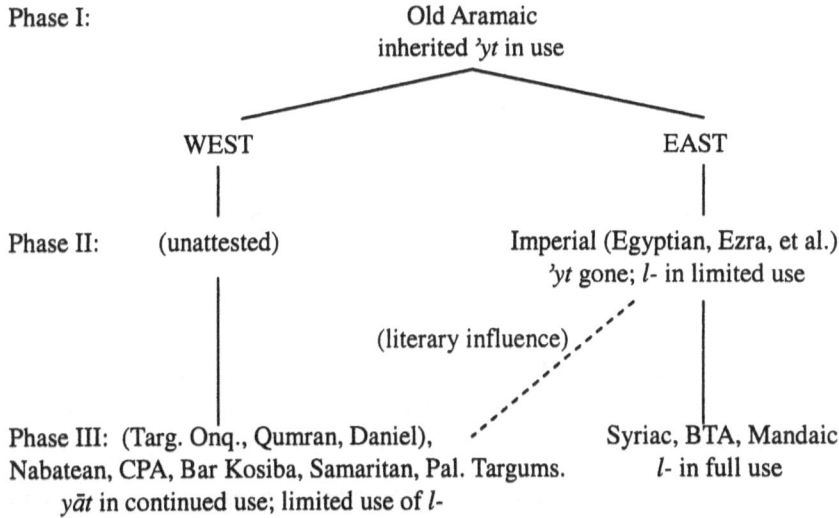

This is not meant to be an accurate tree of genetic relationships, simply a representation based on usage of the direct object marker. It can be summed up verbally as follows:[51] Phase I represents the situation as inherited from Proto-NWS, which is to say there existed a non-obligatory *nota accusativi* '*yt* */ʾiyyāt/.[52] In Phase II, during which time the use of an eastern variety of Aramaic was spread across the Near East by the Assyrian, Babylonian, and especially the Persian empires, '*yt* was lost and *l*- began to appear as the direct object marker. Its early use was mainly limited to the object of participles (which historically, as nominal forms, could not take an object suffix) or when the object was animate. The Imperial form of Aramaic, as a language of state, not surprisingly developed into a literary standard. In Phase III, we find a noticeable split between Eastern and Western dialects. The Western dialects retained a reduced version of the older form, namely, *yāt* (though with dialectal differences, and often only with pronominal suffixes), while in the east the construction with *l*- became widespread. Some texts from the west make extensive use of *l*-, notably the book of Daniel, literary texts from Qumran and a legal contract from the Bar-Kosiba period, and these can be explained as having been composed in (or influenced by) the standard literary language inherited from the Imperial period. In the later dialects of

---

[51]The classic study of this is Kutscher (1960-61). Folmer (1995: 369-71) presents a nice summary, essentially of Kutscher. The present description differs slightly from these previous works.

[52]Presumably, the function of this particle was more than just a direct object marker, since the accusative case was still in use and its use is inconsistent in early dialects like Old Aramaic and Phoenician.

CPA and the Palestinian Targums, *l-* has been incorporated, though only in its limited function with animate nominal objects. Targum Onqelos is a mixed dialect, not composed in a single place, and shows features of east and west.

A final point must be made about Aramaic, namely, the existence of a parallel use of *l-* with genitive phrases. There are three main ways of expressing genitival relationship, though as with the *notae accusativi*, there are diachronic and dialectal differences. Syriac will suffice here as a sample dialect, since these differences are irrelevant for our present purposes. The three methods are:

1. NOUN + NOUN (construct phrase) (e.g., Syriac *bar malkā* 'the son of a/the king)
2. NOUN + GENITIVE EXPONENT + NOUN (*brā d-malkā*, idem)[53]
3. NOUN + possessive suffix + GENITIVE EXPONENT + NOUN (*breh d-malkā* 'the son of the king'; lit., 'his son, of the king')

Method number three is marked as definite, and this serves a useful function in Syriac (and other contemporary Aramaic dialects) in which there is no definite article. Kaufman (1974: 131-32) believes this Aramaic construction to be a calque from Akkadian (e.g., *māršu ša šarri* 'the son of the king'), which likewise has no definite article.[54] This is analogous to the above-mentioned *bnāy l-baytā* construction, in which the object is also marked as definite. However, there is also a fourth method which is extremely rare in all ancient Aramaic dialects, namely:

4. *l-* with anticipatory suffix (e.g., Syriac *breh l-malkā* 'the son of the king')[55]

The derivation of this construction is convincingly explained as an analogy to the prepositional accusative construction. It seems that its rarity in ancient Aramaic dialects (with a handful of attestations from CPA, Samaritan, Mandaic, and Syriac) is attributable to the fact that it was a colloquial form which had not yet become a part of the written language. Hopkins notes modern reflexes of both the objectival and genitival uses of *l-* in the Neo-West Aramaic dialects. For example:

---

[53] See above (section 3.4.3) for a discussion on genitive exponents.

[54] Von Soden (1995: §138j, Anm.) suggests the opposite direction of influence, but the presence of this construction in OB makes this suspect.

[55] In reality, Syriac attests this construction only with the governing noun *šmā* 'name', as first pointed out by Goldenberg (1979: 324). This construction is discussed in detail, and its origins explained, in Hopkins (1997).

NWA (Ma'lula): *faṯhil ṭar'a* 'he opened the door' (cf. Syriac *patḥeh l-tar'ā*); *mōr-əl payṭa* 'master of the house'[56]

5.1.3 Akkadian

In Neo-Assyrian (see 2.1), the preposition *ana* 'to, for', can be used as a *nota accusativi*. In this dialect, unlike earlier dialects of Akkadian, there is only a two-way case distinction, namely, nominative-accusative (*-u*) and genitive (*-i*). Therefore, given that the accusative is no longer unambiguously marked, *ana* may be used to avoid ambiguity or for emphasis of the object.[57] An example is:

Neo-Assyrian: *a-na* PN *id-du-ku* 'they killed PN'

Von Soden (1995: §114e) notes that a similar use of *ana* is also found occasionally in Neo- and Late Babylonian. This use of *ana* in Akkadian can undoubtedly be attributed to Aramaic influence, though the situation of Akkadian at this period (i.e., the lack of an unambiguous accusative case) warranted the adoption of this Aramaism.

5.1.4 Arabic

The use of the preposition *li-* 'to, for' to mark nominal and pronominal direct objects is known from Classical Arabic, where it is almost exclusively used before the objects of verbal nouns and participles.[58] Unlike elsewhere in Semitic, the definiteness or animacy of the object does not seem to have any bearing on the use of *li-*.[59] Examples are:

Classical Arabic: *muṣaddiqan li-mā ma'ahum* 'verifying that which they have' (Sura 2:91); *'in kuntum lir-ru'yā ta'burūna* 'if you can interpret the dream' (Sura 12:43)

In Quranic Arabic, the use of *li-* in conjunction with finite verbs appears only for reasons of syntax or (in poetry) meter or rhyme.[60] In post-Quranic Classical

---

[56] Examples are taken from Arnold (1990: 286, 301-2); further explanations can also be found therein.

[57] Hämeen-Anttila (2000: 77), Parpola (1984: 205 n. 29). Lipiński (1997: §52.10) claims Middle and Neo-Babylonian attestations of this construction, but I have not found support for this elsewhere.

[58] We have seen already above (3.1.2) that *l-* was used after participles—which historically were unable to take an object suffix—in some Aramaic dialects.

[59] A. Fischer (1910) is a detailed study. Also see Brockelmann (1908-13 II: §211a) and Wright (1967 II: §29, §31).

[60] A. Fischer (1910: 184).

Arabic its use can be explained possibly by the weakening of the case system in spoken Arabic, or to Aramaic influence.

In some Middle Arabic dialects, such as that of Christian Palestinian texts, *li-* is used extensively to mark direct objects, in particular when the object precedes the verb.[61] An anticipatory (or, more often, resumptive) verbal object suffix is optional. Unlike in Classical Arabic, however, the Middle Arabic construction is found only with definite direct objects. As Blau (1967: 413) points out, this is almost certainly due to Aramaic substrate influence, as the Middle Arabic syntax in this case does not match that of Classical Arabic but does match that of Aramaic (see above, 5.1.2).

> Middle Arabic (Christian Palestinian): *l-mn trydwn ... nryd l-yšwʿ* 'whom do you want? ... We want Jesus'; *w-l-ʿbdk ywnʾn ʾnzlth* 'and you brought down your servant Jonah'

Some dialects of modern Arabic, including Lebanese, Syrian, Galilean, and Iraqi, employ a construction with the preposition *la-* 'to, for' to mark certain kinds of direct objects. The construction requires an anticipatory pronominal suffix on the verb. For example:

> Lebanese Arabic: *šufto la-najīb* 'I saw Najib' (lit., 'I saw him *la*-Najib')[62]
>
> Iraqi (Christian Baghdadi) Arabic: *qag̱ētūnu ləl-əktēb* 'I read the book' (lit., 'I read it, *la*-the book')[63]

This construction is well known from Aramaic (see above, 5.1.2), and in fact, like the Middle Arabic construction, has most likely arisen in these dialects through Aramaic substrate influence. Some grammars report that the construction is limited to proper names or animate nouns;[64] this does not seem to be fully accurate, at least not for all dialects involved. Levin (1987), on Galilean Arabic, describes a range of usages with both animate and inanimate definite objects, though all in what might be described as "emphatic" contexts. Koutsoudas (1978: 529), on Lebanese, states that all definite nouns are eligible. Blanc (1964: 128-30) and Abu-Haidar (1991: 116), on Baghdadi, also include all definite nouns, though add that the construction is optional. Usage certainly varies by dialect (as noted even by Blanc), but it seems safe to generalize that the construction is on the whole limited to definite nouns, and in some dialects is obligatory with proper names.

A parallel construction, also present in Aramaic and Ethiopic, is found in

---

[61] Blau (1967: 413-23).

[62] Thackston (1996: 38-39), Koutsoudas (1978).

[63] Abu-Haidar (1991: 116).

[64] For example, Thackston (1996: 38-39) on Lebanese, Cowell (1964: 435) on Syrian.

genitival noun phrases, as in:

> Lebanese Arabic: *bayto la-najīb* 'Najib's house'
> Iraqi (Christian Baghdadi) Arabic: *maġtu l-axūyi* 'my brother's wife'

Maltese (see above, 2.4) also marks direct objects with the dative preposition—in this case, *lil*—though unlike in the dialects of Arabic discussed above, anticipatory object marking is not found. The object marker is obligatory when the object is a proper name, stressed personal pronoun, or an animate (human) noun with a possessive pronominal suffix. With definite animate nouns without a possessive suffix, object marking is optional, though more common when the object is human.[65] Examples are:

> Maltese: *Il-tifel ra lil Maria* 'The boy saw Maria'; *Il-tabib bagħat lilu* 'The doctor sent him' (or: 'It was him the doctor sent'); *Il-mara bagħtet 'il binha* 'The woman sent her son' (*'il* < *lil*); *Tereża rat lill-kelb / il-kelb* 'Theresa saw the dog'

It has traditionally been assumed that object marking in Maltese is related to object marking in Levantine dialects, and therefore ultimately stems from Aramaic substrate influence. Borg and Mifsud (2002) question this theory, and suggest that the Maltese construction is instead a product of Romance adstratum (see below, 5.2.1). Both scenarios are plausible, but since Maltese is more closely linked with North African Arabic dialects, Borg and Mifsud have good reason to question the former theory.

5.1.5 Ge'ez

Ge'ez makes use of a construction identical to that of the modern Arabic dialects discussed above. That is to say, the preposition *la-* can be used to mark a direct object, in conjunction with a required anticipatory object suffix on the verb.[66] This construction is also extended to nominal phrases (as in Aramaic and Arabic) and even to prepositional phrases. Examples are:

> Ge'ez: *qatalo la-nəguś* 'he killed the king'; *waldu la-nəguś* 'the son of the king, the king's son'; *dibehomu la-ḥəzb* 'against the people'

---

[65]Borg and Mifsud (2002) provide a detailed account of object marking in Maltese, including a discussion of its origin.

[66]The anticipatory object suffix is omitted in the case of an object following a perfective active participle, as in *qatiləya la-nəguś gʷayayku* 'Having killed the king, I fled'. Because the perfective participle already has a pronominal suffix (its subject), it cannot take another.

The verbal and nominal constructions are extremely common and are often simply referred to by scholars as the *qatalo la-nəguś* and *waldu la-nəguś* constructions, respectively.[67] The *la* of this construction is not always recognized as the preposition, and discussions of it as such are few.[68]

It is essential to note that in Ge'ez, which has no definite article, the *qatalo la-nəguś* construction is marked for definiteness. The simple phrase *qatala nəguśa* may be translated as 'he killed a king' or 'he killed the king', whereas *qatalo la-nəguś* can only be translated as 'he killed the king'. Similarly, *waldu la-nəguś* must mean 'the king's son', while the simple construct phrase *walda nəguś* can mean 'the king's son' or 'a king's son'. So the Ge'ez construction has the same restriction of definiteness we find in all of the above languages, yet it is the construction itself which marks that definiteness, not the form of the noun. Remembering that the loss of accusative case-marking is often cited—here and elsewhere—as the catalyst for the rise of *notae accusativi* in other languages, it is also noteworthy that Ge'ez has a fully functional accusative case, as evidenced by the example *qatala nəguśa* (nom. *nəguś*) above. In Ge'ez it seems the functionality of the construction is in the realm of definiteness, unlike in Canaanite and Arabic dialects, where definiteness is rather a prerequisite to its use, and its functionality is in the marking of the object. It is thus parallel to later Eastern Aramaic dialects (Syriac, BTA, Mandaic) which have no definite article and similarly use this construction to mark definiteness in verbal and nominal phrases.

However, if we look at the Ge'ez accusative marker more closely, we find that it is identical to the morpheme which marks the construct state. This actually can lead to ambiguity, if the direct object is also the first member of a construct. So, in the phrase *qatala nəguśa mədr*, the form *nəguśa* is the first member of a construct phrase and can be interpreted as a nominative or accusative; it may be translated 'he killed the king of the country' or 'the king of the country killed'. So, the prepositional accusative actually does serve to make the accusative more explicit, as in Aramaic, Hebrew, etc.

5.1.6 Tigrinya, Tigré

In Tigrinya, the preposition *nə-* 'to, for' is used for both indirect and definite direct objects.[69] Its use with direct objects seems to be optional, and it is less likely to appear when the object is inanimate. The form may also be used with

---

[67]After Lambdin (1978: 44, 64). Tropper (2002) refers to the *qatalo la-nəguś* (§52.32) and *betu la-nəguś* (§52.43) constructions.

[68]See Testen (1998: 177 n. 54).

[69]Leslau (1941: 42-43). Both Kogan in Hetzron (1997: 432-33) and Melles (2001: 12) provide only very brief comments on *nə-* as a D.O. marker.

pronominal suffixes, in which case the base is nə'a- (variant nə'a-). When nə- is used as a D.O. marker, either with nominal or pronominal objects, the verb usually has an object suffix as well. This is equivalent to the Ge'ez, modern Arabic, and Eastern Aramaic constructions. Unlike in Ge'ez, extended use of nə- in nominal or prepositional phrases is not found. Examples are:

> Tigrinya: 'ətā dəmmu näti ṣäba sätəyato 'the cat drank the milk' (näti < nə + 'əti) (lit., 'the cat nə-the milk drank it'; 'ətom qʷälə'u nə'ay rä'ayuni 'those children saw me' (lit., 'the children nə-me saw me')

In Tigré, the preposition 'əgəl 'to, for' is used "with considerable regularity" to mark the direct object, often with a co-referential verbal suffix.[70] Raz does not say whether the direct object need be definite, but a cursory look at the texts he provides seems to indicate as much; Leslau does indeed specify that this construction is limited to definite objects. Unlike in Tigrinya, and the other languages discussed above, 'əgəl might not be the main indirect object marker. As an indirect object marker, 'əgəl competes with the common 'əl, which is the cognate of the preposition la of the other languages discussed above.[71] And in fact, the base 'əl- is used if the direct object is a pronoun, optionally preceded by 'əgəl. The base 'əgəl- is also found for pronominal objects. It seems that 'əgəl and 'əl are in competition with one another, with the older 'əl being the more restricted morpheme. Examples are:

> Tigré: 'əgəl lä-šakät däfnäya 'he filled up the pit' (lit., ''əgəl the pit, he filled it'); 'əgəlye sä'ami 'kiss me'; ṣäbṭa 'əla 'he attached her'

5.1.7 Summary

The Semitic *notae accusativi* described above can essentially be divided into two groups:

Group 1:
 Hebrew 'et / 'ēt, before suffixes 'ôt- / 'ōt-
 Phoenician 'yt
 Old Aramaic 'yt, Western Aramaic yāt (see table in 5.1.2)

---

[70]Raz (1983: 83). Leslau (1945b: §41) provides a more detailed description.
[71]Raz (1983: 81) claims that the normal indirect object marker is 'əl, but the many examples of 'əgəl in his text contradict this statement. Leslau (1945b: §40) says that 'əgəl is normal, while 'əl is normal with a pronominal indirect object.

Group 2:
>Aramaic *l-* (see table in 5.1.2)
>Late Biblical Hebrew *lə-*
>Akkadian (Neo-Assyrian, Neo- and Late Babylonian) *ana*
>Classical and Middle Arabic *li-*, modern dialectal *la-*
>Ge'ez *la-*
>Tigrinya *nə-*
>Tigré *'əgəl*

In Group 2, each of the *notae accusativi* is identical to the dative/allative preposition 'to, for'. I will therefore refer to this construction as a prepositional accusative. Aramaic *'yt / yāt*, Phoenician *'yt*, and Hebrew *'et*, however, have a less clear etymology that will be discussed below (5.4). Before turning to the history of these particles and constructions, it will be instructive to examine similar constructions in non-Semitic languages.

5.2 On Prepositional Direct Object Marking in Other Languages

One need not look far to find other languages which make use of a prepositional accusative. More importantly, many languages share an important similarity to all the Semitic *notae accusativi*, namely, that there is a distinction in the level of definiteness of the object.

5.2.1 Romance

Probably the best known example of a prepositional accusative comes from Spanish. In the construction often referred to as 'personal *a*', the preposition *a* 'to' must precede any direct object which is a proper name or a pronoun denoting a person.[72]

>*Vi a Juan.* 'I saw Juan.'
>*¿A quién viste?* 'Whom did you see?'
>*No vi a nadie.* 'I didn't see anyone.'

The personal *a* construction may also be found before definite nouns denoting humans, animals, and place names, or even with inanimate nouns when there is a sense of personification, or when there might otherwise be possible confusion with the grammatical subject. For example:

---

[72] See Kattán-Ibarra and Pountain (1997: 127-29), Posner (1996: 121-22), and Harris and Vincent (1990: 106-7) for further details. See Reichenkron (1951) for a more diachronic account of this Spanish construction.

Busco a mi amigo. 'I am looking for my friend.'
Ama a su patria. 'He loves his country.'

An identical construction also exists in Sardinian and in some dialects of Italian and Catalan.[73]

Romanian also employs a similar construction, using the preposition *pe* 'on; for'. The word *pe* derives from Latin *per*, meaning 'for' (along with a host of other meanings). As in Spanish, its use is dependent on the animacy of the direct object, though it is also used to avoid ambiguity. Unlike Spanish, there is normally an anticipatory clitic pronoun on the verb:[74]

Am văzut-o pe Maria. 'I saw Maria.' (lit., 'I have seen her, *pe* Maria.')
L-am văzut pe el. 'I saw him.' (lit., 'Him I have seen, *pe* him.').

5.2.2 Hindi

The Hindi postposition *ko* 'to' is also used to mark animate direct objects; inanimate objects are normally unmarked.[75] The use of *ko* is obligatory with proper names and usually found with any noun referring to a human being:[76]

vah rām ko paṛhātā hai. 'He teaches Ram.' (lit., 'He Ram-*ko* teaches.')

The postposition can optionally be used with definite inanimate objects, in which case it conveys a particularizing or emphatic sense. Note that there is no definite article in Hindi, thus definiteness, which must normally be gleaned from context, can actually be marked by the use of *ko*:

kitāb paṛho. 'Read the book.' or 'Read a book.'
kitāb ko paṛho. 'Read the book.'

The postposition *ko* is also found with independent object pronouns, for example *mujhko*, which can be an indirect object 'to me' or a direct object 'me'. However, the more original accusative pronoun, in this case *mujhe* 'me', is still more common. With the polite pronoun *āp* 'you', *āpko* is the only possible accusative form. This use of *-ko* has parallels in other Indo-Aryan languages, such as Bengali.

---

[73]Harris and Vincent (1990: 336), Posner (1996: 122-23). On Sardinian alone, see Bossong (1982). On Catalan alone, see Wheeler, Yates, and Dols (1999: 242, 462).
[74]Harris and Vincent (1990: 409-10), Posner (1996: 122), Cazacu (1980: 199-200). Cotelnic (2000: 257-58) also provides a nice description, though in Romanian.
[75]The postposition *ko* is itself grammaticalized, cf. Sanskrit *kákṣa* 'armpit' (later Indic > 'side'). See Turner (1966: §14342).
[76]McGregor (1995: 53), Jain (1995: 98-99).

5.2.3 Conclusions

In this small sample of languages we can highlight the following points:

1. In Romance and Hindi, the dative preposition can mark the accusative.
2. The usage is most common with personal names (or animate nouns) and personal pronouns, followed by definite nouns, and may be found with indefinite nouns for emphasis or syntactic clarity.[77]
3. In Hindi, the construction can be used to specify definiteness.
4. In Romanian, a pronominal object is normally employed to anticipate the nominal direct object. (In Spanish, this is possible as well.)
5. In Hindi, we find the dative pronouns acquiring an accusative function.

5.3 On Grammaticalization, DATIVE > ACCUSATIVE

The data on Semitic in section 5.1 have, to my knowledge, never been collected together in one work and described in detail. Yet, except for some minor points, all of the data have been known. In this section I hope to add what has been missing in the past: how and why the prepositional accusative construction came into being.

First let us focus on Aramaic, seeing as in this language we can watch the development of this construction across many centuries. The motivation for grammaticalization is generally thought to be a speaker's desire for expressiveness or explicitness. In the case of Aramaic (and Akkadian and post-Classical Arabic), it is clear what prompted this motivation, namely, the loss of the inherited accusative case. In addition, the use of the prepositional accusative with participial forms has a clear motivation—the partly nominal, partly verbal status of participial forms warrants a more explicit marking of the direct object to make clear a verbal function. The factors which created a favorable environment for the creation of a direct object marker are obvious, but what actually triggered its development? And why should dative/allative preposition come to mark this? Parallels in other languages like Spanish and Hindi show us that this is a widespread phenomenon, but that in itself is not an answer.

Perhaps a clue lies in the early distribution of the construction. Referring back to the summary chart in 5.1.2 above, we see that in the earliest Aramaic dialects to use the prepositional accusative, its use is restricted to animate (specifically, human) objects. Only later is its use extended to definite inanimate objects. This development follows the very well-known principles of animacy hierarchy and definiteness hierarchy. According to these principles, animate

---

[77]See Comrie (1979) for a discussion of animate and definite direct objects.

nouns (especially humans) are more likely to be included in linguistic rules than inanimate ones, and definite nouns are more likely to be included in linguistic rules than indefinite ones.[78] We have seen examples of this in all of the data above, in 5.1 and 5.2.

This leads us to the question of why the construction is limited to animates in the first place. Why would a speaker of Egyptian Aramaic reject an utterance such as 'you struck my wife' and opt instead for 'you struck to/for my wife'? Why did Ezra write literally (5:12) 'our fathers angered to/for the God of heaven'? There are three possible answers. The first has to do with respect. When we address a king as "your majesty", we are doing so to avoid addressing him directly. Spaniards used to address superiors with *vuestra merced* 'your grace', to avoid direct address – this has developed into modern *Usted*.[79] That is to say, direct address is replaced by indirect address. In Aramaic we are perhaps dealing with a similar phenomenon, though with regard to direct objects rather than direct address. The direct object was replaced by an indirect one, when the object was something to be respected, i.e., animate beings. The second possibility has to do with the desire for explicitness with regard to animate beings. That is to say, there is more chance of ambiguity—and more desire to be unambiguous—in a sentence like 'Jack sees Jill' versus 'Jill sees Jack'. There is much less ambiguity in a sentence with only one animate component, like 'Jill sees the building'; with the reverse order, 'the building sees Jill', "the building" can still only be logically interpreted as the direct object.[80] In Aramaic, freer word order and the lack of direct object marker (or any case marking) would create such ambiguity in a sentence like 'Jack sees Jill'. The third possible explanation is that indirect objects are more often humans. That is to say, an indirect object is often connected with a verb of saying, telling, giving, asking, showing, or bringing, and therefore is likely to be human. Once the indirect object marker comes to mark direct objects, this fact would have worked in conjunction with the universal tendency of animacy hierarchy to restrict the direct object marking to human/animate nouns.

For the affect of animacy/respect with regard to case marking, we can observe the development of the Slavic case system. In Russian, for example, the accusative form of masculine nouns is normally identical to the nominative. However, if the noun is animate (human or animal), the accusative is instead equal to the genitive. For example:

---

[78]Lyons (1999: 213-15), Hopper and Traugott (2003: 165-67), Croft (2003: 128-32).
[79]Penny (2002: 138). Some have suggested that Arabic *'ustāð* 'master' was a catalyst for this change.
[80]Comrie (1979: 19) comes to a similar conclusion. He notes that subjects are typically animate, and therefore animate direct objects warrant marking as such.

	'chair'		'boy'	
	sg.	pl.	sg.	pl.
Nom.	*stol*	*stoly*	*mal'čik*	*mal'čiki*
Acc.	*stol*	*stoly*	*mal'čika*	*mal'čikov*
Gen.	*stola*	*stolov*	*mal'čika*	*mal'čikov*

The replacement of the masculine accusative singular forms of human nouns with genitive ones is a common Slavic trait, though the modern Slavic languages differ slightly with regard to the extent which the change has penetrated.[81] For example, Russian has extended it to plural nouns and other non-human animates (i.e., animals), while Czech has extended it to animals, but not to plurals. The motivation in Slavic is thought partly to be a desire for disambiguity. That is to say, once the nominative and accusative endings have become identical, and due to the free word order of Slavic, a need was felt to differentiate between 'Jack sees Jill' and 'Jill sees Jack'. Klenin (1983) has argued for other factors contributing to the change, including genitive verbal government and genitive/accusative syncretism in pronominal paradigms. But the ultimate question—why choose the genitive to replace the accusative?—remains unaddressed.

For our Semitic examples, we can not know for sure the catalyst for the dative to accusative shift, though we are aware of the conditioning factors that would have made such a change desirable. But as to the ultimate question of why the dative preposition was used, there is indeed a simple answer. This preposition is the indirect object marker. For reasons of respect, disambiguity, or due to a general linguistic tendency, the indirect object marker came to mark direct objects. And again, whether for reasons of respect, disambiguity, or because of the distribution of indirect objects, only animate direct objects were originally affected by this shift. Later, the marking of direct objects spread to all definite nouns, and in languages like Ge'ez and Syriac, the construction itself functions as a way to mark definiteness.

I should at this point discuss another possible theory, involving an analogy with the verbal object suffixes. In many of the Semitic languages, the verbal object suffixes, which normally indicate the direct object, can in fact indicate an indirect object. For example:

Biblical Hebrew: *lō(') yākəlû dabbərô lə-šālōm* 'they could not speak peaceably to him' (Gen. 37:4)[82]

---

[81] See Townsend and Janda (1996: 154-55).

[82] See Bogaert (1964) for a discussion of Hebrew, Aramaic, and Ugaritic indirect object suffixes, along with further references.

Ge'ez: *'arxəwana* 'open for us' (Matt. 25:11)[83]
Classical Arabic: *fa-bġinī raġulan* 'seek for me a man'[84]

So, perhaps, the use of the prepositional accusative, which is simply a case of the indirect object marker serving to mark direct objects, developed on analogy to this double function of the verbal object suffixes. We could illustrate this four-part analogy as follows:

PRONOMINAL I.O. : NOMINAL I.O. :: PRONOMINAL D.O. : NOMINAL D.O.
verbal obj. suffix : *l-* + noun :: verbal obj. suffix : X = *l-* + noun

However, this scenario does not seem likely. Most importantly, the dative use of the verbal object suffixes is extremely rare in Aramaic.[85] It is also rare in Hebrew, though the Hebrew data are only indirectly relevant, as the Hebrew prepositional accusative is an Aramaism. In Ethiopic, on the other hand, the object suffixes are often used in a dative sense, but it is very possible that their frequency can be attributed to the prevalence of the prepositional accusative construction.[86] Another problem with this theory is that it does not help explain prepositional accusatives in other languages like Spanish, Romanian, and Hindi, where there remain distinct accusative and dative object pronouns.

Finally, it should be noted, again, that the appearance of a prepositional accusative in Late Biblical Hebrew, Akkadian, Middle and Modern (Colloquial) Arabic, is undoubtedly due to the influence of Aramaic. In Maltese, the influence is possibly from Romance (see above, 5.1.4). The borrowing of such a construction is not unusual; Heine and Kuteva (2005: 150-52) have collected other examples of languages that have borrowed a prepositional accusative construction. The Ethiopic constructions, however, are most likely independent. This development is typologically common enough to make this unremarkable. The Classical Arabic use of *li-* may also be independent, as suggested by its restriction to the objects of verbal nouns and participles.

5.4 On the Origin of Hebrew *'et* / Aramaic *yt* / *yāt*

Waltke and O'Connor (1990: 177) refer to *'et* as "one of the most difficult grammatical morphemes in Biblical Hebrew." Muraoka (1985: 146) notes that

---

[83]Dillmann (1907: §178).
[84]Brockelmann (1908-13 II: §213a).
[85]Bogaert (1964: 227-28).
[86]That is not to say that the dative object suffixes cannot be traced back to Proto-Semitic. They are indeed Proto-Semitic (Gensler 1998), but their relative infrequency in Aramaic, and possibly in Ge'ez, make them an unlikely analogical source of the prepositional accusative.

"[n]o single particle has given rise to more widespread and also mutually more contradictory discussion than the so-called *nota accusativi*." However, most of the problems pertaining to *'et* are in connection with its exact synchronic semantic and syntactic function(s). Here we shall focus on the origin of the particle and grammaticalization.[87]

Are Hebrew *'et*, Phoenician *'yt*, and Aramaic *yāt* examples of grammaticalization? To answer this question, we must uncover the source of the particles; unfortunately, this may be impossible. Even the source form—that is to say, the phonological shape, with no regard to its meaning—is difficult to pin down.

The logical first place to look for the source of *'et* in Hebrew would be the homophonous preposition *'et* 'with'; however this scenario can be ruled out rather easily. When these words take suffixes, we find that they employ two different bases:

	'et (acc.)	*'et* ('with')
1cs	*'ōtî*	*'ittî*
2ms	*'ōtəkā*	*'ittəkā*
2fs	*'ōtāk*	*ittāk*
3ms	*'ōtô*	*'ittô*
3fs	*'ōtāh*	*'ittāh*
1cp	*'ōtānû*	*'ittānû*
2mp	*'etkem*	*'ittəkem*
2fp	(wanting)	(wanting)
3mp	*'ōtām* (or *'ethem*)	*'ittām*
3fp	*'ethen* (or *'ōtān*)	(wanting)

The preposition *'et* has good cognates in Semitic, specifically, Phoenician *'t*, Akkadian *itti* 'with'.[88] In Phoenician, the preposition *'t* is distinct from the accusative marker, which usually appears as *'yt*. Furthermore, many problems arise when comparing this PS preposition to the Phoenician and Aramaic form of the object marker, which contain a consonantal *y*. Finally, there are likely cognate

---

[87] I refer the reader to Khan (1984), Garr (1991), and the standard Hebrew grammars for discussion of the syntax.
[88] Possibly also Geʻez *'enta* 'through; via; by; at' (so Praetorius 1873: 643, Nöldeke 1886: 738; Leslau 1987: 33 is unsure). Far less likely as a cognate is Arabic *'inda* 'at, by'. Some would derive (via grammaticalization) the Hebrew preposition *'et* and its cognates from the PS word **yad-* 'hand' (cf. Eitan 1928: 48-50); this is simply conjecture and would exclude the Geʻez form, though it may work for the Arabic *'inda < **'an + yad-*.

accusative particles in Arabic and Ethiopic, namely *iyyā-* and *kiyā-*, which make such a connection even less likely. We can rule out any known preposition as the source of the *nota accusativi*.

For the Hebrew particle, the suffixal base *'ōt-* allows us to reconstruct an original **'āt-*, with the expected Canaanite shift *ā* > *ō*. The original **'āt-* was shortened to **'at-* before the heavy (2pl. and 3pl.) suffixes, and this later became *'et-*. The independent form must also come from a similar closed-syllable shortening of **'āt* to **'at*, and later reduction to *'et* due to its unstressed position.[89] The non-clitic (stressed) form *'ēt* developed secondarily from the unstressed form.[90] This development, originally suggested by Praetorius in 1901, has long been accepted, though by no means universally.[91] So, this leaves us with an original Hebrew **'āt*, presumably a reduced form of the particle *'yt* */'iyyāt/* evidenced in Aramaic and Phoenician. The reduction is paralleled in Aramaic, which itself reduces the particle to *yāt*. The loss of the initial syllable is perhaps due to a metanalysis of the type promoted by both Bravmann and Correll (see below, 5.4.2). For example, in Hebrew, a possible source would be the 1cs perfect form, as in:

*qaṭāltī 'iyyāt X 'I killed X' > **qaṭāltī(y)āt X* > **qaṭāltī 'āt X*.

However, such a suggestion is not necessary; we have seen how grammaticalization and cliticization commonly lead to irregular phonetic reductions.

5.4.1 Some Older Etymological Proposals

The Hebrew and Aramaic *notae accusativi* have long been connected with the independent object pronouns found in Ethiopic (*kiyā-* < **kīyā-*)[92] and Arabic (*iyyā-*).[93] Both the Ethiopic and Arabic forms occur exclusively with pronominal suffixes, and serve as secondary, emphatic accusative pronouns; pronominal objects are normally suffixed directly to the verb. Some nineteenth-century Semitists assumed the Ethiopic form, or something close to it, to be the original.

---

[89] For a similar development, compare *yād* 'hand', with 2fp possessive suffix *yedken* (Ezek. 13:21), both < **yad*.
[90] Recall that the unstressed form occurs roughly eight times more often than the stressed form (see note 2 of this chapter).
[91] Praetorius (1901: 369-70), Gesenius (§103b), Bauer-Leander (1927: §81k').
[92] Ge'ez *i* must derive from PS **ī*. See Tropper (2002: 46) for the full declension of *kiyā-*.
[93] See Wright (1971 I: §188) or W. Fischer (2002: §272) for the full declension of the Arabic form. Note that Wright transliterates this form as *īyā*. According to Hirschfeld (1918: 32-33; 1926: 16), the connection between the Hebrew and Arabic forms of the *notae accusativi* was first made by the Karaite scholar Al-Qirqisani in the tenth century.

Böttcher, for example, derives Hebrew 'et from an original *kəwat.[94] Wright (1890: 112) assumes a weakening of *kīyā > Arabic dialectal hīyā- > Classical Arabic 'iyyā-, to which the NWS languages have appended the feminine marker -(a)t. He assumes Phoenician to represent this stage ('īyāt-), that a weakening to yāt accounts for the Aramaic, and a further weakening to 'āt (with the subsequent Canaanite shift of ā > ō) accounts for the Hebrew. Praetorius (1873: 640) likewise derives the Arabic from the Ethiopic, but believes the Canaanite and Aramaic *notae accusativi* to be unrelated. Remarkably, Praetorius derives the Ethiopic form from kʷəlyāt, the plural of kʷəlit 'kidney'. This would certainly be a nice example of grammaticalization, but should undoubtedly be rejected. He sees the Canaanite and Aramaic forms as derivatives of a noun meaning 'sign', as in Hebrew 'ôt, Arabic 'āya(t). Others scholars have also seen this lexeme (or its root) as the source for the Hebrew form (cf. König 1881-97 II: 294-95; Klein 1987: 60). Another possible source for the Ethiopic form is suggested by Dillmann (1907: §65). He presumes a noun kiyāt as an abstract 'self', derived from the first and second person verbal suffixes ku, ka, ki.

Presumably recognizing the problems inherent in positing an Ethiopic-like form as the source, Brockelmann (1908-13 I: §106b-c) views the Arabic 'iyyā- as original. He suggests that Ethiopic has preposed a demonstrative element k-, while the NWS forms have added the feminine ending -(a)t. Brockelmann's view is still endorsed by some today (cf. Tropper 2002a: 46 n. 59).

Barth (1913: 91-95) has a more complicated theory, essentially deriving the respective accusative markers from various combinations of Semitic deictic elements. For example, he assumes Hebrew 'et is composed of *'ī + t, while the suffixal base 'ōt- derives from *wāt (comparing an "Old Aramaic" form <wth>; but see above, 5.1.2). He derives Arabic 'iyyā < *'ī + yā, Ethiopic kiyā < *k + iy + yā, and Aramaic < yā + t. Similar in this piecemeal approach is Eitan (1928: 50-51); an exception is his explanation of the Hebrew form, which he derives from supposed asseverative t-.

In a short 1914 article, H. Bauer proposed a very clever etymology for these *notae accusativi*. He recognized the connection between the Canaanite, Arabic, Aramaic, and Ethiopic forms, but believed that no single proto-form could be reconstructed. He also noted—with a keen sense for grammaticalization—that other languages have developed case markers from verbs.[95] He suggested that the verbal root √'ty 'to come', used in a hendiadys construction, weakened to become a *nota accusativi*. The variant forms shown by the languages are a result

---

[94]Böttcher (1866-68 II: 57). The transliteration is mine; Böttcher gives the form in Hebrew characters.

[95]Bauer's examples (1914: 369 n. 1) are Chinese bă 'take' > direct object marker, Chinese gei 'give' > dative, and Ewe ná 'give' > dative; these same examples are given in Heine and Kuteva (2002: 153, 289).

of different underlying verbal forms. For example, he believes that Hebrew *'*āt*- comes from a first person imperfect (**'a'ti* > **'āti*), while Aramaic *yāt* derives from a third person imperfect form (**ya'ti* > **yāti*). Wary of Praetorius' explanation of Hebrew *'et* < *'āt* (see above), Bauer suggests that *'et* may come from the imperative form *'iti* 'come!'. Bauer's theory is important, because he recognizes that this grammatical particle should have developed from a lexical item, and he supports his theory with parallels from other known instances of case-marker development. However, as much as he is to be commended for this, the theory seems highly unlikely.

5.4.2 Some Recent Etymological Proposals

Bravmann (1977: 182-85) believes that the Arabic object pronouns derive from a metanalysis of the first person object suffixes, when used in conjunction with a second person object suffix. For example, the Classical Arabic form of 'he gave me it' is *'aṭānīhi*, which can be broken down into *'aṭā* 'he gave' + 1cs object suffix *-nī* + 3ms object suffix *-hi* (< *hu*). Because the 1cs possessive suffix *-ī* sometimes appears as *-iya* (cf. Brockelmann 1908-13 I: §105c), Bravmann assumes that the 1cs object suffix was earlier *-niya*. Thus, 'he gave me it' would have earlier been *'aṭāniyahu*. It is from this form that he suggests a reanalysis to *'aṭāni + (i)yahu*, this second element subsequently becoming a new independent object pronoun. This is very clever, but excludes any connection with the forms in other Semitic languages.

Correll (1994) offers a solution reminiscent of that of Bravmann. He posits the Akkadian independent object pronouns, specifically 1cs *yāti* and 2cs *kuāti*, as the source for the WS object markers.[96] A phrase like *qaṭalani yāti* 'he killed me', with an emphatic independent object pronoun, could be reanalyzed in various ways. He thinks that Old Aramaic and Phoenician reanalyzed it as *-ni + iyāti*, other dialects of Aramaic as *-ni + yāti*, and Hebrew as *-niy + āti*, thus explaining the attested *notae accusativi*. He explains the initial *k-* of the Ethiopic forms as being from the second person object suffixes, and explains the lack of a final *-t* in Arabic and Ethiopic via other metanalyses. This is another clever theory, though one which seems implausible; the construction *qaṭalani yāti* 'he killed me' (with an emphatic redundant object pronoun) would have been relatively rare and, moreover, the development of an entire paradigm out of the 1cs form seems unlikely.

In a long article dealing mainly with the syntax of direct object markers,

---

[96]The connection of the Akkadian independent direct object pronoun was suggested already by P. Haupt, as noted by Brockelmann (1908-13 I: §106d) and Bauer (1914: 369). Mention should also be made of Garr's derivation (1985: 116) of the Sam'alian form *wt* from the WS 3ms object pronoun **huwati*.

Khan (1984: 495) suggests a connection with the particle of existence, Hebrew *yeš*, Aramaic *'īt*, etc. (see above, 3.4.5.1). This is problematic phonologically (namely, that the final consonants of Hebrew *'et* and *yeš* cannot derive from the same source), and Khan presents no good argument for the semantic shift. His theory also leaves wanting any explanation of the Arabic and Ethiopic forms.[97]

Testen (1997), like Bauer, Correll, and others, seeks a regularity in the seemingly disparate phonological forms of the direct object markers. After a complex and very insightful analysis, Testen is led to reconstruct an original shape **ʾiwy-ay, from which the Canaanite, Aramaic, Arabic, and Ethiopic forms derive. He then speculates that this form is a manifestation of either the root *√hwy* 'to be' or *√ḥwy* 'to live'; this lexeme **iwy-ay* should then have a meaning 'being, essence', and therefore we are dealing with a grammaticalization similar to that found with the reflexive pronouns (see above, 3.1.3). Testen's phonological explanation is brilliant, and the meaning of his reconstructed source lexeme would fit nicely; however, he is using several very hypothetical steps to reconstruct a noun pattern evidenced by only one other Arabic word (*'iḥdā* 'one (f.)'). Therefore, his theory remains doubtful.

Finally, we should mention the discussion found in Lipiński (1997: §52.10). Somewhat reminiscent of Brockelmann, he assumes an original **ʾiyyat, with a loss of *t* and restriction to pronominal use in Arabic. He makes no mention of the Geʻez forms, but does note the MSA object pronouns with initial *t-* (see below, 5.6.2). Oddly, he connects (§36.31) the *nota accusativi* with the Middle Babylonian possessive adjective *attu-* < **aytu*.

5.4.2 Conclusions on *'et* / *yāt*

The ultimate source of these forms is indeed problematic to isolate. For our purposes, however, it is sufficient to note that the change of PREPOSITION > OBJECT MARKER can be ruled out. Of the above theories, several involve grammaticalization, including those of Praetorius, Bauer, and Testen. Others, such as those of Correll and Bravmann, involve analogical restructuring, but no grammaticalization. Many others, most importantly Brockelmann, Barth, Eitan, reconstruct PS elements with no apparent meaning.

I maintain that there is no need to find regularity in the development of the various *notae accusativi* in terms of their phonological development. These are clitic words which have been subject to restructuring of usage, and which are likely the product of grammaticalization. Complex attempts to prove their "regular" derivations, such as those of Bauer, Testen, and Correll, are perhaps unnecessary.

---

[97]Similarly, Blake (1915: 378) assumes a connection between Hebrew *'et* and Aramaic *'īt*. See also Blake (1953: 7-8).

Not only is the source disputed, but also its function. It is unclear whether the original use was limited to pronominal objects, as in Arabic and Ethiopic (and see below, 5.6.2, on MSA), or whether it originally preceded nouns as well. What we can say for certain is that, whatever the source, it is reconstructable to Proto-West Semitic. If Arabic and Ethiopic reflect the original situation, then the use of the particle before nouns is simply an analogical extension.

The problem must remain unsolved for now, and may remain so indefinitely. This particle was excluded from the discussion of the history of the prepositional direct object markers above (5.3); however, as Hebrew *'et* and Aramaic *yāt* undergo further semantic developments, they will be discussed in the framework of re-grammaticalization below.

5.5 On Re-grammaticalization of the *Nota Accusativi 'et / yāt*

The *nota accusativi l-*, which derives from a dative/allative preposition, provides an interesting, though not particularly unusual, example of grammaticalization. On the other hand, the origins of Hebrew *'et* and Aramaic *yāt* are shrouded in obscurity, and we can only hypothesize that they arose via grammaticalization. However, these forms are themselves further grammaticalized in some unexpected ways.

5.5.1 Syriac *yāt* as a Reflexive

As already noted above (5.1.2), Syriac has essentially lost *yāt* in its function as a direct object marker. Its few attestations, all but one of which are in the Peshitta, are readily explained as archaisms or Hebraisms. However, there exists a form *yāt-* in Syriac, used with pronominal suffixes as a reflexive pronoun, synonymous with the more common *napš-* and *qnom-* (see above, 3.1.3). Examples are:

> Syriac: *nāṣe 'am yāteh* 'is at variance with himself'; *pgar yāteh* 'his own body'; *d-hī mdabbrā napšāh wa-mṭakksā yātāh* 'who guides herself and rules herself'

Nöldeke (1904a: §223) derives this reflexive word from the noun *yātā* 'nature, essence', and explicitly states (§287 n. 1) that reflexive *yāt-* is not to be connected with the accusative marker *yāt*. Brockelmann (1908-13 I: §106c), on the other hand, does see a connection, as does Wright (1890: 112-13). Brockelmann believes that the reflexive usage is an extension of its original use as an accusative pronoun, and that the noun *yātā* is actually a back-formation from the reflexive usage of *yāt-*, on analogy with the nominal bases of the other reflexive pronouns *napšā* 'soul' and *qnomā* 'person, existence'.[98]

A preference for Nöldeke's theory versus that of Brockelmann might seem somewhat subjective. According to the former, the noun gave rise to the reflexive, while according to the latter, the reflexive gave rise to the noun. Brockelmann believes that the noun was formed on analogy with the other reflexives, but if the noun already existed as Nöldeke believes, we could explain its reflexive use on analogy with the same forms. It cannot be said for sure which did indeed come first. But there are several arguments which suggest that Brockelmann's theory is the correct one:

> 1. The extension of the object pronoun to reflexive pronoun is paralleled elsewhere (cf. Latin, Romance, German, and Swedish, where they are identical for first and second persons).
>
> 2a. *yāt* is extended to other pronominal functions in other dialects of Aramaic (see below, 5.5.2).
>
> 2b. The extended *yāt* of other Aramaic dialects has the meaning 'that very, the same'; on the semantic proximity of reflexives and words meaning 'same', see 5.5.2.
>
> 3. There is no other good etymology of the independent noun *yātā*.

The situation in Syriac thus provides an nice example of Kuryłowicz's fourth law of analogy: the function of the older direct object marker, *yāt-*, has become limited (to reflexive use), while the newer marker, based on the preposition *l-*, has taken over the broader function (direct object marking).

5.5.2 Accusative > Demonstrative

In Mishnaic Hebrew and in the contemporary neighboring dialects of Christian Palestinian, Samaritan, and (very rarely) Jewish Palestinian Aramaic, the accusative marker *'et / yāt* has acquired a new demonstrative function. The form appears with third person pronominal suffixes, and functions as a demonstrative adjective. In Mishnaic Hebrew alone, *'et* without suffixes may also be used as a demonstrative pronoun, before a relative clause.[99] In JPA, the suffixed form is also attested as a demonstrative pronoun. This new demonstrative can have a general meaning 'that', or a more emphatic meaning 'that very, this very, that same', as illustrated by the following examples:

---

[98] Brockelmann's inclusion of the corresponding Akkadian form (presumably he means *yâti* 'me'), which can signify genitive as well as accusative, is not necessary.

[99] Found already in LBH; cf. Eccles. 4:3.

Mishnaic Hebrew: *'et še-lipnê ham-miṭṭā wə-'et še-lə-'aḥar ham-miṭṭā* 'those before the bier and those behind the bier'; *bə-'ôtāh šāʿā* 'in that moment'; *'ôtô hay-yôm* 'that day, this very day'[100]

JPA: *ythwn l' hnyyn ly* 'those are not pleasing to me'; *by-yth qyqylth* 'in that ruin'; *yth 'ḥwnn* 'that brother of ours'[101]

CPA: *b-ywm' yth* 'on that day' (= Heb. *bay-yôm ha-hû(')*, 1 Sam. 6:15); *b-yth zbn'* 'at that time'; *yth lyly'* 'that same night' (Exod. 12:42); *b-hw ywm' yth* 'that very day' (= Heb. *bə-ʿeṣem hay-yôm haz-ze*, Exod. 12:51)[102]

Samaritan Aramaic: *b-yth ywmh* 'on that day' (= Heb. *bay-yôm ha-hû(')*, Deut. 31:17); *lgw yth mqwmh* 'in that place'[103]

This shift from accusative marker to demonstrative seems to be due to a reanalysis. Recalling the example of French *pas*, discussed above (1.1), we can trace the development of *'et* in Hebrew through a similar cycle of grammaticalization and reanalysis:

Stage 1. *'et* is an object marker, for nouns and pronouns

Stage 2. *'et* with suffixes develops an emphatic, appositional use:
rā'îtî 'ôtô, hā-'îš še-rā'îtā 'I saw him, the man you saw'

Stage 3. *'et* with suffixes is reanalyzed as a demonstrative (recall the almost total lack of *'et* used for pronominal objects in Mishnaic Hebrew, though its non-suffixed form remains productive):
rā'îtî 'ôtô hā-'îš še-rā'îtā 'I saw that very man that you saw'

Stage 4. *'et* with suffixes is grammaticalized in this function as evidenced by its use in non-objectival position and the redundant use of object-marking *'et* (see 5.5.3).[104]

Given that this shift occurs in Mishnaic Hebrew as well as in neighboring Aramaic dialects, it seems certain that there was influence or borrowing in one direction. So we must determine which language was the innovator and which was the borrower. Nöldeke (1868a: 471 n. 2) and Wright (1890: 13) believe that the

---

[100]Segal (1927: §§75, 416-17), Pérez Fernández (1999: 23). For this last example, Segal translates 'that day', while Pérez Fernández translates 'this very day'; this illustrates how the English translations can be quite subjective.

[101]Dalman (1905: §17.8), Sokoloff (2002a: 246). Both authors emphasize the rarity of this construction.

[102]Müller-Kessler (1991: 72).

[103]Macuch (1982: 135). Macuch translates *yt* simply as *derselbe*, but based on the examples, the range of meaning seems to be the same as the other languages.

[104]A Modern Hebrew speaker sees the use of objectival *'et / 'oto* as completely distinct from demonstrative *'oto*.

Mishnaic use is a borrowing from Aramaic. Segal (1927: 202 n. 1) disagrees, noting that the relative rarity in Jewish Palestinian Aramaic suggests that CPA and Samaritan have borrowed from Mishnaic.[105] It seems to me that Mishnaic Hebrew was the innovator, as I have already assumed in the outline of development above. The decisive factor seems to me to be the near absence of *'et* as a pronominal object marker, while in these Aramaic dialects *yāt* retains its older function as well as its demonstrative function. Admittedly, the development of *yāt* as a reflexive in Syriac suggests a native (Aramaic) development, rather than a borrowing. Perhaps it is best to simply call this re-grammaticalization of the *nota accusativi* an areal phenomenon.

Waltke and O'Connor (1990: 178) discuss another theory which would explain the demonstrative use of *'et*, which hypothesizes that the particle originally (in pre-Hebrew) had an emphatic/reflexive meaning similar to Latin *ipse*. They believe that the Mishnaic demonstrative usage strengthens this hypothesis, yet this seems to me rather backward. If such a usage is absent from Biblical Hebrew,[106] why should Mishnaic Hebrew preserve a meaning from more than a thousand years earlier? The development outlined above satisfactorily explains the shift from an accusative marker to a demonstrative.

Above (5.5.1) it was noted that this development strengthens the argument that Syriac reflexive *yāt* comes from the accusative marker, rather than from an independent source. Consider CPA *b-ywm' yth* 'on that (very) day'; how different is this in meaning from Syriac *bə-yawmā yāteh* 'on the day itself'? In fact, there is a close relationship between reflexive pronouns and demonstratives, as can be seen elsewhere in Semitic. For example, in the Biblical Hebrew expression *bə-'eṣem hay-yôm haz-ze* 'on this very day', the word *'eṣem* is the normal reflexive pronoun (see above, 3.1.3). In a similar vein, the Tigrinya and Amharic reflexive pronouns have become third person personal pronouns (*nəssu* and *əssu* respectively; see above, 3.1.5); third person personal pronouns are often closely connected with demonstratives. Consider also the Latin reflexive/emphatic pronoun *ipse*, which has become the Spanish demonstrative *ese* (Latin *ipse rēx* 'the king himself', Spanish *ese rey* 'that king').

Finally, it must be noted that we also find a parallel development in Ge'ez, with the independent accusative pronoun *kiyā-* being used as a demonstrative.[107]

---

[105] As Segal (1927: 202 n. 1) points out, Nöldeke (1868a: 513, 522) gives other examples of MH influence on CPA.

[106] See Muraoka (1985: 146-58) for a discussion of "emphatic" uses of *'et* in BH. He claims there are none. Gesenius (§117i) lists some possible examples, though these are all from LBH, suggesting an earlier phase of the shift which led to the Mishnaic situation.

[107] Dillmann (1907: §150a), Tropper (2002: §52.21f).

Ge'ez: *kiyāhā lelita* 'on that (same) night' (Exod. 12:42, cf. CPA above); *ba-kiyāhon mawā'əl* 'in those days' (Judith 4:6).

5.5.3 "The Same"

In Modern Hebrew, *'et* with suffixes is still found used as a demonstrative, though with the emphatic meaning 'that very', as in:

Modern Hebrew: *'oto 'iš yašav šam* 'that very man sat there'

The construction itself also has the meaning 'the same', in which capacity it is far more common.[108] The definite article is optional with the governing noun:

Modern Hebrew: *ze 'oto ha-'iš še-ra'iti 'etmol* 'this is the same man I saw yesterday'; *'oto davar qara* 'the same thing happened'; *qarati ('et) 'oto ha-sefer* 'I read the same book'

Note in the final example that the use of *'et* to mark the object is historically redundant, but, while still optional, has been accepted as correct in Modern Hebrew.

From the perspective of an English speaker, there are two separate meanings of *'oto ha-'iš*: one translates into English as a demonstrative phrase 'that man', while the other translates as an adjectival phrase 'the same man'. But in fact, the meanings occupy the same semantic realm in Hebrew and derive from the same historical function. Hebrew dictionaries do not distinguish between the two (different from our perspective) meanings.

Note that in Modern Hebrew *'et* with suffixes is the normal way of expressing a pronominal object, the verbal object suffixes having become obsolete in speech, or at least relegated to a high speech register. But the coexistence of pronominal *'oto* and demonstrative *'oto* is due to the intentional conflation of Biblical and Mishnaic Hebrew that has made up the revival of the Modern Hebrew language. Historically, they are not coexistent in common use (though in CPA and Samaritan Aramaic they are).

Worth including here are other examples of 'same' which derive from pronominal forms (i.e., emphatic/reflexive pronouns). Above (5.5.2) we saw examples of reflexives becoming demonstratives. There are also examples of reflexives used to mean 'same', most notably Arabic *nafs l-* 'the same'. For example:

Syrian Arabic: *nafs əl-wa't* 'the same time' (vs. *əl-wa't nafso* 'the time itself')[109]

---

[108] On both of these Modern Hebrew uses of *'et ('oto)*, see Glinert (1989: §9.2, §9.5-6).
[109] Cowell (1964: 468).

From outside of Semitic, we can add here French *même* 'same; self', German *(der)selbe* 'same' and the related *selbst* 'self'. The implications of this are that 'self' and 'same' can be closely related, as are 'same' and 'that very'. Via syllogism we can thus equate 'self' and 'that very', which we saw already in the example of Latin *ipse* > Spanish *ese*. Thus, in Aramaic, the Syriac use of *yāt* as a reflexive and the CPA/Samaritan use of *yāt* as a demonstrative are easily relatable.

5.6 Appendix: Other Semitic Direct Object Markers

In addition to the languages discussed above, some other Semitic languages possess direct object markers. It seems appropriate that there should be some discussion of these here, however brief.

5.6.1 The Amharic Direct Object Marker

In Amharic, a definite direct object is marked by a suffix *-(ə)n*.[110] The etymology of this particle is uncertain. Leslau (1987: 380) and Dillmann (1907: 376), following Praetorius (1879: 197), suggest a connection with the rather rare Ge'ez directional morpheme *-ne*, as in *yāstagābə'omu* ... *'aḥatta-ne* 'he will gather them into one' (John 11:52). If this suggestion is correct, we would be facing a situation somewhat similar to that of the prepositional accusative of Ge'ez, Aramaic, etc. However, the rarity of the Ge'ez particle and the absence of an Amharic counterpart are problematic. Perhaps, instead, we might look to the Tigrinya preposition *nə-* 'to' as a possible cognate. In fact, D. Appleyard has recently argued (2004) that the particle is cognate with the Tigrinya particle, as well as with Ge'ez *la-*. These theories will not be taken up further here; suffice it to say that the object marker is almost certainly the result of grammaticalization. Recalling the developments of other Semitic languages, and the grammaticalization tendencies there and in the other languages discussed above, a prepositional source—especially one with a dative/allative meaning—is a good place to begin.

5.6.2 Modern South Arabian Object Pronouns

In addition to the above survey of Hebrew *'et* and its cognates, it should be noted that the object pronouns in the Modern South Arabian languages have an initial element *t-*. For example:

---

[110] See Leslau (1995: 181-90) for a detailed discussion on its use.

Soqotri: *šīnək teh* 'I saw him'[111]
Harsūsi: *šēnek tūk* 'I saw you'[112]

This has long been noticed (cf. Brockelmann 1908-13 II: 324), but is usually absent from discussions of the *notae accusativi* (two exceptions are Bauer 1914, Lipiński 1997: §52.10). I have omitted these forms from the discussion here as well, for three reasons. First, our knowledge of Modern South Arabian historical grammar is only in its early stages. Second, the fact that we are dealing with just a single consonant *t-*, along with the fact that *t* is a very common element in so much of Semitic morphology, makes the probability of chance similarity to Hebrew *'et* and its cognates too great. Third, even if we could say for certain that the MSA form is cognate with Hebrew, it would not contribute to our investigation of its ultimate source.

---

[111] Simeone-Senelle in Hetzron (1997: 389).
[112] Johnstone (1977: 126).

Chapter 6

Present Tense Markers

6.1 Introduction

As the Semitic languages developed, so did their systems of verbal tenses and aspects. The overall tendency was toward a tense-based system, as found in the modern languages, and as opposed to the aspectual system reconstructed for Proto-Semitic and present in Akkadian. Inherited verbal forms took on new functions to accommodate these changes, and, in addition, compound tenses developed with the help of auxiliaries, just as we find in modern Germanic or Romance languages. Sometimes these auxiliary verbs or particles remained independent, while some have become cliticized or affixed. Some have been grammaticalized to the point that they are no longer transparent. Many of these have already been discussed above in section 3.2. This chapter will focus on one small subset of these, namely the present tense markers found in modern Aramaic and Arabic dialects, the origins of which have been the source of some disagreement, and whose developments have never been clearly described.[1] In the cases taken up in this chapter, grammaticalization has resulted in a phonetic alteration which has obscured the derivation of the particle, as well as a complete fusion of the particle with the verb. The designation 'present tense' is rather broad, and in reality can include more than one English tense. In this chapter, I use the term 'present tense' in its widest sense, to cover the general present and any present habitual/progressive/continuous aspects.

---

[1] For general discussions on these types of markers in Modern Arabic, see Durand (1992) and Eksell (1995), or the shorter treatment of Fischer and Jastrow (1980: 75). W. Heinrichs (2002) provides an excellent discussion of many such Neo-Aramaic forms; a brief overview can be found in S. Fox (1994).

6.2 Aramaic *qā, k(V)-*

In Jewish Babylonian Aramaic, the particle *qā*, written <q'> or (rarely) as a prefixed <q->, appears before participles. Margolis (1910: 81) simply says that the particle *qā* "strengthens" the participle, which on its own has come to be used as a present tense; this is a vague statement, but suggests that *qā* can be omitted without any alteration in meaning. Kutscher (1971: 282) maintains that it denotes a continuous or habitual action. Breuer (1997), in the most comprehensive and up-to-date discussion of the topic, claims that the particle is used to denote continuous action. Other examples I have seen outside of Breuer's article support his conclusion, so it seems that this construction roughly corresponds to an English present progressive. Margolis also notes that the participle with *qā* can have a conative meaning, i.e., 'about to' do something. The construction can also be combined with a form of the past-tense copula to express a progressive aspect in the past tense.[2] Examples are:

BTA: *q' mšm' ln* 'he informs us'; *hwt q' mḥmy' tnwr'* 'she was heating up the oven'; *ytyb ... q' 'kyl nhm'* 'he sat down ... and ate bread' (lit., 'eating bread'); *q' qṭly lyh* 'they were about to kill him'

In Mandaic, a particle *q'-* (variants *qy-, q-*) is used in the same fashion, though in the Classical language it seldom appears.[3] Examples are:

Mandaic: *q-'ty'* 'he comes'; *mwd q'-h'z't* 'what do you see?'

These Jewish Babylonian and Mandaic particles undoubtedly derive from *qā'ē* (< *qā'ēm*), the masculine singular active participle of the root √*qwm* 'to stand'.[4] The simple participial form can be seen in the following examples:

BTA: *q'y bry '-'ygr'* 'my son is standing on the roof'; *'t' 'lyhw w-q'y '-ptyḥ'* 'Elijah came and was standing at the entrance'

---

[2]Sokoloff (2002b: 976-77) provides the most detailed range of meanings, with abundant examples. In addition to the references given above, see also the brief discussion in Schlesinger (1928: 34-35, 40-46), as well as the study of Golomb (1989).
[3]Nöldeke (1875: 379), Macuch (1965: 105, 280, 433). Macuch is vague, but he notes that in modern Mandaic the construction *qV* + PARTICIPLE has completely replaced the inherited imperfect (i.e., the prefix-conjugation).
[4]The letter *m* drops in many forms of this root, especially in final position. See Sokoloff (2002: 992) or Margolis (1910: 10) for forms. Also see Boyarin (1976), who discusses the common loss of final consonants in BTA. The loss of the final *m*, i.e., *qā'ē < qā'ēm*, is due to a phonetic change (as discussed in Boyarin), and not to the grammaticalization which causes further weakening of this form (*qā'ē > qā*).

This etymology seems to have been first noted by Luzzatto (1836: 176);[5] it was supported by Geiger (1863: 422),[6] and it eventually became standard (cf. Brockelmann 1908-13 II: §84f). A key piece of evidence which secures this etymology, already pointed out by Luzzatto, is the occasional parallel use of the full form *qā'ēm* (and its inflected forms) in Jewish Palestinian Aramaic:[7]

> JPA: *w-hwh qyym dyyn ḥd lysṭys* 'he was judging a robber'; *ql ṭlyy' qyymyn mdḥkyn* 'the voice of the children laughing'

Before continuing with this etymological discussion, let us examine several dialects of Neo-Aramaic which mark the present indicative by means of a prefix *k(V)-*. This prefix is attached to a present "base", which was historically the active participle. For example, in the NENA dialect of Qaraqosh, the present tense marker is *k-* and the present tense base of the root √*ptx* 'open' is *paṭəx* (cf. Syriac *pātaḥ*); thus the 3ms present tense is *k-paṭəx* 'he opens'.[8] The bare present tense base, i.e., without the prefix *k-*, is essentially equivalent to the Arabic jussive and subjunctive moods, used for wishes and negative commands and in purpose clauses, as in *paṭəx* 'let him open'. Other examples with the prefixed *k-* are:

> NENA (Qaraqosh): *la k-ədən* 'I don't know'; *k-raqḏax 'u-k-mwunsax 'u-k-zamrax* 'we dance, have a good time, and sing'; *'ana g-bi'ən xamra* 'I want wine' (*gb* < *kb)

The situation in Turoyo is essentially the same, though the prefix is *ko-*.[9] An example of the bare present tense base can be seen in *lazəm d-šəm'ina* 'it is necessary that we hear'. Examples of the present tense with the prefix *ko-* are:

> Turoyo: *ko-šəm'ina mede* 'we hear something'; *koxəl* 'he is eating' (< **ko-'oxəl*)

Other modern dialects which exhibit a form of this particle include the NENA dialects of Urmia (*či*, written <ki->) and Sardarid (*či-* < **ki-*).[10] In other Neo-Aramaic dialects, such as that of Jewish Arbel, the particle *k-* is used, though

---

[5] See also the more available Luzzatto (1865: 64).
[6] Geiger points out Luzzatto's work in a review of Nöldeke (1862); Nöldeke had remarked (p. 44) that the "Ursprung ... ist ganz dunkel."
[7] See Sokoloff (2002a: 480).
[8] Khan (2002: 97-98, 299-310).
[9] Jastrow (1985: 145-48).
[10] On Urmian, see Nöldeke (1868: 294) and Tsereteli (1978: 58); on the dialect of Sardarid, see Younansardaroud (2001: 199-200).

only before certain verbal roots containing an initial glottal stop.[11]

As with Jewish Babylonian *qā*, Neo-Aramaic *k-* can in some dialects be used in conjunction with a past-tense copula to express a past progressive or habitual aspect:

> NENA (Qaraqosh): *kə-mšagəl-wa b-baġdedə* 'he used to work in Baghdad'[12]

Already in the mid-nineteenth century, Nöldeke (1868b: 294) traced this particle *k(V)-* back to the earlier particle *qā* that appears in Jewish Babylonian Aramaic and Mandaic. Brockelmann (1908-13 II: §84f) followed suit. Lipiński (1997: §42.19), on the other hand, derives the modern *ki-* from an earlier *kīn*, a participial form of the root √*kwn* 'to be, exist'. As W. Heinrichs (2002: 247) notes, the biggest hindrance to connecting the modern and classical forms would seem to be the phonetic correspondence of *qā* and *k(i)*. One can explain the loss of the emphatic feature (i.e., *q* > *k*; see below, 6.2.3), but it is crucial to note that forms with initial *k-* are actually attested in pre-modern times. There are, in fact, a few examples in Jewish Babylonian of a form *kā* (written <k'> or as a prefix <k->), as noted in Sokoloff (2002a: 549). In addition, Eastern (Nestorian) Syriac has a particle *kā*, though it is attested only in the thirteenth-century grammar of Bar Hebraeus, where it is also the subject of discussion.[13] Bar Hebraeus identifies this particle as an Eastern colloquialism.[14] There is no evidence to support Lipiński's suggestion.

To summarize, the etymology from the verb 'stand' is secure for the classical and modern particles. The early evidence for the consonant shift *q* > *k*, along with the parallel distribution of the particles (i.e., before participles and optionally in combination with the past copula) leaves little doubt that the modern forms are to be equated with the classical ones.[15] At this point, the grammatical-

---

[11] See Khan (1999: 96) on Arbel; also Khan (2004: 102). See W. Heinrichs (2002) for an overview of the dialect distribution of this prefix, and an explanation of its restriction in some dialects.

[12] Khan (2002: 310-11).

[13] Brockelmann (1928: 314).

[14] The reference in Bar Hebraeus (206: 13) can be found in Moberg (1922: 205; in translation, 1907-13 I: 30). It is worth noting, for historical interest, that Bar Hebraeus himself derives the present tense marker from the deictic particle *hā*. See W. Heinrichs (2002: 249) for further discussion.

[15] Mention should be made of the recently published discussion by A. Tezel (2003: 35-36). In a brief note, Tezel suggests that a possible source for Turoyo *ko-* is the Aramaic particle *kad* 'when, while'. This is a clever suggestion, reminiscent of the possible development of Arabic *b-* < *baynā* 'while' (see below, 6.6); however, it seems unlikely in this case.

ization itself remains to be discussed.

That a verb 'to stand' should be grammaticalized and impart an actual present tense meaning is not unusual. We will discuss the process of grammaticalization, but first let us look at parallels in other languages.

6.2.1 Spanish, Italian, Portuguese (Brazilian), and Swedish

In Spanish, the progressive aspect consists of an appropriate form of the verb *estar* 'to be' + GERUND, for example:[16]

Ahora estoy viviendo en Boston. 'Now I'm living in Boston.'
Ella estaba cocinando cuando él llegó. 'She was cooking when he arrived.'

On the surface, it seems that Spanish behaves exactly like English, that is to say, it uses a form of 'to be' + GERUND to indicate progressive aspect. But it is important to recognize that Spanish *estar* derives from Latin *stare* 'to stand'. *Estar* is only one of two verbs meaning 'to be' in Spanish, and, in fact, still retains in meaning 'to stand' in context. The other verb, *ser*, is the more basic copula. Therefore, the construction is not quite parallel to English, and is in fact analogous to that of Aramaic.

The situation in Italian mirrors that of Spanish; the verb *stare* 'to be; to stand' + GERUND expresses progressive aspect:[17]

Adesso sta leggendo il giornale. 'She is reading the newspaper now.'
I contadini stavano discutendo. 'The peasants were arguing.'

Brazilian Portuguese (though not Continental; see below 6.5.2) provides another parallel from Romance:[18]

Estou trabalhando. 'I am working.'

The Scandinavian languages exhibit a construction that is slightly different, in that the construction is not as fully grammaticalized as in Romance. In this case, the construction is not regularly used and the verb 'stand' is limited in its use, sharing its role with the verbs 'sit' and 'lie'.[19] For example, in Swedish one can say:

---

[16]Kattán-Ibarra and Pountain (1997: 105-6).
[17]Maiden and Robustelli (2000: 302-4) have a detailed presentation of this construction.
[18]Harris and Vincent (1988: 162).
[19]Haugen (1982: 157-58). See Kuteva (1999; modified and expanded in 2001: 43-74) for a lengthy discussion on the grammaticalization of 'sit/stand/lie' in Scandinavian and a variety of other languages. Also see Heine and Kuteva (2002: 280-82) for other examples of 'stand' becoming the marker of the present continuous.

Du står och ljuger. 'You are lying.' (lit., 'You are standing and lying.')
Maten står och kallnar. 'The food is getting cold.'

However, the simple phrases *Du ljuger* and *Maten kallnar* are identical in meaning, save perhaps for a minor semantic nuance: the compound phrase is only an actual present, while the simple one can be an actual or a general present. In Swedish (as well as in Norwegian and Danish), grammaticalization has occurred, though it remains in the earliest phase. The meaning of the auxiliary (in this case 'stand') has been bleached, but its form and inflection remain intact, and its use optional.

6.2.2 Conclusions

The grammaticalization of 'stand' as evidenced in its early phase by Jewish Palestinian Aramaic has a parallel in Scandinavian. The more complete grammaticalization of 'stand' as a present tense marker is parallel to the Romance examples above, with the difference that Neo-Aramaic does not make the same aspectual distinctions. That is to say, Spanish clearly distinguishes *trabajo* 'I work' from *estoy trabajando* 'I am working (right now)', while Neo-Aramaic does not. The situation in Jewish Babylonian Aramaic is more or less parallel to the Spanish, with the particle *qā* marking a progressive only.

The grammaticalization in Aramaic has had the following three consequences, all of which are consistent with the general tendencies of the process:

1. Gender and number distinction has been neutralized, and only the m.sg. form *qā'ē* acquired a grammatical function.
2. There has been an irregular phonetic reduction of *qā'ē > qā*.
3. There has been a weakening of the emphatic velar $q > k$ (or, if q was a uvular, there was a change in place of articulation).

Even without the evidence of a shift $q > k$ in Jewish Babylonian and the Syriac evidence, we could comfortably assume that such a change took place for the Neo-Aramaic forms; however, the evidence from the classical dialects certainly strengthens the case that the Neo-Aramaic forms are to be derived from *qā'ē*. In fact, we have a nice parallel to this weakening of the emphatic, from within the history of Aramaic.[20] We saw above (3.2.5) that the past tense marker *kəm-*,

---

[20]There are also other examples of word-initial $q > k$ in Neo-Aramaic, as pointed out by Contini (1997: n. 29). This fact was noted already by Nöldeke (1868: §20), and is discussed in other Neo-Aramaic grammars (cf. Jastrow 1988: 7; Khan 2002: 43). However, this seems to me weak evidence to support our theory here. This sporadic change is usually rare and varies by dialect, so to hinge an argument on such an irregular, unpredict-

which appears in some NENA dialects, derives from a grammaticalized form of the root √qdm.[21]

In some Neo-Aramaic dialects there has been another consequence of grammaticalization, which is really a repetition of number two above:

4. There have been further phonetic reductions > k-.

Turoyo is not included in number four, as the form ko- can be traced back to an earlier kā by regular sound change.[22] The prefix ki- found in some NENA dialects should most likely be derived from the prefix kā + the copula *iṯ-.[23] For the dialects which simply have k-, it is impossible to determine if these derived directly from kā, or if they went through a stage ki-; perhaps both developments are attested.

Why was the verb 'stand' grammaticalized as a present tense marker? The proximate reasons are obvious from the discussion above. The verb 'stand' was used in a hendiadys construction (as in JPA and Swedish) whose usage became so common that its meaning was eventually bleached and its form grammaticalized. But for the ultimate cause, one must ask why a verb meaning 'stand' was used in the first place. According to Kuteva (1999), the answer to this question, at least for many languages which have grammaticalized a verb 'stand', seems to hinge on the use of the word 'stand' in describing spatial position. For example, in English we say, 'the chair is in the corner', but in Swedish one says *stolen står i hörnet* 'the chair stands in the corner'. This copula-like use of the verb 'stand' in the expression of spatial position seems to be the forerunner to its grammaticalization. Aramaic does not fit perfectly into this scheme, however, as the verb 'stand' is not usually used to describe spatial position as in Swedish. However, there are two points which suggest that an explanation of this type is correct. First, the root √qwm does have the additional meaning of 'exist, be present, be located', as in:

---

able sound change is rather unsound. It seems more secure to consider the change qā- > ko- as independent within the framework of grammaticalization.

[21] Another example of an emphatic losing its emphatic quality when grammaticalized is the Geʿez preposition wəsta 'in, into' < waṣṭ 'interior', along with its probable Akkadian cognate ištu 'from, out of' (see above, 3.3.2).

[22] For the change ā > o, cf. Syriac ḥmārā, Turoyo ḥmoro 'donkey'. Jastrow (1978: 301) has a completely different interpretation of Turoyo ko-. He sees it is as a borrowing of the qəltu-Mesopotamian Arabic deictic particle kū ~ kwā (the source of the present tense marker in Anatolian Arabic; see below, 6.4.2). Contini (1997: 158) disagrees with Jastrow, but suggests the possibility that the Anatolian form influenced the change q- > k- in Turoyo; this suggestion is plausible, but unnecessary.

[23] Other dialects simply have i-, from *iṯ-, marking the present tense. See W. Heinrichs (2002: 247-49) for a discussion of the development outlined here.

Syriac: *kul d-qāʾem* 'everything that is'
JPA: *w-hwh ʾḥytwpl qʾm tmn* 'Ahitophel was there'
BTA: *tnʾ hykʾ qʾy* 'where is the *Tanna* located?'

So, there is clear usage of 'stand' with a locational, copula-like meaning. For Semitic, this is the crucial point, rather than its use to express spatial relations. Recall the examples from Romance, where 'stand' has become a true copula, one used to denote location (cf. Spanish *estar* vs. *ser*).[24] Second, the true copula is non-existent in the present tense in Aramaic, as elsewhere in Semitic. Thus, any explicit expression of the copula—and we might call an auxiliary present tense marker explicit—must rely on other verbs, in this case 'stand'.

Finally, we should address Margolis's note, mentioned above (6.2), on the conative use of the Jewish Babylonian particle *qā*, translatable as 'about to'. I see this as separate from present-marking function of *qā*; that is to say, while the etymology and phonetic development are the same, I think that its function is from its original meaning 'stand', and not an innovative by-product of the present-tense usage. For the use of 'stand' to denote a conative action, compare Modern Hebrew *ʿomed lə-* (*ʿomed* 'stands'), which can mean 'about to' or 'supposed to'. Or, to use Romance once again, compare Italian *stare per* or Spanish *estar por* 'to be about to'.[25] As in Aramaic, the conative use of Italian *stare per* and Spanish *estar por* certainly derives from its original meaning 'stand'. Examples from these languages are:

Modern Hebrew: *hu ʿamad li-hyot ʾav* 'he was about to be a father'
Italian: *sta per piovere.* 'it's about to rain.'

In fact, the conative *qā* may even come from the past tense *qām*, rather than the participle *qāʾē(m)*. This could explain its past tense meaning in the conative example given above, and in the other example given in Margolis (1910: 81):

BTA: *qʾ blʿh l-spyntʾ* 'it was about to swallow the ship'[26]

6.3 Arabic *da-, qa(d)-, gāʿid*

In the Muslim Arabic dialect of Baghdad, the construction *da* + NON-PAST is

---

[24]Kuteva (1999: 206) notes that the development of Spanish is not quite the same as in the Scandinavian languages.
[25]Maiden and Robustelli (2000: 290).
[26]I have been unable to verify this passage. I found a close match in Baba Batra 74b, *ʾtʾ qʾ bʿy blʿh l-spyntʾ* 'he came, wanting to swallow the ship', but in this case *qʾ* is functioning as a present tense marker. However, Sokoloff (2002b: 221) gives for this same passage *qʾ blʿ l-spyntʾ*.

used to express a present progressive/continuous/habitual tense.[27] For example:

Muslim Baghdadi Arabic: š-da-təsawwi 'what are you doing?'; da-yiktib maktūb 'he is writing a letter'; da-yəʿāwinhum ihwāya 'he helps them a lot'

Jewish and Christian Baghdadi Arabic, on the other hand, employ the prefixes qad- (allomorph qa-) and qa-, respectively, with the same function:[28]

Jewish Baghdadi Arabic: qad-amši 'I'm walking'; qa-yġīd yəmši 'he wants to walk'

Christian Baghdadi Arabic: qa-ṭəṭbəx ṭabīx 'she's cooking a stew'

Both of these prefixes, Muslim Baghdadi da- and Jewish/Christian Baghdadi qa(d)-, derive from *qāʿid, the m.sg. active participle of the root √qʿd 'to sit'.[29] In fact, the full form is occasionally used in Muslim Baghdadi, for example:

Muslim Baghdadi Arabic: fašši zēn ʾanta ma-gāʿəd tətqaddara 'something good that you don't appreciate' (note q > g in this dialect, in most environments)[30]

In Kuwaiti Arabic, we find a construction with the fully inflected form of the participle, gāʿid (< *qāʿid), with a present progressive or habitual meaning.[31]

Kuwaiti Arabic: rifīji gāʿid yišrab wiski 'my friend is drinking whiskey'; maryam gāʿda tinjaḥ kil sina 'Maryam succeeds every year'

The situation in Chadian Arabic is identical to that of Kuwaiti, with the exception that that the meaning seems to be more restricted. Jullien de Pommerol gives 'être en train de' as the only meaning. Examples are:[32]

---

[27]Erwin (1963: 139); Blanc (1964: 115-16).
[28]Blanc (1964: 115-16). Specifically on Christian Baghdadi, see Abu-Haidar (1991: 88).
[29]D. Cohen (1986: 293) derives da- from either the root √dwm 'to continue, persist' or √dwr (dialectally) 'to do'. This seems unlikely given the other evidence for a source qāʿid, though admittedly the a-vowel of da- is curious. For the reduction of qāʿid > da-, in which the first syllable is lost and an a-vowel is added to the end, we can compare the Egyptian future tense marker ḥa < rāyiḥ (see above, 3.2.7.1).
[30]Blanc (1964: 26-27) notes that in Muslim Baghdadi Arabic, q > g is common, but not obligatory. In our example here, it is retained in the form tətqaddara, perhaps due to the preceding voiceless stop or to contamination (or borrowing) from the standard written language.
[31]Al-Najjar (1984: 126-39), Brustad (2000: 248).
[32]Jullien de Pommerol (1999: 66, 208).

Chadian Arabic: *al-wilēd gāʾid yabki* 'the child is crying'; *intu gāʾidīn tifakkuru šunū* 'what are you (pl.) thinking about?'

Finally, in Sudanese Arabic, *gāʿid* is even more restricted, imparting solely a continuous aspect ('keep on'). For example:

Sudanese Arabic: *gāʿid tarāsil 'ahalak* 'do you keep in touch with your family?' (lit., 'keep on corresponding with')[33]

6.3.1 Other Languages

We will see below that the grammaticalization of 'sit' essentially parallels that of 'stand' discussed above (6.2), so we do not need to use examples from other languages to illustrate our argument. Examples can be found in Heine and Kuteva (2001: 276-77). Here we will just repeat that in the Scandinavian languages, as noted above, the verb 'sit' is used along with the verbs 'stand' and 'lie' as optional markers of the present continuous. An example is:

Swedish: *vi satt och pratade* 'we were talking' (lit., 'we sat and talked')

6.3.2 Conclusions

There is a structural difference between the Arabic grammaticalization of 'sit' and the Aramaic grammaticalization of 'stand'. The Aramaic construction began as PARTICIPLE + PARTICIPLE, whereas the Arabic is PARTICIPLE + NON-PAST. In Aramaic, the participle itself (as a category) had already become a present tense. When the new progressive tense with auxiliary 'stand' arose, it naturally grew out of this earlier present tense (= participle). In Arabic, on the other hand, the participle was and is more restricted in use, with the Semitic prefix conjugation (imperfect) being used as the general non-past.[34] Therefore, when the dialects developed a new present tense based on 'sit', the original non-past form served as its basis. The grammaticalization can be outlined as follows:

1. The meaning of the participle was bleached and acquired a continuous aspect (Sudanese) or progressive tense meaning (Kuwaiti, Chadian).
2. Gender and number distinction was neutralized, thus only the m.sg. form *qāʿid* (*gāʿəd*) came to be used in the grammatical function (Muslim Baghdadi).

---

[33] Bergman (2002: 41).
[34] A future meaning could be made explicit with an auxiliary *sawfa* or *sa-*, see above (3.2.7.3).

3. There has been an irregular phonetic reduction of *qāʿid* > *qad-*, *qa-*, *da-*, as a result of cliticization (Baghdadi, all dialects).

We saw above that 'stand' had some ancillary, more copula-like meanings, which likely influenced its choice as an auxiliary. The verb 'sit' in Arabic can also have such meanings, namely 'remain, stay'. In fact, in Chadian Arabic, the root is used as a locational verb 'to be present', for example:[35]

Chadian Arabic: *mūsa gāʾid* 'Moussa is there'

We should also include here a mention of Yemeni Arabic, which utilizes another root meaning 'sit' as an auxiliary, namely *jilis* (variant *jiss*), with the meaning 'to continue, keep doing, remain' (cf. Sudanese, above). It is fully conjugated, and therefore the grammaticalization is at an early stage.[36] Examples are:

Yemeni Arabic: *yijiss yizʿij* 'he is annoying'; *bī-jlisū yiʿayyidū* 'they keep on celebrating'

Finally, it should be noted that the verb 'sit' is found with an inchoative ('begin to') use in Tunisian Arabic, possibly elsewhere.[37] This can be connected with the inchoative use of 'stand' in Tunisian and other Arabic dialects, including Kuwaiti, Chadian, and Yemeni.[38] This development is separate from the use of 'sit' and 'stand' as present tense markers.

6.4 Arabic *k-*

6.4.1 North African

In many dialects of Moroccan Arabic, the prefix *ka-* marks the present progressive, habitual present, or even general present tense.[39] For example:

---

[35] Jullien de Pommerol (1999: 66).
[36] Watson (1993: 158-59).
[37] D. Cohen (1975: 136), Singer (1984: 310).
[38] See Al-Najjar (1984: 97) on Kuwaiti, Jullien de Pommerol (1999: 207) on Chadian, Watson (1993: 157) on Yemeni. Compare also the Syrian ingressive usage of *ʾām* (< **qām* 'stand') (Ambros 1977: 76).
[39] Harrell (1962: 176), Caubet (1993 I: 32; II: 184-86, 226-27), Heath (2002: 209-11). I am not including here the prefixes *ta-* and *la-* of other Moroccan dialects, which are probably Berber loans (Colin 1935: 134-34; D. Cohen 1985: 292). Contrarily, Durand (1992: 10) derives the prefix *ta-* from *tālī*, the active participle from the root √*tlw* 'to follow').

> Moroccan Arabic: *ka-nmši ʿandha kull nhāṛ* 'I go to her place every day'; *āš ka-tdīr hna* 'what are you doing here?'; *ka-nxāf mən əl-klāb* 'I am afraid of dogs'

This prefix surely comes from a form of the root √*kwn* 'to be'.[40] The most likely form, phonologically and semantically, would be *kā'in*, the active participle. However, evidence from other dialects requires a different solution. In some Moroccan and Algerian dialects, the prefix *ka-* appears only on third person forms, while *ku-* appears in conjunction with the first and second persons.[41] For example:

> Algerian Arabic (Djidjelli): *ku-nəbīʿ u-nəšri* 'I buy and sell' (i.e., 'I do business'); *ka-iḥəbb kəll-ən-nās* 'He likes everyone'[42]

This has led scholars to suggest that the source is the perfect tense, which has the base *kān-* for the third person forms (e.g., Moroccan *kān* 'he was'), and *kun-* for the other persons (e.g., *kunt* 'I was'). In written Arabic, the verb *kāna* is in fact used in conjunction with the imperfect tense, and expresses a past continuous or habitual.[43] For example:

> Classical Arabic: *kāna yarkabu fī kulli yawmin* 'he used to ride out every day'; *rijālun kānū yakūnūna maʿa (')l-mulūki* 'men who lived (used to live) with the princes'

> Modern Standard Arabic: *kuntu 'adrusu fī (')l-jāmiʿati ʿinda-mā...* 'I was studying at the university when...'; *kāna dā'iman yatakallamu ʿanka* 'He was always talking about you'

However, despite the attestation of this construction (which itself is an example grammaticalization, of the type discussed in 3.2.3.1), the development of an auxiliary marking past tense into a prefix marking the present tense is fairly strange. G. Colin (1935: 134) has suggested that the Moroccan construction has been influenced by a Berber one, but this does not seem to solve the problem.

---

[40]Kampffmeyer (1899; 1900) disagrees. He suggests as the source the CA particles *ka'an* 'as if' (normally followed by a dependent verb) or *ka'anna* 'it is as if' (normally followed by an independent nominal sentence).
[41]Noted in M. Cohen (1924: 68-71), D. Cohen (1985: 292). On Moroccan, see Heath (2002: 209-11).
[42]Marçais (1952: 151-52, 615-16).
[43]Classical: Wright (1967 II: §9); Modern Standard: Mace (1998: 34). As Wright notes, this construction often translates a Greek or Latin imperfect.

6.4.2 Anatolian

A prefix *kū-* is found in *qəltu-*Arabic dialects of Northern Iraq and Southeastern Turkey.[44] The particle denotes an actual present as opposed to a general one, roughly equivalent to the English present progressive. Examples are:

> Jewish Arbel Arabic: *kū-təšrab* 'you are drinking' (cf. *təšrab* 'you drink')[45]
>
> *qəltu-*Arabic (Kinderib): *kū-təqša'ūn ṣīyād-ana* 'you (pl.) see that I am a hunter'[46]
>
> *qəltu-*Arabic (Azex): *kū-nəktəb* 'we are writing'[47]

Jastrow (1978: 300) derives this particle from a series of forms he calls the demonstrative copula. These dialects have a grammaticalized pronominal series, formed with the demonstrative element *k-* plus the independent personal pronouns, and used as a locational copula (cf. Spanish *está* as opposed to *es*). For example, in the dialect of Kinderib we find *kūwe* 'he is' (< **k-* + *hūwe*), *kənt* 'you (m.sg.) are' (< **k-* + *ənt*), *kana* 'I am' (< **k-* + *ana*).[48] The use of this series is illustrated in the following examples:

> *qəltu-*Arabic (Qartmin): *əbnu kū qəddām əmmu* 'his son is (standing) in front of his mother' (*kū* < **k-* + *hū*); *ana kana xalf əd-dawāb* 'I am behind the pack-animal'

Jastrow's derivation is quite satisfactory, and will be discussed further below (6.4.3), but it seems to me that there is at least one other possibility for the source of this prefix *kū*. It may simply derive from the non-past forms of the root √*kwn* 'to be' (3ms *yakūnu*).[49] This would make the Anatolian construction very similar to the English present progressive 'to be doing'.

6.4.3 Conclusions

The North African and Anatolian present tense markers may or may not derive from the same source lexeme. The North African forms *ka-* or *ku-* certainly derive from the root √*kwn*, though exactly which form of the root is unclear. We

---

[44]Jastrow (1978: 300-2).
[45]Jastrow (1990: 62-63).
[46]Jastrow (1999: 46).
[47]Jastrow (1978: 301).
[48]See above (3.2.8.2) for other similar examples of grammaticalization.
[49]This is the position taken by Lipiński (1997: §38.24), Khan (1999: 112), and, strangely, Fischer and Jastrow (1980: 75).

have the following options:

1. If the participle *kāʾin* is the source, we need only assume a phonetic reduction, due to grammaticalization, to explain the prefix *ka-*; it would remain difficult to explain the allomorph *ku-* present in some dialects.

2. If we assume that the past tense *kāna* (conjugated for person) is the source, then the dialects which have *ka-* ~ *ku-* have simply undergone phonetic reduction. In the dialects which only have *ka-*, distinction for person has then been neutralized, as per the tendency of grammaticalization.

If this root is also the source of the Anatolian present tense marker, we also only need assume phonetic reduction (*yakūnu* > *kū-*), possibly following the neutralization of person/number/gender distinction; positing this earlier step avoids having to posit the reduction of longer forms like 2mp *takūnūna*. The grammaticalization of 'be' as an auxiliary is extremely common, and has already been discussed above (3.2.3.1), so it will not be discussed further here.

If the Anatolian forms do in fact come from the so-called demonstrative copula, and I suspect they do, we are then dealing with a grammaticalization which corresponds very nicely to the type of grammaticalization discussed in 6.2 and 6.3, namely, a locational verb (here, pseudo-verb) coming to mark the present tense. It also exactly reminiscent of the situation in Algerian dialects in which the copula *ṛā-* (+ object suffixes) has come to mark the present progressive (3.2.8.2). It will be recalled that the Algerian copula has roughly the meaning 'to be situated, located', exactly like the Anatolian copula *k-*. I would hold that it is this locational meaning of the copula which has led to its grammaticalization as a present tense marker, not simply its function as a general copula. In Anatolian, once the demonstrative copula series was grammaticalized, all distinctions for person, gender, and number were lost, with the 3ms form *kū-* having been generalized. In some Anatolian dialects, the form of the prefix does show variation, but this is most likely due to later phonetic change and not the original paradigm of the copula. For example, Azex *kū-nəktəb* 'we are writing', but *k-īktəb* 'he is writing' (< **kū-yəktəb*), *k-aktəb* 'I am writing' (< **kū-aktəb*).

6.5 Aramaic *b-*

Many dialects of North-Eastern Neo-Aramaic form a present continuous tense with a prefix *b-*, though there is variation in the form of the construction and usage. All constructions essentially take the form *b-* + INFINITIVE + COPULA (or COPULA + *b-* + INFINITIVE). A past tense copula can be used to indicate a past progressive. The dialects of Bespen and Sardarid will serve as representative NENA dialects here:

NENA (Bespen): *holi b-ktawa / b-ktawɛ-wən* 'I am writing'; *holɛ bi-taya* 'they are coming'; *bi-xalɛ-wa* 'she was eating'[50]

NENA (Sardarid): *bï-dmä:x-ïlï* 'he is sleeping'[51]

This prefix *b-* undoubtedly is identical to the common Semitic preposition *b-* 'in, at'. One factor which supports this claim is that this prefix governs a nominal form (i.e., the infinitive), which would be expected following a preposition. As an aside, it is worth noting that in some of these NENA dialects, the preposition *b-* is often replaced by another preposition in its locative (but not its instrumental) meaning. For example:

NENA (Bespen): *go bayta* 'in the house'

Possibly the partial replacement of prepositional *b-* was motivated by its grammaticalized use within the verbal system.

6.5.1 Dutch, German, and English

Dutch has a progressive aspect, used to indicate an action that is currently in progress. The construction consists of the appropriate form of *zijn* 'to be' + *aan* 'on; at' + *het* 'the' + INFINITIVE.[52] For example:

Ik ben (een brief) aan het schrijven. 'I am writing (a letter).'
Wij zijn voetbal aan het spelen. 'We are playing football.'
Hij was haring aan het eten. 'He was eating herring.'

In colloquial German, one finds the exact same construction:

Ich bin am Essen. 'I am eating.' (*am* < *an* + *dem*)

English attests, or at least attested in older dialects, a similar construction with *on*, or less often *upon* or *in*. Unlike in Dutch and German, English lacks the definite article and uses the gerund instead of the infinitive. Jespersen gives the following examples:[53]

Whyle Torrent an huntyng wase 'While Torrent was hunting' (*an* = 'on')

---

[50] Sinha (2000: 131). Notice from the first example that the copula can precede (when independent) or follow (when enclitic), with no functional difference.
[51] Younansardaroud (2001: 87-88). For other dialects, see Maclean (1895: 82), Tsereteli (1978: 59), S. Fox (1997: 32), W. Heinrichs (2002).
[52] Shetter and Van der Cruysse-Van Antwerpen (2002: 141-42).
[53] Jespersen (1949: 168-77).

I am upon writing a little treatise.
Whyl this yeman was thus in his talking 'While this yeoman was talking'

Much more often, the preposition *on* was shortened to *a*:

They had ben a fyghtyng. 'They had been fighting.'
I'm a-goin' to tell you.
What are you a talking on?[54]

What these Germanic forms have in common is the combination of a copula plus locative preposition and a nominal form of the verb to indicate a progressive aspect. Note that the tense itself it determined by the appropriate form of the verb 'to be' in all of the above examples.

6.5.2 Portuguese (Continental) and Italian

Continental Portuguese uses a construction very similar to the type found in the German and Dutch, namely the appropriate form of the verb *estar* 'to be; to stand' + *a* 'to, at' + INFINITIVE:[55]

Está a escrever. 'He is writing.'
Estou a trabalhar. 'I am working.'

Italian possesses the same construction, *stare a* + INFINITIVE, though with a more durative nuance and different (and more limited) usage than the usual progressive tense, which is *stare* + GERUND:[56]

Stettero tutta la giornata a pescare. 'They were (busy) fishing all day.'

6.5.3 Conclusions

The above examples from Germanic, Portuguese, and Italian exactly parallel the construction found in Neo-Aramaic dialects. The use of a COPULA + LOCATIVE PREPOSITION is essentially the same as a locative/copular verb, so this grammaticalization can be compared to that of 'sit' and 'stand' above. The major difference is that the "main verb" in this construction is not actually a finite verb, but rather a nominal form (i.e., infinitive). This is expected, since a preposition normally takes a noun as its head.

This means that this Aramaic construction is not to be directly connected

---

[54]These final two examples are from Charles Dickens, *The Pickwick Papers* and *David Copperfield*, respectively.
[55]Harris and Vincent (1988: 162), Posner (1996: 175).
[56]Maiden and Robustelli (2000: 305).

with the temporal construction *b-* 'in, at' + INFINITIVE that is attested elsewhere in Semitic, for example:

Biblical Hebrew: *wa-yəhî bə-nosʿām miq-qedem way-yimṣəʾû biqʿā* 'and as they migrated east, they came across a valley' (lit., 'in their migrating') (Gen. 11:2)

That is to say, while the constructions themselves are identical and certainly relatable, I do not believe that the Neo-Aramaic present tense has developed out of a subordinate temporal construction of the type found in Hebrew. Rather, I think that the Aramaic present tense is parallel to the examples from Germanic, Portuguese, and Italian. It is the locative meaning of the preposition which has led to the formation of a present tense. This locative preposition can be compared with the locative verbs ('stand', 'sit', 'be located') which developed into tense-markers as described above (6.2 - 6.4).

6.6 Arabic *b-*

Several Arabic dialects, including those of Syria-Palestine and Egypt, indicate the present indicative tense by means of a prefixed *b(i)-*, attached to the historical non-past (imperfect) tense.[57] Usage varies slightly between the dialects.[58] In Egyptian it is used with all present tense meanings; the same is true in Syria and Lebanon, though the present progressive is often expressed by an additional auxiliary (*ʿam/ʿamma*).[59] For example:

Egyptian Arabic: *uxti b-tidris dilwaʾti* 'my sister is studying now'; *uxti b-tidris b-il-lel* 'my sister studies at night'

Syrian Arabic: *mā b-aʿrəf.* 'I don't know.'; *ž-žāžāt b-ibīḍu bēḍ.* 'Hens lay eggs.'[60]

Lebanese Arabic: *ma b-tišrab šāy?* 'you don't drink tea?'; *b-yiktub maktūb kull jumʿa* 'he writes a letter every week'

---

[57] See Abdel-Massih et al. (1979: 268-69) on Egyptian, Cowell (1964: 324-29) and Ambros (1977: 75) on Syrian, Thackston (1996: 54-55) on Lebanese.
[58] See Brustad (2000: 248-53) for a discussion.
[59] This particle *ʿam(ma)* derives from the root √*ʿml* 'to do' and is connected with the Egyptian auxiliary form *ʿammāl*, meaning 'continue, keep on', as in *qalbi ʿammāl yitaktik* 'my heart keeps on ticking' (Hinds and Badawi 1986: 602; see also Brustad 2000: 246-47). Feghali (1928: 22) is uncertain about this etymology.
[60] Cowell (1964: 326) gives the form *žāžat*, but this is a misprint for *žāžāt* (as correctly printed on p. 215).

What is the origin of this particle *b(i)-*? This question will be addressed in the following section.

6.6.1 Yemeni Arabic *bi-* and its Origin

The most obvious suggestion would be the preposition *b-*, which, as we saw above (6.5), is the source for the present-tense marker of several Neo-Aramaic dialects. However, there is good evidence which suggests otherwise. Yemeni (San'ani) Arabic also uses a prefix *bi-* to indicate the present indicative, though again with slight differences in distribution from the other dialects discussed above.[61] Crucially, the prefix has the form *bayn-* before the 1sg. form. Examples are:

> Yemeni (San'ani) Arabic: *mā bayn-afham-š* 'I don't understand'; *lilmā bi-ta'kal* 'why are you limping?'

In some Northern Yemeni dialects, the prefix *bayn-* (variants *bēn-*, *bin-*) appears before all persons.[62]

> Northern Yemeni Arabic: *wēš bēn-tisawwī* 'what are you doing?'

This Yemeni prefix certainly derives from Classical Arabic *baynā* (< *bayna-mā*) 'while', which was used to form circumstantial clauses. For example:

> Classical Arabic: *bayna-mā naḥnu namši 'ið 'araḍa rajulun* 'while we were walking, a man appeared'; *baynā nasūsu n-nāsa* 'while we govern the people'[63]

We can assume that the imperfective nature of this circumstantial construction came to indicate a progressive or actual present tense, in an utterance like:

> 'Not understanding, I cannot answer' → 'I don't understand, I can't answer'

This reinterpretation led to grammaticalization of the particle *baynā*, its eventual extension to all (non-circumstantial) present tense expressions, and finally its phonetic erosion.

6.6.2 A Proto-Central-Semitic Parallel to Yemeni?

The extension of an original circumstantial verbal form may have a parallel at

---

[61] Watson (1991:72-76, 78-83).
[62] Behnstedt (1987: 53, 161).
[63] Wright (1967 II: §67 note), W. Fischer (2002: §444).

the Proto-Central-Semitic level, in the development of the CS *yaqtulu* form. The Proto-Semitic imperfective/durative tense had the form *yVqattVl* as evidenced by Akkadian (*iparras*), Ethiopic (*yənabbər*), and Modern South Arabian (Mehri *yəkōtəb*). In the Central Semitic languages, this form is absent, having been replaced by the form *yaqtulu*; in fact, this shared innovation is the defining feature of CS.[64] Assuming that this is correct, that an indicative present tense form *yaqtulu* was indeed a CS innovation, one must then ask what its relationship is to the Akkadian subordinating morpheme *-u*.[65] In Akkadian, the subordinating marker *-u* is attached to any finite verb form which appears in a subordinate (i.e., dependent) clause.[66] For example:

Akkadian: *Enkidu ša aramm-u* 'Enkidu, whom I loved'; *balāṭam ša tasaḫḫur-u* 'the life that you seek'; *aššum uštamaḫḫar-u ittīka* 'because he will rival you'; *imtaši ašar iwwald-u* 'he has forgotten the place where he was born'[67]

It is generally assumed that the Akkadian subordination marker *-u* is related to the final *-u* of the CS *yaqtulu* form, but there is little consensus on exactly how this relationship works.[68] A. Hamori (1973) has suggested a very plausible theory, according to which the CS *yaqtulu* developed via an analogy. Consider the following two hypothetical sentences, using Akkadian forms for convenience:

(A) **mutam iqabbi āmur*
 'I saw a man speaking' (*iqabbi* = imperfective)

(B) *mutam ša iqbû āmur*
 'I saw a man who spoke' (*iqbû* < **iqbi-u*; *iqbi* = preterite)

Type (A) is ungrammatical in Akkadian, but I assume, as Hamori does (p. 321), that this type of relative clause existed in Proto-Semitic. Hamori assumes that in Proto-Semitic, a relative particle was redundant, and therefore unnecessary, in construction (B), as the final *-u* was a sufficient marker of subordination. Thus,

---

[64]This classification and criterion was first suggested by Hetzron (1976). See also Huehnergard (2005).

[65]The Akkadian *-u* is often referred to as the subjunctive marker. This term is misleading and is best avoided (von Soden 1995: §81a).

[66]Huehnergard (1997: §§19.2-3). Note that this suffix does not appear when there is already a verbal ending present (i.e., a feminine, plural, or ventive morpheme).

[67]OB Gilgameš Sippar ii: 2, iii:2; OB Gilgameš Penn ii:1, ii:5.

[68]Note that in the Old Assyrian dialect of Akkadian, there is an additional subordination marker *-ni*, used when the verb has another suffix and so cannot take *-u*, for example., *ša iprusū-ni* (Huehnergard 1997: 602). This *-ni* is undoubtedly related to the ending of CS *yaqtulūna*, the plural of *yaqtulu*. Thanks to J. Huehnergard for bringing this to my attention.

using again Akkadian for convenience, we can posit an original construction of the type:[69]

(C) *mutam iqbû āmur
'I saw a man who spoke'

In West Semitic, since the inherited past tense *yaqtul* had already been supplanted by the verbal adjective *qatala*, with *qatala* becoming the normal West Semitic past tense, the subordinate *yaqtulu* form was reinterpreted as an imperfective form, based on the more or less equivalent meanings of sentences types (A) and (C). That is to say, the following semantic equation was made:

(A) *mutam iqabbi āmur = (C) *mutam iqbû āmur
'I saw a man speaking' = 'I saw a man who spoke'

This led to the reinterpretation and extension of the *yaqtulu* form, and its complete replacement of the inherited *yVqattVl* imperfective.

So, both in Proto-Central-Semitic and in Yemeni, there has been a grammaticalization which has resulted in the extension of a dependent verbal form to general present tense use. We can also compare the development of the Ethiopic perfective active participle (*nabiro*) in Tigrinya, discussed above (3.2.4).

6.6.3 On the Origin of the Syro-Palestinian and Egyptian *b-*

The derivation of the Yemeni prefix *bayn-/bi-* from Classical Arabic *baynā* is rather secure. But does the prefix *b-* of Egyptian and Syro-Palestinian dialects need to be connected with the Yemeni forms? Of course, this is possible, likely even, but unfortunately cannot be proven. There is no evidence in these dialects that this *b-* goes back to an earlier *bayn-*, so we must still look for other possibilities. As already noted (6.6.1), the most obvious source would be the preposition *b-*.[70]

If the Syro-Palestinian prefix *b-* does indeed derive from the preposition *b-*, we are faced with a problem. The form following this prefix is a finite verb, namely, the Arabic imperfect (non-past). We would expect a nominal form to follow a preposition, simply because a preposition normally governs a nominal form. This is also what we find in the Aramaic, Germanic, and Portuguese examples above (6.5). There are two solutions to this problem. The first hinges on

---

[69]This construction is attested in Arabic, as in *rajul-un yaktub-u* 'a man writing'. Hamori believes this is an archaic construction which Arabic preserves.

[70]See also Kampffmeyer (1900) for a review of nineteenth-century theories, including derivations from the verbs *'abā* 'to refuse', *biddi* 'want', *bā'a* 'to come', and the OSA present tense marker *b-*.

the fact that the Arabic imperfect can have a participial function, as in the phrase *rajulun yaktubu* 'a man writing'. We might suggest that this verbal form was able to take a preposition because it is filling the same slot as a nominal form (i.e., the participle *kātibun*). The second solution centers on the fact that Arabic has no regular gerundive or infinitival form. There exist the various verbal nouns, but these are unpredictable in formation, and so would hardly lend themselves to the creation of a new tense. We should also note that the Arabic imperfect is used with other tense-marking prefixes, like the modern (dialectal) future particle *raḫ-* and Classical *sa-* (see above, 3.2.7.1 and 3.2.7.3, respectively); perhaps this played a role.[71]

Perhaps this is not a problem at all. In fact, several prepositions can be used in conjunction with the Arabic imperfect tense. We saw above (3.2.7.4) that two future tense markers in Arabic dialects can be traced back the prepositions *ḥattā* and *li-*.[72] Constructions with these two prepositions, denoting purpose, are attested in Classical and Modern Standard Arabic, so their derivation as future tense markers in clear. The preposition *b-* is not attested this way in either phase of Arabic, so we would have to hypothesize its use in Arabic temporal clauses of the type attested with *baynā*; however, elsewhere in Semitic this preposition is attested in this way (cf. the Biblical Hebrew examples above, 6.5.3).[73]

An additional piece of evidence yet to be considered is the appearance of a seemingly identical prefix *b-* in the Qatabanic and, very rarely, Minaic dialects of OSA. As in Syro-Palestinian and Egyptian Arabic, this prefix appears before all imperfect indicative forms. Examples are:

OSA (Qatabanic): *kl mngw b-yktrbwn* 'all things that they will request'; *kbrm bykbr* 'a kabir who holds office'[74]

In the past, some scholars have taken this OSA particle as the source for the Arabic ones.[75] They assume that it was borrowed into Arabian dialects (by which they presumably mean Yemeni), and then spread north. This is quite prob-

---

[71]As a parallel, we might recall also the Arabic future construction *sawfa / sa-* + IMPERFECT (a verbal form) and the (rare) Mishnaic Hebrew future construction *sôp* + INFINITIVE (a nominal form), both of which were discussed above (3.2.7.3).

[72]This argument is sufficient to satisfy Nöldeke (1904b: 64) regarding a derivation from the preposition.

[73]J. Huehnergard has kindly pointed out that the Akkadian preposition *ina* 'in' can also introduce a temporal clause, though rarely, and only with verbal adjectives and forms of the verb *edûm* 'to know'. For example, *ina lā īdû* 'while he was unaware; unknowingly'. Incidentally, *edûm* only occurs in the preterite (as a finite verb). See von Soden (1995: §170b), Huehnergard (1997: §26.2a).

[74]Texts AM 757/11 and R 3688/2, respectively. See Nebes (2004: §4.3.2.3) and Beeston (1984: §Q5.7a).

[75]See Kampffmeyer (1900). Also noted in Nöldeke (1910: 65).

lematic. If Yemeni borrowed the OSA particle, how do we explain the form *bayn-* and its variants? Would we even expect that a verbal prefix can be borrowed in this way?[76] If we assume, as I have above, that the Yemeni forms are derived from *baynā*, could then a particle from OSA have bypassed Yemen and made its way to Syro-Palestine? This scenario seems highly implausible; however, we still must look at the OSA form itself. It is quite possible that the OSA *b-* derives from the preposition *b-*.[77] If we also assume that the Syro-Palestinian and Egyptian *b-* derives from the preposition, we thus have a possible parallel.

The ultimate source of the Syro-Palestinian and Egyptian present tense marker *b-* remains uncertain. The debate can be summarized as follows:

Arguments that *b-* derives from *baynā*:
1. The grammaticalization of *baynā* > *b-* is attested in Yemeni dialects.
2. *baynā*, as a subordinating particle, is attested before the imperfect tense in Classical and Modern Standard Arabic.
3. *b-*, as a preposition or subordinator, is not attested before verbal forms in Arabic.

Arguments that *b-* derives from the preposition *b-*:
1. This is the simplest derivation phonologically.
2. Other grammaticalized verbal particles, used in conjunction with the imperfect, derive from prepositions.
3. A preposition 'in' or 'on' is commonly grammaticalized as a present tense marker.

The evidence seems to me to favor the derivation from *baynā*, but by no means is this assured. Recent scholarship remains divided.[78] Even if the source is the preposition *b-*, we can still assume that the present tense function stems from its use in a temporal clause, and not from its locative prepositional function.[79] This would be unlike the situation in Neo-Aramaic, where the locative meaning is crucial.

Finally, mention should be made of the Kuwaiti verbal prefix *bi-*, which is not to be connected with forms of the other dialects treated above. As already discussed (3.2.7.2), the Kuwaiti particle indicates future tense and is derived

---

[76] It has been suggested earlier in this chapter (n. 39) that some dialects of Moroccan Arabic have borrowed such prefixes from neighboring Berber dialects.

[77] D. Cohen (1985: 293: n. 44) suggests that OSA form derives from the Arabic. This seems highly unlikely, given the age of the OSA texts; also unlikely is the early date he suggests for the reduction of *baynā* > *b-*.

[78] Cf. Fischer and Jastrow (1980: 75), Durand (1992: 6).

[79] It is the use of *b-* in temporal clauses elsewhere in Semitic that convinces M. Cohen (1924: 64-65) of the derivation from the preposition.

from a form *yabi* 'wants' (< CA *yabġi*).[80]

6.7 Chapter Conclusions

From the above data, we can classify the present tense markers of Arabic and Aramaic into two main types:

Type 1: Aramaic *qā*, *k(V)-* < *qā'ēm* 'stand'
Arabic *da-*, *qa(d)-*, *gā'id* < *gā'id* 'sit'
North African Arabic *k-* < √*kwn* 'be'
Anatolian Arabic *k-* < *kūwe* 'he is (located)'; (or, < √*kwn* ?)
Aramaic *b-* < *b-* 'in, at'

Type 2: Yemeni Arabic *b-* < *baynā* 'while'
Syro-Palestinian and Egyptian Arabic *b-* < (*baynā* 'while' ?); (or, < *b-* 'in, at' ?)

In Type 1, the present tense originates in a locative construction. In all but one case, the present tense marker derives from an auxiliary verb. This auxiliary may originally be a verb 'be', 'sit', or 'stand'. As was shown, these verbs share a common trait, namely, that they can all be used to describe locative position, translatable as 'to be present'. The exception in this group is Aramaic *b-*, which derives from a preposition; however, it is a locative preposition, and therefore fits very well semantically within this category.

In Type 2, the present tense marker derives from a subordinating particle marking a temporal clause; the particle itself ultimately derives from a preposition. Of course, with the Syro-Palestinian and Egyptian forms, we are speculating, as the etymology is unclear. It does seem, though, that one of the two etymologies proposed here is very likely correct. It is worth noting again that if the form does indeed derive from the preposition *b-*, the Aramaic *b-*, while sharing the same source lexeme, developed quite differently. The finite verbal form following the Arabic *b-* suggests that we must be dealing with an original subordinate clause which has taken on the function of a main verb, while the Aramaic stems from an original locative construction.

The type of grammaticalization exemplified in Type 1 is extremely common in the languages of the world. I have given examples from a handful of non-Semitic languages above; others can be found in Heine and Kuteva (2002) and Bybee et al. (1994: 128-29).[81] The type of grammaticalization represented by Type 2, on the other hand, is far less common cross-linguistically. However, the

---

[80] Al-Najjar (1984: 86-90), including a discussion of grammaticalization.
[81] Bybee et al. also provide some very good discussion of this type of grammaticalization. See especially pp. 127-33.

extension of a verb in a subordinate temporal clause to the main clause is paralleled in both Proto-Central Semitic and Ethiopic.

Several of the cases discussed above, most clearly Aramaic *qā* / *k(V)-*,[82] demonstrate another very common cross-linguistic grammaticalization, namely, the development of a progressive/continuous tense into a general present. See Bybee et al. (1994: 140-44) and Heine and Kuteva (2002: 93-94) for discussion and further references.

---

[82]Discussed in detail by W. Heinrichs (2002).

Chapter 7
Summary

In the previous four chapters we have investigated a large number of examples of grammaticalization in Semitic, and have seen how widespread changes of this type are. In Chapters 4, 5, and 6, we closely examined three categories of grammaticalization in a way that had not been previously done for the Semitic languages, with the hope of satisfactorily explaining some problematic developments.

In Chapter 4, we looked at the Central Semitic definite article, perhaps the most heavily debated topic included in this treatment. We saw that cross-linguistic evidence points overwhelmingly to a demonstrative origin for definite articles. Likely demonstrative sources can be found for the CS definite articles, and their developments can be explained through grammaticalization and its characteristic tendencies. In the appendix to this chapter, we saw that parallel developments have occurred in some modern Semitic languages (e.g., Tigrinya), but that the histories of other Semitic definite articles (e.g., in Amharic and Mehri) remain to be adequately explained.

In Chapter 5, we provided a rather comprehensive description of direct object markers in the Semitic languages. Two types of direct object markers can be found. The first, which derives from an original dative/allative preposition, seems to have been an innovation of both Aramaic and Geʻez, which later spread to some neighboring Semitic languages. This is not surprising, for, as we saw, this type of grammaticalization is quite common cross-linguistically. The second type of direct object marker, reflected in Hebrew *'et* and Aramaic *'yt / yāt*, is of obscure origin, but this particle has itself later been grammaticalized in interesting ways.

Finally, in Chapter 6, we examined a number of prefixes which have come to mark the present tense in modern Arabic and Aramaic dialects. All of the prefixes we investigated have their origins either in a locative verb (or construction) or, in one or two cases, in a temporal subordinate clause. More importantly, the development of these prefixes, why they were grammaticalized, and how they attained the forms attested, were explained with the help of grammaticalization theory and cross-linguistic parallels.

These examples of grammaticalization in Semitic, along with those discussed in Chapter 3, are, of course, not exhaustive. There remain many more examples to be collected, and, more importantly, thoroughly investigated. The many examples which appear in Chapter 3 also need to be explored in greater detail; some are rather straightforward (reflexive pronouns, for example), but others (future tense markers, derived stems, existential particles) would make the subject of very interesting and rewarding further research.

The study of grammaticalization as a specific linguistic change or process can lead to valuable insights into the history of the Semitic languages. At the same time, the Semitic languages, with their over four thousand years of attested history, provide a goldmine of examples for the study of grammaticalization itself.

Bibliography

In the bibliography, only the following abbreviations are used: *BSOAS* (*Bulletin of the School of Oriental and African Studies*), *JAOS* (*Journal of the American Oriental Society*), *JNES* (*Journal of Near Eastern Studies*), *JSS* (*Journal of Semitic Studies*), and *ZDMG* (*Zeitschrift der Deutschen Morgenländischen Gesellschaft*).

Aartun, Kjell. 1959. Zur Frage des bestimmten Artikels im Aramäischen. *Acta Orientalia* 24:5-14.

Abboud, Peter F., and Ernest N. McCarus. 1983. *Elementary Modern Standard Arabic, Part 1*. Cambridge: Cambridge University Press.

Abdel-Massih, Ernest T., Zaki N. Abdel-Malek, and El-Said M. Badawi. 1979. *A Comprehensive Study of Egyptian Arabic. Volume 3: A Reference Grammar of Egyptian Arabic*. Ann Arbor: Center for Near Eastern and African Studies, The University of Michigan.

Abu-Haidar, Farida. 1991. *Christian Arabic of Baghdad*. Wiesbaden: Harrassowitz.

Allan, Robin, Philip Holmes, and Tom Lundskær-Nielsen. 2000. *Danish: An Essential Grammar*. London: Routledge.

Al-Najjar, Balkees. 1984. The Syntax and Semantics of Verbal Aspect in Kuwaiti Arabic. Ph.D. diss., University of Utah.

Alting, Jacob. 1686. *Fundamenta punctationis linguae sanctae*. 4th ed. Frankfurt: J.G. Fabri.

Ambros, Arne. 1977. *Damascus Arabic*. Malibu: Undena.

_____. 1998. *Bonġornu, Kif Int? Einführung in die maltesische Sprache*. Wiesbaden: Reichert.

Andersen, Henning. 1995. *Historical Linguistics 1993*. Amsterdam: Benjamins.

Anttila, Raimo. 1989. *Historical and Comparative Linguistics*. 2d ed. Amsterdam: Benjamins.

Appleyard, D. L. 1977. A Comparative Approach to the Amharic Lexicon. *Afroasiatic Linguistics* 5/2:1-67.

_____. 2004. Some thoughts on the Origin of the Amharic Object Marker - —, -[ə]n. In *Studia Aethiopica: In Honour of Siegbert Uhlig on the Occasion of his 65th Birthday*, ed. Verena Böll, Denis Nosnitsin, Thomas Rave, Wolbert Smidt and Evegenia Sokolinskaia, 291-301. Wiesbaden: Harrassowitz.

Arnold, Werner. 1990. *Das Neuwestaramäische*. Vol. 5, *Grammatik*. Wiesbaden: Harrassowitz.

Badawi, Elsaid, M.G. Carter, and Adrian Gully. 2004. *Modern Written Arabic: A Comprehensive Grammar*. London: Routledge.

Barth, Jakob. 1896. Zwei Pronominale Elemente. *American Journal of Semitic Languages* 13:1-13.

_____. 1905a. Zum semitischen ḏ. *ZDMG* 59:159-62.

———. 1905b. Ursemit. *e*, zum Demonstrativ *ḏ.*, *tī* und Verwandtes. *ZDMG* 59:633-43.

———. 1907-11. *Sprachwissenschaftliche Untersuchungen zum Semitischen.* 2 vols. Leipzig: J. C. Hinrichs.

———. 1913. *Die Pronominalbildung in den semitischen Sprachen.* Leipzig: J.C. Hinrichs.

Bauer, H. 1914. Semitische Sprachprobleme. *ZDMG* 68:365-72.

Bauer, Hans, and Pontus Leander. 1922. *Historische Grammatik der hebräischen Sprache des Alten Testamentes.* Halle: Niemeyer.

———. 1927. *Grammatik des Biblisch-Aramäischen.* Halle: Niemeyer.

Beeston, A.F.L. 1973. The Inscription Jaussen-Sauvignac 71. *Proceedings of the Seminar for Arabian Studies* 3:69-72.

———. 1981. Languages of Pre-Islamic Arabia. *Arabica* 28:178-86.

———. 1984. *Sabaic Grammar.* Manchester: Journal of Semitic Studies.

Behnstedt, Peter. 1987. *Die Dialekte der Gegend von Ṣaʻdah (Nord-Jemen).* Wiesbaden: Harrassowitz.

Bennett, Stephen Frank. 1984. Objective Pronominal Suffixes in Aramaic. Ph.D. diss., Yale University.

Benveniste, Emile. 1966. *Problèmes de linguistique générale.* Paris: Gallimard.

Bergman, Elizabeth M. 2002. *Spoken Sudanese Arabic: Grammar, Dialogues, and Glossary.* Springfield, VA: Dunwoody.

Blake, Frank. 1915. Studies in Semitic Grammar I. *JAOS* 35:375-85.

———. 1942. Studies in Semitic Grammar II. *JAOS* 62:109-18.

———. 1953. Studies in Semitic Grammar V. *JAOS* 73:7-16.

Blanc, Haim. 1964. *Communal Dialects of Baghdad.* Cambridge: Harvard University Press.

Blau, Joshua. 1966-67. *A Grammar of Christian Arabic.* 3 vols. Louvain: Secrétariat du CorpusSCO.

———. 1972. Marginalia Semitica II. *Israel Oriental Studies* 2:57-82.

Bloch, Alfred. 1946-49. Kleine Beiträge zur Arabistik. *Anthropos* 41-44:723-36.

Bogaert, M. 1964. Les suffixes verbaux non accusatifs dans le sémitique nord-occidental et particulièrement en hébreu. *Biblica* 45:220-47.

Borg, Albert, and Manwel Mifsud. 2002. Maltese Object Marking in a Mediterranean Context. In *Mediterranean Languages: Papers from the MEDITYP Workshop, Tirrenia, June 2000.* Paolo Ramat and Thomas Stolz, 33-46. Bochum: N. Brockmeyer.

Bossong, Georg. 1982. Der präpositionale Akkusativ im Sardischen. In *Festschrift für Johannes Hubschmid zum 65. Geburtstag*, ed. Otto Winkelman and Maria Braisch, 579-99. Bern: Francke.

———. 1985. Zur Entwicklungsdynamik von Kasussystemen. *Folia Lingua Historica* 6:285-321.

Böttcher, Friedrich. 1866-88. *Ausführliches Lehrbuch der hebräischen Sprache.* 2 vols. Edited by Ferdinand Mühlau. Leipzig: Johann Ambrosius Barth.

Boyarin, Daniel. 1976. The Loss of Final Consonants in Babylonian Jewish Aramaic (BJA). *Afroasiatic Linguistics* 3/5:19-23.

_____. 1981. An Inquiry into the Formation of Middle Aramaic Dialects. In *Bono Homini Donum: Essays in Historical Linguistics in Memory of J. Alexander Kerns, Part II*, ed. Yoël L. Arbeitman and Allan R. Bomhard, 613-49. Amsterdam: Benjamins.

Bravmann, M.M. 1977. *Studies in Semitic Philology*. Leiden: Brill.

Breuer, Johanan. 1997. The Function of the Particle 'qā' in Babylonian Aramaic [in Hebrew]. *Lešonenu* 60:73-94.

Brock, Sebastian P. 2001. *The Hidden Pearl: The Syrian Orthodox Church and Its Ancient Aramaic Heritage*. 3 vols. With the assistance of David G. K. Taylor. Rome: Trans World Films Italia.

Brockelmann, Carl. 1908-13. *Grundriss der vergleichenden Grammatik der semitischen Sprachen*. 2 vols. Berlin: von Reuther.

_____. 1910. *Précis de linguistique sémitique*. Translated by W. Marçais and M. Cohen. Paris: Geuthner.

_____. 1928. *Lexicon Syriacum*. 2d ed. Halle: Niemeyer.

_____. 1968. *Syrische Grammatik*. 11th ed. Leipzig: VEB.

Brown, Francis, S. R. Driver, and Charles Briggs. 1906. *A Hebrew and English Lexicon of the Old Testament*. Boston: Houghton Mifflin.

Brustad, Kristen E. 2000. *The Syntax of Spoken Arabic*. Washington, DC: Georgetown University Press.

Bunis, David M. 1999. *Judezmo: An Introduction to the Language of the Sephardic Jews of the Ottoman Empire* [in Hebrew]. Jerusalem: Magnes.

Buxtorf, Johannes. 1620. *Thesaurus grammaticus linguae sanctae*. 3d ed. Basel: Ludovici Regis.

Bybee, Joan, Revere Perkins, and William Pagliuca. 1994. *The Evolution of Grammar: Tense, Aspect, and Modality in the Languages of the World*. Chicago: University of Chicago Press.

Campbell, A. 1959. *Old English Grammar*. Oxford: Clarendon.

Campell, Lyle. 2001. What's Wrong with Grammaticalization? *Language Sciences* 23: 113-61.

Campbell, Lyle, and Richard Janda. 2001. Introduction: Conceptions of Grammaticalization and Their Problems. *Language Sciences* 23:93-112.

Cantineau, J. 1930. *Inventaire des inscriptions de Palmyre*. Fasc. 3: *La Grande Colonnade*. Beirut: Imprimerie Catholique.

_____. 1930-32. *Le Nabatéen*. 2 vols. Paris: Ernest Leroux.

_____. 1935. *Grammaire du palmyrénien épigraphique*. Cairo: L'Institut Français d'Archéologie Orientale.

Caquot, André, Maurice Sznycer, and Andrée Herdner. 1974. *Textes ougaritiques. Tome I: Mythes et légendes*. Paris: du Cerf.

Caquot, André, Jean-Michel de Tarragon, and Jesús-Luis Cunchillos. 1989. *Textes ougaritiques. Tome II: Textes religieux et rituels, correspondance*. Paris: du Cerf.

Caskel, Werner. 1954. *Lihyan und Lihyanisch*. Vol. 4 of *Arbeitsgemeinschaft für Forschung des Landes Nordrhein-Westfalen*. Köln: Westdeutscher.

Caubet, Dominique. 1991. The Active Participle as a Means to Renew the Aspectual System: A Comparative Study in Several Dialects of Arabic. In *Semitic Studies in Honor of Wolf Leslau*, vol. 1, ed. Alan S. Kaye, 209-24. Wiesbaden: Harrassowitz.
_____. 1993. *L'arabe marocain*. 2 vols. Louvain: Peeters.
Chaker, Salem. 1997. Quelques faits de grammaticalisation dans le système verbal berbère. In *Grammaticalisation et Reconstruction*. Mémoires de la Société de Linguistique de Paris, Nouvelle Série, Tome V, 103-21. Paris: C. Klincksieck.
Chamora, Berhanu, and Robert Hetzron. 2000. *Inor*. Munich: Lincom Europa.
Christophersen, Paul. 1939. *The Articles: A Study of their Theory and Use in English*. Copenhagen: Munksgaard.
Cohen, C. 1983. Expressing the Pronominal Object in Mishnaic Hebrew [in Hebrew]. *Lešonenu* 47:208-18.
Cohen, David. 1975. *Le parler arabe des juifs de Tunis. Tome II: Étude linguistique*. Paris: Mouton.
_____. 1984. *La phrase nominale et l'évolution du système verbal en sémitique: Études de syntaxe historique*. Leuven: Peeters.
Cohen, Marcel. 1912. *Le parler arabe des juifs d'Alger*. Paris: H. Champion.
_____. 1924. *Le système verbal sémitique et l'expression du temps*. Paris: Imprimerie Nationale.
_____. 1947. *Essai comparatif sur le vocabulaire et la phonétique du chamito-sémitique*. Paris: Ancienne Honoré Champion.
Colin, Georges S. 1935. L'opposition du réel et de l'éventuel en arabe marocain. *Bulletin de la Société de Linguistique de Paris* 36:133-40.
Comrie, Bernard. 1979. Definite and Animate Direct Objects: A Natural Class. *Linguistica Silesiana* 3:13-21.
Contini, Riccardo. 1997. Alcuni casi di grammaticalizzazione (e degrammaticalizzazaione) in Ṭūrōyō. In *Afroasiatica Neapolitana*, ed. Alessandro Bausi and Mauro Tosco, 151-68. Naples: Istituto Universitario Orientale.
Cook, Edward M. 1992. Qumran Aramaic and Aramaic Dialectology. In *Abr-Nahrain Supplement 3, Studies in Qumran Aramaic*, ed. T. Muraoka, 1-21. Louvain: Peeters.
Cook, John A. 2001. The Hebrew Verb: A Grammaticalization Approach. *Zeitschrift für Althebraistik* 14:117-43.
Correll, Christoph. 1994. Ein neuer Anlauf zur Erklärung der Herkunft der 'Notae accusativi' in den klassischen semitischen Sprachen. In *Festschrift Ewald Wagner zum 65. Geburtstag. Band I: Semitische Studien unter besonderer Berücksichtigung der Südsemitistik*, ed. Wolfhart Heinrichs and Gregor Schoeler, 21-43. Beirut: Steiner.
Cotelnic, Teodor, ed. 2000. *Gramatica uzuală a limbii române*. Chişnău, Moldova: Litera.
Cowell, Mark W. 1964. *A Reference Grammar of Syrian Arabic*. Washington, DC: Georgetown University Press.
Croft, William. 2003. *Typology and Language Universals*. 2d ed. Cambridge: Cambridge University Press.

Cross, Frank Moore. 2003. Some Problems in Old Hebrew Orthography with Special Attention to the Third Person Mascline Singular Suffix on Plural Nouns [-âw]. In idem, *Leaves from an Epigrapher's Notebook*, 351-56. Winona Lake: Eisenbrauns.

Cull, Richard. 1872. The Assyrian Verbs *basu*, "to be;" *qabah*, "to say;" and *isu*, "to have," Identified as Variant Forms of Verbs Having the Same Significance in the Hebrew Language. *Transactions of the Society of Biblical Archaeology* 1:281-93.

Dalman, Gustaf H. 1905. *Grammatik des jüdisch-palästinischen Aramäisch*. 2d ed. Leipzig: J.C. Hinrichs.

Degen, Rainer. 1969. *Altaramäische Grammatik*. Wiesbaden: Franz Steiner.

Diem, W. 1974. A Historical Interpretation of Iraqi Arabic ʾaku "there is". *Orbis: Bulletin international de documentation linguistique* 23:448-53.

Diessel, Holger. 1999. *Demonstratives: Form, Function, and Grammaticalization*. Philadelphia: Benjamins.

Dietrich, Manfried, Oswald Loretz, and Joaquin Sanmartín. 1995. *The Cuneiform Alphabetic Texts from Ugarit, Ras Ibn Hani and Other Places*. 2d ed. Münster: Ugarit-Verlag.

Dillmann, August. [1907] 1974. *Ethiopic Grammar*. 2d ed. Revised and edited by Carl Bezold. Translated by James A. Crichton. Reprint, Amsterdam: Philo.

Dodi, Amos. 1981. The Grammar of Targum Onqelos: According to Geniza Fragments [in Hebrew]. Ph.D. diss., Bar-Ilan University.

Donner, Herbert, and Wolfgang Röllig. 2002. *Kanaanäische und aramäische Inschriften: Band 1*. 5th ed. Wiesbaden: Harrassowitz.

Doss, Madiha. 1987. Further Remarks on the Use of B-Imperfect in Spoken Literary Arabic. *Zeitschrift der arabischen Linguistik* 17:93-95.

Durand, Olivier. 1992. I preverbi dell'imperfettivo in arabo dialettale. *Rivista degli Studi Orientali* 65:1-11.

Eitan, Israel. 1928. Hebrew and Semitic Particles. *American Journal of Semitic Languages* 45:48-63.

Eksell, Kerstin. 1995. Complexity of Linguistic Change as Reflected in Arabic Dialects. In *Dialectologia arabica: A Collection of Articles in Honour of the Sixtieth Birthday of Professor Heikki Palva*. Studia Orientalia 75:63-73.

Ember, Aaron. 1917. Kindred Semitic Words. *Zeitschrift für ägyptische Sprache und Altertumskunde* 53:83-90.

———. 1930. *Egypto-Semitic Studies*. Leipzig: Asia Major.

Epstein, Richard. 1995. The Later Stages in the Development of the Definite Article: Evidence from French. In *Historical Linguistics 1993*, ed. Henning Andersen, 159-75. Amsterdam: Benjamins.

Erwin, Wallace M. 1963. *A Short Reference Grammar of Iraqi Arabic*. Washington, DC: Georgetown University Press.

Faber, Alice. 1991. The Diachronic Relationship Between Negative and Interrogative Markers in Semitic. In *Semitic Studies in Honor of Wolf Leslau on the Occasion of His Eighty-fifth Birthday*, vol. 1, ed. Alan S. Kaye, 411-36. Wiesbaden: Harrassowitz.

Fassberg, Steven E. 1990. *A Grammar of the Palestinian Targum Fragments from the Cairo Genizah.* Atlanta: Scholars.
Feghali, Michel. 1928. *Syntaxe des parlers arabes actuels du Liban.* Paris: Imprimerie Nationale.
Firmage, Edwin. 2002. The Definite Article in Phoenician. *Maarav* 9: 33-52.
Fischer, A. 1905a. Redakteurglossen. I. Zu J. Barth, 'Zum semitischen Demonstrativ $\underline{d}$.'. *ZDMG* 59:443-48.
_____. 1905b. Ursemit. *e*, zum Demonstrativ $\underline{d}$., *tī* und Verwandtes. *ZDMG* 59:644-71.
_____. 1910. Auflösung der Akkusativrektion des transitiven Verbs durch die Präposition *li* im klassischen Arabisch. *Berichte über die Verhandlung der Königlichen Sächsischen Gesellschaft der Wissenschaften zu Leipzig: Philologisch-historische Klasse* 62:161-88.
Fischer, Wolfdietrich. 1959. *Die demonstrativen Bildungen der neuarabischen Dialekte: Ein Beitrag zur historischen Grammatik des Arabischen.* The Hague: Mouton.
_____, ed. 1982. *Grundriss der arabischen Philologie.* Wiesbaden: Ludwig Reichert.
_____. 2002. *A Grammar of Classical Arabic.* 3d ed. Translated by Jonathan Rodgers. New Haven: Yale University Press.
Fischer, Wolfdietrich, and Otto Jastrow, eds. 1980. *Handbuch der arabischen Dialekte.* Wiesbaden: Harrassowitz.
Fitzmyer, Joseph A. 1971. *The Genesis Apocryphon of Qumran Cave I.* 2d ed. Rome: Pontificio Istituto Biblico.
_____. 1979. *A Wandering Aramean: Collected Aramaic Essays.* Missoula: Scholars.
_____. 1995. *The Aramaic Inscriptions of Sefire.* 2d ed. Rome: Pontificio Istituto Biblico.
Fitzmyer, Joseph A., and Daniel J. Harrington. 1978. *A Manual of Palestinian Aramaic Texts.* Rome: Pontificio Istituto Biblico.
Folmer, M. L. 1995. *The Aramaic Language in the Achaemenid Period: A Study in Linguistic Variation.* Leuven: Peeters.
Fox, Joshua. 2003. *Semitic Noun Patterns.* Winona Lake: Eisenbrauns.
Fox, Samuel Ethan. 1994. The Relationships of the Eastern Neo-Aramaic Dialects. *JAOS* 114:154-62.
_____. 1997. *The Neo-Aramaic Dialect of Jilu.* Wiesbaden: Harrassowitz.
Frank, Yitzḥak. 1995. *Grammar for Gemara: An Introduction to Babylonian Aramaic.* Jerusalem: Ariel.
Friedrich, Johannes and Wolfgang Röllig. 1999. *Phönizisch-Punische Grammatik.* 3d ed. Revised by Maria G. Amadasi Guzzo. Rome: Pontificio Istituto Biblico.
Furlani, Giuseppe. 1919. La *nota accusativi* את in Ebraico. *Rivista degli Studi Orientali* 8:213-31.
von der Gabelentz, Georg. 1891. *Die Sprachwissenschaft. Ihre Aufgaben, Methoden, und bisherigen Ergebnisse.* Leipzig: Weigel.
Gai, Amikam. 1984. Predicative State and Inflection of the Nominal Predicate in Akkadian and Syriac. *Afroasiatic Linguistics* 9/1:83.
Garr, W. Randall. 1985. *Dialect Geography of Syria-Palestine, 1000-586 B.C.E.* Philadelphia: University of Pennsylvania Press.

———. 1991. Affectedness, Aspect, and Biblical Hebrew ʾet. *Zeitschrift für Althebraistik* 4:119-34.
Geiger, A. 1863. Review of *Über die Mundart der Mandäer*, by Theodor Nöldeke. *ZDMG* 42:420-23.
Gelb, I. J. 1955. *Old Akkadian Inscriptions in the Chicago Natural History Museum: Texts of Legal and Business Interest.* Chicago: Chicago Natural History Museum.
———. 1970. *Sargonic Texts in the Ashmolean Museum, Oxford.* Chicago: University of Chicago Press.
Gensler, Orin D. 1998. Verbs with Two Object Suffixes: A Semitic Archaism in Its Afroasiatic Context. *Diachronica* 15:231-84.
Gesenius: see Kautzsch 1910.
Gildea, Spike, ed. 2000. *Reconstructing Grammar: Comparative Linguistics and Grammaticalization.* Philadelphia: Benjamins.
Givón, Talmy. 1991. The Evolution of Dependent Clause Morpho-syntax in Biblical Hebrew. In Traugott and Heine 1991, vol. 2, 257-310.
Glaser, Eduard. 1897. Ursprung des arabischen Artikels ال. *ZDMG* 51:166-67.
Glinert, Lewis. 1989. *The Grammar of Modern Hebrew.* Cambridge: Cambridge University Press.
Gogel, Sandra Landis. 1998. *A Grammar of Epigraphic Hebrew.* Atlanta: Scholars.
Goldenberg, Gideon. 1979. Review of *The Ethiopians: An Introduction to Country and People*, by Edward Ullendorff. *JSS* 24:321-26.
———. 1991. "Oneself", "One's Own" and "One Another" in Amharic. In *Semitic Studies in Honor of Wolf Leslau*, vol. 1, ed. Alan S. Kaye, 531-49. Wiesbaden: Harrassowitz.
Golomb, David M. 1985. *A Grammar of Targum Neofiti.* Chico, CA: Scholars.
———. 1989. Contrasting Forms Within the Verbal System of Babylonian Talmudic Aramaic. Typescript.
Gordon, Amnon. 1982. The Development of the Participle in Biblical, Mishnaic, and Modern Hebrew. *Afroasiatic Linguistics* 8/3:121-79.
Gordon, E.V. 1962. *An Introduction to Old Norse.* 2d ed. Revised by A.R. Taylor. Oxford: Clarendon.
Grand'henry, Jacques. 1972. *Le parler arabe de Cherchell (Algérie).* Louvain-La-Neuve: Institut Orientaliste.
Greenberg, Joseph H. 1978. How Does a Language Acquire Gender Markers? In *Universals of Human Language*, vol. 3, ed. Joseph H. Greenberg, 47-82. Stanford: Stanford University Press.
Grotzfeld, Heinz. 1965. *Syrisch-arabische Grammatik (Dialekt von Damaskus).* Wiesbaden: Harrassowitz.
Hackett, Jo Ann. 2004. Phoenician and Punic. In *Cambridge Encyclopedia of the World's Ancient Languages*, ed. Roger Woodard, 365-85. Cambridge: Cambridge University Press.
Halévy, J. 1891. L'article hébreu. *Revue des Études Juives* 23:117-21.
Hämeen-Anttila, Jaakko. 2000. *A Sketch of Neo-Assyrian Grammar.* Helsinki: Neo-Assyrian Text Corpus Project of the University of Helsinki.

Hamori, Andras. 1973. A Note on *yaqtulu* in East and West Semitic. *Archiv Orientální* 41: 319-24.
Harning, Kerstin Eksell. 1980. *The Analytic Genitive in the Modern Arabic Dialects.* Stockholm: Acta Universitatis Gothoburgensis.
Harrell, Richard S. 1962. *A Short Reference Grammar of Moroccan Arabic.* Washington, DC: Georgetown University Press.
Harris, M. 1980. The Marking of Definiteness in Romance. In *Historical Morphology*, ed. J. Fisiak, 141-56. Mouton: The Hague.
Harris, Martin, and Nigel Vincent, eds. 1988. *The Romance Languages.* New York: Oxford University Press.
Harviainen, Tapani. 1983. Diglossia in Jewish Eastern Aramaic. *Studia Orientalia* 55:97-113.
Hasselbach, Rebecca. 2003. The Pronominal Suffixes of the Third Person Masculine Singular in Hebrew. *Harvard Working Papers in Linguistics* 8:45-66.
⎯⎯⎯⎯. 2004. A Historical and Comparative Study of Sargonic Akkadian. Ph.D. diss., Harvard University.
Haugen, Einar. 1982. *Scandinavian Language Structures: A Comparative Historical Survey.* Minneapolis: University of Minnesota Press.
Haupt, Paul. 1906. Semitic Verbs Dervied from Particles. *American Journal of Semitic Languages* 22:257-61.
Hayward, Richard J. 2000. Afroasiatic. In *African Languages: An Introduction*, ed. Bernd Heine and Derek Nurse, 74-98. Cambridge: Cambridge University Press.
Heath, Jeffrey. 2002. *Jewish and Muslim Dialects of Moroccan Arabic.* London: RoutledgeCurzon.
Heine, Bernd. 1993. *Auxiliaries: Cognitive Forces and Grammaticalization.* Oxford: Oxford University Press.
⎯⎯⎯⎯. 1997a. Grammaticalization and Language Universals. In *Grammaticalisation et Reconstruction*. Mémoires de la Société de Linguistique de Paris, Nouvelle Série, Tome V, 11-23. Paris: C. Klincksieck.
⎯⎯⎯⎯. 1997b. *Possession: Sources, Forces, and Grammaticalization.* Cambridge: Cambridge University Press.
Heine, Bernd, and Tania Kuteva. 2002. *World Lexicon of Grammaticalization.* Cambridge: Cambridge University Press.
⎯⎯⎯⎯. 2005. *Language Contact and Language Change.* Cambridge: Cambridge University Press.
Heine, Bernd, Ulrike Claudi, and Friederike Hünnemeyer. 1991. *Grammaticalization: A Conceptual Framework.* Chicago: University of Chicago Press.
Heinrichs, H.M. 1954. *Studien zum bestimmten Artikel in den germanischen Sprachen.* Giessen: Schmitz.
Heinrichs, Wolfhart. 2002. Peculiarities of the Verbal System of Senāya within the Framework of North Eastern Neo-Aramaic (NENA). In *"Sprich doch mit deinen Knechten aramäisch, wir verstehen es!". 60 Beiträge zur Semitistik: Festschrift für Otto Jastrow zum 60. Geburtstag*, ed. Werner Arnold and Hartmut Bobzin, 237-68. Wiesbaden: Harrassowitz.

Hetzron, Robert. 1969. Third person singular pronoun suffixes in Proto-Semitic. *Orientalia Suecana* 18:101-27.
_____. 1972. *Ethiopian Semitic: Studies in Classification*. Manchester: Manchester University Press.
_____. 1976. Two Principles of Genetic Classification. *Lingua* 38:89-108.
_____, ed. 1997. *The Semitic Languages*. London: Routledge.
Hillers, Delbert R., and Eleonora Cussini. 1996. *Palmyrene Aramaic Texts*. Baltimore: Johns Hopkins University Press.
Hinds, Martin, and El-Said Badawi. 1986. *A Dictionary of Egyptian Arabic*. Beirut: Librairie du Liban.
Hirschfeld, Hartwig. 1918. *Qirqisāni Studies*. London: Oxford University Press.
_____. 1926. *Literary History of Hebrew Grammarians and Lexicographers*. London: Oxford University Press.
Hopkins, Simon. 1997. On the Construction šmēh l-ġaḇrā "the Name of the Man" in Aramaic [in Hebrew]. *Massorot: Studies in Language Traditions and Jewish Languages* 9-11:349-61.
Hopper, Paul J., and Elizabeth Closs Traugott. 1993. *Grammaticalization*. Cambridge: Cambridge University Press.
_____. 2003. *Grammaticalization*. 2d ed. Cambridge: Cambridge University Press.
Huehnergard, John. 1983. Asseverative *la and Hypothetical *lu/law in Semitic. *JAOS* 103:569-93.
_____. 1986. On Verbless Clauses in Akkadian. *Zeitschrift für Assyriologie* 76:218-49.
_____. 1987. "Stative," Predicative Form, Pseudo-Verb. *JNES* 46:215-32.
_____. 1995. What Is Aramaic? *Aram* 7:261-82.
_____. 1997. *A Grammar of Akkadian*. Atlanta: Scholars Press.
_____. 2004. Afro-Asiatic. In *Cambridge Encyclopedia of the World's Ancient Languages*, ed. Roger Woodard, 138-59. Cambridge: Cambridge University Press.
_____. 2005. Features of Central Semitic. In *Biblical and Oriental Essays in Memory of William L. Moran*, ed. Agustinus Gianto, 155-203. Rome: Pontificio Istituto Biblico.
_____. Forthcoming. On the Etymology of the Hebrew Relative še-. In *Biblical Hebrew in Its Northwest Semitic Setting: Typological and Historical Perspectives*, ed. Avi Hurvitz and Steven E. Fassberg. Jerusalem: Magnes.
Hug, Volker. 1993. *Altaramäische Grammatik der Texte des 7. und 6. Jh.s. v. Chr.* Heidelberg: Heidelberger Orientverlag.
von Humboldt, Wilhelm. 1825. Über das Entstehen der grammatikalischen Formen und Ihren Einfluß auf die Ideenentwicklung. *Abhandlungen der Königlichen Akadamie der Wissenschaften zu Berlin*:401-30.
Isaaksson, Bo. 1994-95. Arabic Dialectology: The State of the Art. *Orientalia Suecana* 43-44:115-32.
Jain, Usha R. 1995. *Introduction to Hindi Grammar*. Berkeley: Center for South and Southeast Asia Studies.
Jastrow, Otto. 1978. *Die mesopotamisch-arabischen qəltu-Dialekte. Band I: Phonologie und Morphologie*. Wiesbaden: Steiner.

_____. 1981. *Die mesopotamisch-arabischen qəltu-Dialekte. Band II: Volkskundliche Texte in elf Dialekten*. Wiesbaden: Steiner.

_____. 1985. *Laut- und Formenlehre des neuaramäischen Dialekts von Mīdin im Ṭūr ʿAbdīn*. 3d ed. Wiesbaden: Harrassowitz.

_____. 1988. *Der neuaramäische Dialekt von Hertevin (Provinz Siirt)*. Wiesbaden: Harrassowitz.

_____. 1990. *Der arabische Dialekt der Juden von ʿAqra und Arbīl*. Wiesbaden: Harrassowitz.

_____. 1992. *Lehrbuch der Ṭuroyo Sprache*. Wiesbaden: Harrassowitz.

_____. 1999. Verbformen und ihre Funktionen im arabischen Dialekt von Kəndērīb (Südostanatolien). In *Tempus und Aspekt in den semitischen Sprachen: Jenaer Kolloquium zur semitischen Sprachwissenschaft*, ed. Norbert Nebes, 43-53. Wiesbaden: Harrassowitz.

Jaussen, A. and M.-R. Sauvignac. 1914. *Mission archéologique en Arabie II*. Paris: Paul Geuthner.

Jespersen, Otto. 1949. *A Modern English Grammar on Historical Principles*. Vol. 4. Copenhagen: Einar Munksgaard.

Johnstone, T.M. 1970. A Definite Article in the Modern South Arabian Languages. *BSOAS* 33:295-307.

_____. 1977. *Ḥarsūsi Lexicon*. London: Oxford University Press.

_____. 1987. *Mehri Lexicon and English-Mehri Word-List*. London: School of Oriental and African Studies.

Joüon, Paul. 1913. Études de philologie sémitique (suite). *Mélanges de l'Université Saint-Joseph* 6:121-46.

_____. 1996. *A Grammar of Biblical Hebrew*. 2 vols. Revised and translated by T. Muraoka. Rome: Pontificio Istituto Biblico.

Jullien de Pommerol, Patrice. 1999. *Grammaire pratique de l'arabe tchadien*. Paris: Karthala.

Kampffmeyer, G. 1899. Beiträge zur Dialectologie des Arabischen. *Wiener Zeitschrift für die Kunde des Morgenlandes* 13:1-34.

_____. 1900. Die arabische Verbalpartikel *b* (*m*). *Mittheilungen des Seminars für Orientalische Sprachen zu Berlin: Westasiatische Studien* 3:48-101.

Kattán-Ibarra, Juan, and Christopher J. Pountain. 1997. *Modern Spanish Grammar*. London: Routledge.

Kaufman, Stephen A. 1974. *The Akkadian Influences on Aramaic*. Chicago: University of Chicago Press.

Kautzsch, E., ed. 1910. *Gesenius' Hebrew Grammar*. 2d ed. Revised and translated by A.E. Cowley. Oxford: Clarendon.

Khan, Geoffrey. 1984. Object Markers and Agreement Pronouns in Semitic Languages. *BSOAS* 47:468-500.

_____. 1999. *A Grammar of Neo-Aramaic: The Dialect of the Jews of Arbel*. Leiden: Brill.

_____. 2001. The Use of the Indefinite Article in Neo-Aramaic. In *New Data and New Methods in Afroasiatic Linguistics: Robert Hetzron in Memoriam*, ed. Andrzej Zaborski, 85-94. Wiesbaden: Harrassowitz.

———. 2002. *The Neo-Aramaic Dialect of Qaraqosh*. Leiden: Brill.
———. 2004. *The Jewish Neo-Aramaic Dialect of Sulemaniyya and Ḥalabja*. Leiden: Brill.
Klein, Ernest. 1987. *A Comprehensive Etymological Dictionary of the Hebrew Language for Readers of English*. New York: Macmillan.
Klenin, Emily. 1983. *Animacy in Russian: A New Interpretation*. Columbus, Ohio: Slavica.
König, Ekkehard, and Johan Van der Auwa. 1994. *The Germanic Languages*. London: Routledge.
König, Ekkehard, and Peter Siemund. 2000. Intensifiers and Reflexives: A Typological Perspective. In *Reflexives: Forms and Functions*, ed. Zygmunt Frajzyngier and Traci S. Curl, 41-74. Philadelphia: Benjamins.
König, Fr. Eduard. 1881-97. *Lehrgebäude der hebräischen Sprache*. 3 vols. Leipzig: J.C. Heinrichs.
Koutsoudas, Andreas. 1978. Doubled Nominals in Lebanese. In *Readings in Arabic Linguistics*, ed. Salman H. Al-Ani, 527-41. Bloomington: Indiana University Linguistics Club. First published in *Glossa* 1 (1967):33-48.
Kouwenberg, N.J.C. 1997. *Gemination in the Akkadian Verb*. Assen: Van Gorcum.
———. 2000. Nouns as Verbs: the Verbal Nature of the Akkadian Stative. *Orientalia* 69:21-71.
Krahmalkov, Charles R. 1992. Phoenician 'YT and 'T. *Rivista di Studi Orientali* 66:227-31.
———. 2001. *A Phoenician-Punic Grammar*. Leiden: Brill.
Krotkoff, Georg. 1982. *A Neo-Aramaic Dialect of Kurdistan*. New Haven: American Oriental Society.
Kuryłowicz, J. 1950. La mimation et l'article en arabe. *Archiv Orientální* 18:323-88.
———. [1965] 1975. The Evolution of Grammatical Categories. Reprinted in *Esqisses linguistiques II*, 38-54. Munich: Fink.
Kuteva, Tania A. 1999. On 'sit'/ 'stand'/'lie' Auxiliation. *Linguistics* 37:191-213.
———. 2001. *Auxiliation: An Enquiry Into the Nature of Grammaticalization*. Oxford: Oxford University Press.
Kutscher, E.Y. 1960-61. The Language of the Hebrew and Aramaic Letters of Bar-Kosiba and his contemporaries [in Hebrew]. *Lešonenu* 25:117-33.
———. 1969. Two 'Passive' Constructions in Aramaic in the Light of Persian. In *Proceedings of the International Conference on Semitic Studies*. Jerusalem: Israel Academy of Sciences and Humanities.
———. 1971. Aramaic. In *Encyclopaedia Judaica*, vol. 3, 259-87. Jerusalem: Keter.
———. 1982. *A History of the Hebrew Language*. Ed. Raphael Kutscher. Jerusalem: Magnes.
Lambdin, Thomas O. 1971a. The Junctural Origin of the West Semitic Definite Article. In *Near Eastern Studies in Honor of William Foxwell Albright*, ed. Hans Goedicke, 315-33. Baltimore: Johns Hopkins University Press.
———. 1971b. *Introduction to Biblical Hebrew*. New York: Scribner's.
———. 1978. *Introduction to Classical Ethiopic (Ge'ez)*. Atlanta: Scholars.

Laury, Ritva. 1995. On the Grammaticalization of the Definite Article SE in Spoken Finnish. In *Historical Linguistics 1993*, ed. Henning Andersen, 239-50. Amsterdam: Benjamins.
Lazar, Moshe. 2000. *The Ladino Scriptures: Constantinople-Salonica (1540-1572)*. Lancaster, CA: Labyrinthos.
Lehmann, Christian. 1995. *Thoughts on Grammaticalization*. Munich: Lincom Europa.
Leiss, E. 1994. Die Entstehung des Artikels im Deutschen. *Sprachwissenschaft* 19:307-19.
Leslau, Wolf. 1941. *Documents tigrinya*. Paris: C. Klincksieck.
―――. 1945a. *Gafat Documents: Records of a South Semitic Language*. New Haven: American Oriental Society.
―――. 1945b. Grammatical Sketches in Tigré (North Ethiopic): Dialect of Mensa. *JAOS* 65:164-203.
―――. 1948. Supplementary Observations on Tigré Grammar. *JAOS* 68:127-39.
―――. 1950. *Ethiopic Documents: Gurage*. New York: Viking Fund.
―――. 1979. *Etymological Dictionary of Gurage (Ethiopic)*. 3 vols. Wiesbaden: Harrassowitz.
―――. 1987. *Comparative Dictionary of Ge'ez*. Wiesbaden: Harrassowitz.
―――. 1995. *Reference Grammar of Amharic*. Wiesbaden: Harrassowitz.
―――. 1997. *Ethiopic Documents: Argobba: Grammar and Dictionary*. Wiesbaden: Harrassowitz.
―――. 1999. *Zway Ethiopic Documents: Grammar and Dictionary*. Wiesbaden: Harrassowitz.
Levin, Aryeh. 1987. The Particle LA as an Object Marker in Some Arabic Dialects of the Galilee. *Zeitschrift für arabische Linguistik* 17:31-40.
Levinson, Jay Harry. 1974. The Nabatean Aramaic Inscriptions. Ph.D. diss., New York University.
Lieberman, Stephen J. 1986. The Afro-Asiatic Background of the Semitic N-Stem: Toward the Origins of the Semitic and Afro-Asiatic Verb. *Bibliotheca Orientalis* 43: 578-628.
Lipiński, Edward. 1997. *Semitic Languages: Outline of a Comparative Grammar*. Leuven: Peeters.
Littmann, Enno. 1904. *Semitic Inscriptions*. New York: The Century Co.
Livingstone, Alasdair. 1997. An Early Attestation of the Arabic Definite Article. *JSS* 42: 259-61.
Lockwood, W.B. 1968. *Historical German Syntax*. Oxford: Clarendon.
Loprieno, Antonio. 1995. *Ancient Egyptian*. Cambridge: Cambridge University Press.
Luzzatto, Samuel D. 1836. Letter 30 [in Hebrew]. *Kerem Ḥemed* 2:174-83.
―――. 1865. *Elementi grammaticali del caldeo biblico e del dialetto talmudico babilonese*. Padova: A. Bianche.
Lyons, Christopher. 1999. *Definiteness*. Cambridge: Cambridge University Press.
Macdonald, John, ed. and trans. 1963. *Memar Marqah: The Teaching of Marqah*. 2 vols. Berlin: Alfred Töpelmann.
Macdonald, M. C. A. 1998. Some Reflections on Epigraphy and Ethnicity in the Roman Near East. *Mediterranean Archaeology* 11:177-90.

———. 2000. Reflections on the linguistic map of pre-Islamic Arabia. *Arabian Archaeology and Epigraphy* 11:28-79.
———. 2004. Ancient North Arabian. In *Cambridge Encyclopedia of the World's Ancient Languages*, ed. Roger Woodard, 488-533. Cambridge: Cambridge University Press.
Mace, John. 1998. *Arabic Grammar: A Reference Guide*. Edinburgh: Edinburgh University Press.
Măcelaru, Adrian. 2003. Proto-Semitic *yš: Problems and Possible Solutions. In *Afrasian: Selected Comparative-Historical Linguistic Studies in Memory of Igor M. Diakonoff*, ed. M. Lionel Bender, David Appleyard, and Gábor Takács, 233-40. Munich: Lincom Europa.
Maclean, Arthur John. 1895. *Grammar of the Dialects of Vernacular Syriac*. Cambridge: Cambridge University Press.
Macuch, Rudolf. 1965. *Handbook of Classical and Modern Mandaic*. Berlin: de Gruyter.
———. 1982. *Grammatik des samaritanischen Aramäisch*. Berlin: de Gruyter.
Maiden, Martin, and Cecilia Robustelli. 2000. *A Reference Grammar of Modern Italian*. Chicago: NTC.
Malaika, Nisar. 1963. *Grundzüge der Grammatik des arabischen Dialektes von Bagdad*. Wiesbaden: Harrassowitz.
Mansour, Jacob. 2001. The Particles *'aš/'eš* and *'ášu* in the Jewish Arabic of Baghdad. *Zeitschrift für arabische Linguistik* 39:84-89.
Marçais, Philippe. 1952. *Le parler arabe de Djidjelli*. Paris: Maisonneuve.
Margolis, Max L. 1910. *A Manual of the Aramaic Language of the Babylonian Talmud*. New York: G.E. Stechert.
Marrassini, Paolo. 1996. Considerazioni sull'articolo determinativo in semitico nordoccidentale. In *Alle soglie della classicità: Il mediterraneo tra tradizione e innovazione: Studi in onore di Sabatino Moscati*, vol. 3, ed. Enrico Acquaro, 1185-92. Pisa/Rome: Istituti Editoriali e Poligrafici Internazionali.
Mason, John. 1996. *Tigrinya Grammar*. Lawrenceville, NJ: Red Sea.
McMahon, April M.S. 1994. *Understanding Language Change*. Cambridge: Cambridge University Press.
Meillet, Antoine. 1912. L'évolution des formes grammaticales. *Scientia (Rivista di Scienza)* 12, No. 26/6. Reprinted in Meillet 1948, 130-48.
———. 1948. *Linguistique historique et linguistique générale*. Paris: Champion.
Melles, Mulugeta Girmay. 2001. *Tigrinya Grammar and Reader*. Springfield, VA: Dunwoody.
Miller, Cynthia. 1996. *The Representation of Speech in Biblical Hebrew Narrative: A Linguistic Analysis*. Atlanta: Scholars.
Mitchell, T.F., and Shahir El-Hassan. 1994. *Modality, Mood and Aspect in Spoken Arabic*. London: Kegan Paul International.
Moberg, Axel. 1907-13. *Buch der Strahlen: Die grössere Grammatik des Barhebräus*. 2 vols. Leipzig: Harrassowitz.
———. 1922. *Le Livre des splendeurs: La grande grammaire de Grégoire Barhebraeus*. Lund: C.W.K. Gleerup.
de Moor, Johannes C. 1965. Frustula Ugaritica. *JNES* 65:355-64.

Moscati, Sabatino, ed. 1964. *An Introduction to the Comparative Grammar of the Semitic Languages.* Wiesbaden: Harrassowitz.

Müller-Kessler, Christa. 1991. *Grammatik des christlich-palästinisch-Aramäischen. Teil 1: Schriftlehre, Lautlehre, Formenlehre.* Hildesheim: Olms.

────── . 2003. Aramaic *'k'*, *lyk'* and Iraqi Arabic *'aku*, *māku*: The Mesopotamian Particles of Existence. *JAOS* 123:641-46.

Müller-Kessler, Christa, and Michael Sokoloff. 1997. *A Corpus of Christian Palestinian Aramaic, Volume 1: The Christian Palestinian Aramaic Old Testament and Apocrypha Version from the Early Period.* Groningen: Styx.

Muraoka, T. 1972. Notes on the Aramaic of the Genesis Apocryphon. *Révue de Qumran* 8: 7-51.

────── . 1985. *Emphatic Words and Structures in Biblical Hebrew.* Jerusalem: Magnes.

Muraoka, Takamitsu, and Bezalel Porten. 2003. *A Grammar of Egyptian Aramaic.* 2d ed. Leiden: Brill.

Nebes, Norbert, and Peter Stein. 2004. Epigraphic South Arabian. In *Cambridge Encyclopedia of the World's Ancient Languages*, ed. Roger Woodard. Cambridge: Cambridge University Press.

Nöldeke, Theodor. 1862. Über die Mundart der Mandäer. *Ablandung der Königlichen Gesellschaft der Wissenschaften zu Göttingen: Historisch-philologischen Classe* 10:81-160.

────── . 1868a. Über den christlich-palästinischen Dialekt. *ZDMG* 22:443-527.

────── . 1868b. *Grammatik der neusyrischen Sprache am Urmia-See und in Kurdistan.* Leipzig: T. O. Weigel.

────── . 1875. *Mandäische Grammatik.* Halle: Buchhandlung des Waisenhauses.

────── . 1881. Review of *Der neu-aramäische Dialekt von Ṭûr 'Abdîn*, by Eugen Prym and Albert Socin. *ZDMG* 35:218-35.

────── . 1886. Review of *Proglomena eines neuen hebräisch-aramaischen Wörterbuchs zum Alten Testament*, by Friedrich Delitzsch. *ZDMG* 40:718-43.

────── . 1904a. *Compendious Syriac Grammar.* 2d ed. Translated by James A. Crichton. London: Williams and Norgate.

────── . 1904b. *Beiträge zur semitischen Sprachwissenschaft.* Strassburg: Karl J. Trübner.

Nordheimer, Isaac. 1838-41. *Critical Grammar of the Hebrew Language.* 2 vols. New York: Wiley and Putnam.

Obler, Loraine Katherine. 1975. Reflexes of the Classical Arabic *šay'un* 'Thing' in the Modern Dialects: A Study in Patterns of Language Change. Ph.D. diss., University of Michigan.

Owens, Jonathan. 1984. *A Short Reference Grammar of Eastern Libyan Arabic.* Wiesbaden: Harrassowitz.

Pagliuca, William, ed. 1994. *Perspectives on Grammaticalization.* Philadelphia: Benjamins.

Parpola, Simo. 1984. Likalka Ittatakku: Two notes on the morphology of the verb alāku in Neo-Assyrian. *Studia Orientalia* 55:185-209.

Payne Smith, R. 1903. *A Compendious Syriac Dictionary.* Ed. J. Payne Smith. Oxford: Oxford University Press.

Pennacchietti, Fabrizio A. 1968. *Studi sui pronomi determinativi semitici.* Naples: Istituto Orientale di Napoli.
———. 1994. Il preterito neoaramaico con pronome oggetto. *ZDMG* 144:259-83.
———. 1997. On the Etymology of the Neo-Aramaic Particle *qam/kim-* [in Hebrew]. *Massorot: Studies in Language Traditions and Jewish Languages* 9-11:475-82.
Penny, Ralph. 2002. *A History of the Spanish Language.* 2d ed. Cambridge: Cambridge University Press.
Pérez Fernández, Miguel. 1999. *An Introductory Grammar of Rabbinic Hebrew.* Translated by John Elwolde. Leiden: Brill.
Philippaki-Warburton, Irene, David Holton, and Peter Mackridge. 1997. *Greek: A Comprehensive Grammar of the Modern Language.* London: Routledge.
Polzin, Robert. 1976. *Late Biblical Hebrew: Toward an Historical Typology of Biblical Hebrew Prose.* Missoula: Scholars.
Posner, Rebecca. 1996. *The Romance Languages.* Cambridge: Cambridge University Press.
Praetorius, Franz. 1873. Zur aethiopisch-arabischen Grammatik. *ZDMG* 27:639-44.
———. 1879. *Die amharische Sprache.* Halle: Buchhandlung des Waisenhauses.
———. 1901. Zur hebräischen und aramäischen Grammatik. *ZDMG* 55:359-70.
Prochazka, Theodore, Jr. 1988. *Saudi Arabian Dialects.* London: Kegan Paul International.
Prokosch, E. 1938. *A Comparative Germanic Grammar.* Baltimore: Linguistic Society of America.
Puech, Émile. 1982. Note sur la particule accusativale en Phénicien. *Semitica: Cahiers publiés par l'Institut d'études sémitiques du Collège de France* 32:51-55.
Qafisheh, Hamdi A. 1992. *Yemeni Arabic Reference Grammar.* Kensington, MD: Dunwoody.
Qimron, Elisha. 1986. *The Hebrew of the Dead Sea Scrolls.* Atlanta: Scholars.
Rabin, C. 1951. *Ancient West-Arabian.* London: Taylors.
Raz, Shlomo. 1983. *Tigre Grammar and Texts.* Malibu: Undena.
———. 1991. Semitic South-Ethiopic: The Definite Future Revisited. In *Semitic Studies in Honor of Wolf Leslau,* vol. 2, ed. Alan S. Kaye, 1248-64. Wiesbaden: Harrassowitz.
Reichenkron, Günter. 1951. Das präpositionale Akkusativ-Object im ältesten Spanisch. *Romanische Forschungen* 63:342-97.
Rendsburg, Gary A. 2002. *Israelian Hebrew in the Book of Kings.* Bethesda, MD: CDL.
Rosenthal, Franz. 1963. *A Grammar of Biblical Aramaic.* 2d ed. Wiesbaden: Harrassowitz.
Rössler, Otto. 1971. Das Ägyptische als semitische Sprache. In *Christentum Am Roten Meer,* ed. Franz Altheim and Ruth Stiehl. Berlin: de Gruyter.
Rubba, Jo. 1994. Grammaticalization as Semantic Change: A Case Study in Preposition Development. In Pagliuca 1994:81-101.
Rubin, Aaron. 1999. An Introduction to the Comparative Grammar of Egyptian and Semitic. Master's thesis, University of Pennsylvania.

_____. 2004. An Outline of Comparative Egypto-Semitic Morphology. In *Egyptian and Semito-Hamitic (Afro-Asiatic) Studies in Memoriam Werner Vycichl*, ed. Gábor Takács, 454-86. Leiden: Brill.
Rundgren, Frithiof. 1955. *Über Bildungen mit s/š und n-t-Demonstrativen im Semitischen*. Uppsala: Almqvist and Wiksell.
_____. 1989. The Form of the Definite Article in Arabic. In *Studia semitica necnon iranica: Rudolopho Macuch septuagenarico ab amicis et discipulis dedicata*, ed. Maria Macuch, Christa Müller-Kessler, and Bert G Fragner, 257-69. Wiesbaden: Harrassowitz.
Ryckmans, J. 1956. Aspects nouveaux du problème thamoudéen. *Studia Islamica* 5:5-17.
Sabar, Yona. 2002. *A Jewish Neo-Aramaic Dictionary*. Wiesbaden: Harrassowitz.
Sáenz-Badillos, Angel. 1993. *A History of the Hebrew Language*. Translated by John Elwolde. Cambridge: Cambridge University Press.
Scheil, Vincent, ed. 1913. *Textes élamites-sémitiques, cinquième série*. Paris: E. Leroux.
Schladt, Mathias. 2000. The Typology and Grammaticalization of Reflexives. In *Reflexives: Forms and Functions*, ed. Zygmunt Frajzyngier and Traci S. Curl, 103-24. Philadelphia: Benjamins.
von Schlegel, August Wilhelm. 1818. *Observations sur la langue et littérature provençales*. Paris: Librairie Grecque-Latine-Allemande.
Schlesinger, Michel. 1928. *Satzlehre der aramäischen Sprache des babylonischen Talmuds*. Leipzig: Asia Major.
Schrader, Eberhard. 1872. Die assyrisch-babylonischen Keilinschriften. *ZDMG* 26:1-392.
Schultens, Albert. 1737. *Institutiones ad fundamenta linguae hebraeae*. Leiden: J. Luzac.
Schulthess, Friedrich. 1924. *Grammatik des christlich-palästinischen Aramäisch*. Ed. Enno Littmann. Tübingen: J.C.B. Mohr.
Segal, M. H. 1927. *A Grammar of Mishnaic Hebrew*. Oxford: Clarendon.
Segert, S. 1958. Aramäische Studien V. *Archiv Orientální* 26:578-84.
Shetter, William Z., and Inge Van der Cruysse-Van Antwerpen. 2002. *Dutch: An Essential Grammar*. 8th ed. London: Routledge.
Sihler, Andrew L. 1995. *New Comparative Grammar of Greek and Latin*. Oxford: Oxford University Press.
Sima, Alexander. 1999. *Die lihyanischen Inschriften von al-'Uḏayb (Saudi-Arabien)*. Rahden: Marie Leidorf GmbH.
_____. 2002. Der bestimmte Artikel im Mehri. In *"Sprich doch mit deinen Knechten aramäisch, wir verstehen es!". 60 Beiträge zur Semitistik: Festschrift für Otto Jastrow zum 60. Geburtstag*, ed. Werner Arnold and Hartmut Bobzin, 647-68. Wiesbaden: Harrassowitz.
Simeone-Senelle, Marie-Claude, and Martine Vanhove. 1997. La formation et l'évolution d'auxiliaires et particules verbales dans des langues sémitiques (langues sudarabiques modernes et maltais). In *Grammaticalisation et Reconstruction. Mémoires de la Société de Linguistique de Paris, Nouvelle Série, Tome V*, 85-102. Paris: C. Klincksieck.
Sinaceur, Zakia Iraqui. 1994. *Le dictionnaire Colin d'arabe dialectal marocain*. 8 vols. Rabat: Al Manahil.

Singer, Hans-Rudolf. 1958. *Neuarabische Fragewörter*. Ph.D. diss., Friedrich-Alexander-Universität zu Erlangen.
_____. 1984. *Grammatik der arabischen Mundart der Medina von Tunis*. Berlin: de Gruyter.
Sinha, Jasmin. 2000. *Der neuostaramäische Dialekt von Bespən (Provinz Mardin, Südosttürkei): Eine grammatische Darstellung*. Wiesbaden: Harrassowitz.
von Soden, Wolfram. 1965-81. *Akkadisches Handwörterbuch*. 3 vols. Wiesbaden: Harrassowitz.
_____. 1995. *Grundriss der akkadischen Grammatik*. 3d ed. With the assistance of W. Meyer. Rome: Pontificio Istituto Biblico.
Sokoloff, Michael. 2002a. *A Dictionary of Jewish Palestinian Aramaic*. 2d ed. Baltimore: Johns Hopkins University Press.
_____. 2002b. *A Dictionary of Jewish Babylonian Aramaic*. Baltimore: Johns Hopkins University Press.
von Sonnenfels, Aloys. 1757. *Even Bohan, Lapus Lydius, Prüfstein*. Vienna: J. T. Trattner.
Sperber, Alexander. [1959-73] 1992. *The Bible in Aramaic*. 4 vols. Leiden: Brill.
Stevenson, William B. 1962. *Grammar of Palestinian Jewish Aramaic*. 2d ed. Revised by J.A. Emerton. Oxford: Clarendon.
Streitberg, Wilhelm. 1974. *Urgermanische Grammatik*. Heidelberg: Carl Winter.
Takács, Gábor. 1999. *An Etymological Dictionary of Egyptian, Volume I: A Phonological Introduction*. Leiden: Brill.
Tal, Abraham. 1980. *The Samaritan Targum of the Pentateuch: A Critical Edition* [in Hebrew]. 2 vols. Tel Aviv: Tel Aviv University.
_____. 1986. The Dialects of Jewish Palestinian Aramaic and the Palestinian Targum of the Pentateuch. *Sefarad* 46:441-48.
_____. 2000. *A Dictionary of Samaritan Aramaic*. 2 vols. Leiden: Brill.
Tapiéro, Norbert. 2002. *Manuel d'arabe algérien moderne*. Paris: Klincksieck.
Testen, David. 1985. The Significance of Aramaic $r < *n$. *JNES* 44:143-46.
_____. 1997. The Phoenician Direct-Object Marker in the Inscription of Yḥwmlk. *Ugarit-Forschungen* 29:655-60.
_____. 1997-98. Morphological Observations on the Stems of the Semitic 'Nota accusativi'. *Archiv für Orientforschung* 44-45:215-21.
_____. 1998. *Parallels in Semitic Linguistics*. Leiden: Brill.
_____. 2000. Conjugating the "Prefixed Stative" Verbs of Akkadian. *JNES* 59:81-92.
Tezel, Aziz. 2003. *Comprative Etymological Studies in the Western Neo-Syriac (Ṭūrōyo) Lexicon*. Uppsala: Uppsala University.
Thackston, W.M, Jr. 1996. The Vernacular Arabic of Lebanon. Unpublished ms, Harvard University.
Torrego, Esther. *The Dependencies of Objects*. Cambridge, MA: MIT Press.
Townsend, Charles E., and Laura A. Janda. 1996. *Common and Comparative Slavic: Phonology and Inflection*. Columbus, OH: Slavica.
Traugott, Elizabeth Closs, and Bernd Heine, eds. 1991. *Approaches to Grammaticalization*. 2 vols. Amsterdam: Benjamins.
Tropper, Josef. 1993. *Die Inschriften von Zincirli*. Münster: Ugarit-Verlag.
_____. 1994. Present *$*yaqtulum$ in Central Semitic. *JSS* 39:1-6.

―――――. 1995. Die semitische "Suffixkonjugation" im Wandel. In *Vom alten Orient zum Alten Testament: Festschrift für Wolfram Freiherrn von Soden zum 85. Geburtstag am 19. Juni 1993*, ed. Manfried Dietrich and Oswald Loretz, 491-516. Neukirchen-Vluyn: Neukirchener.

―――――. 2000. *Ugaritische Grammatik*. Münster: Ugarit-Verlag.

―――――. 2001. Die Herausbildung des bestimmen Artikels im Semitischen. *JSS* 46:1-31.

―――――. 2002a. *Altäthiopisch: Grammatik des Ge'ez mit Übungstexten und Glossar*. Münster: Ugarit-Verlag.

―――――. 2002b. Die hebraïsche Partikel *hinnē^h* "siehe!". *Kleine Untersuchungen zur Sprache des Alten Testaments und seiner Umwelt* 3:81-121.

―――――. 2002c. *Ugaritisch: Kurzgefasste Grammatik mit Übungstexten und Glossar*. Münster: Ugarit-Verlag.

―――――. 2003. Sekundäres wortanlautendes Alif im Arabischen. In *Studia Semitica*, ed. Leonid Kogan. *Orientalia: Papers of the Oriental Institute* 3, 190-216. Moscow: Russian State University for the Humanities.

Tsereteli, K.G. 1978. *The Modern Assyrian Language*. Moscow: Nauka.

Turner, R.L. 1966. *A Comparative Dictionary of the Indo-Aryan Languages*. 2 vols. London: Oxford University Press.

Ullendorff, Edward. 1965. The Form of the Definite Article in Arabic and Other Semitic Languages. In *Arabic and Islamic Studies in Honor of Hamilton A.R. Gibb*, ed. George Makdisi, 631-37. Leiden: Brill.

Ultan, R. 1978. On the Development of a Definite Article. In *Language Universals*, ed. H. Seiler, 249-65. Tübingen: Narr.

Ungnad, A. 1906. Über Analogiebildungen im hebräischen Verbum. *Beiträge zur Assyriologie* 5:233-78.

―――――. 1907. Der hebräische Artikel. *Orientalistische Literaturzeitung* 10:210-11.

―――――. 1908. Die Grundform des hebräischen Artikels. *ZDMG* 62:80-82.

Vaillant, André. 1958. *Grammaire comparée des langues slaves. Tome II: Morphologie*. Lyon: IAC.

Vanhove, Martine. 1993. *La langue maltaise: Études syntaxiques d'un dialecte arabe »périphérique«*. Wiesbaden: Harrassowitz.

Verhaar, John W. M. 1995. *Toward a Reference Grammar of Tok Pisin: An Experiment in Corpus Linguistics*. Honolulu: University of Hawai'i Press.

Vernus, Pascal. 1997. La grammaticalisation en égyptien ancienne: phrase nominale et morphogenèse de l'inaccompli et du futur. In *Grammaticalisation et Reconstruction*. Mémoires de la Société de Linguistique de Paris, Nouvelle Série, Tome V, 63-83. Paris: C. Klincksieck.

Versteegh, Kees. 1997. *The Arabic Language*. Edinburgh: Edinburgh University Press.

Voigt, Rainer. 1995. Akkadisch *šumma* 'wenn' und die Konditionalpartikeln des Westsemitischen. In *Vom Alten Orient Zum Alten Testament. Festschrift für Wolfram Freiherrn von Soden zum 85. Geburtstag am 19. Juni 1993*, ed. Manfried Dietrich and Oswald Loretz, 517-28. Neukirchen-Vluyn: Neukirchener.

―――――. 1998. Der Artikel im Semitischen. *JSS*, 43:221-58.

_____. 1999. Die Präpositionen im Semitischen — Über Morphologisierungsprozesse im Semitischen. *In Tradition and Innovation: Norm and Deviation in Arabic and Semitic Linguistics*, ed. Lutz Edzard and Mohammed Nekroumi, 22-43. Wiesbaden: Harrassowitz.
de Vries, Jan. 1962. *Altnordisches Etymologisches Wörterbuch*. Leiden: Brill.
Vycichl, Werner. 1957. Trois notes de linguistique amharique. *Annales d'Éthiopie* 2:167-70.
_____. 1983. *Dictionnaire étymologique de la langue copte*. Leuven: Peeters.
Waltke, Bruce K. and M. O'Connor. 1990. *An Introduction to Biblical Hebrew Syntax*. Winona Lake: Eisenbrauns.
Watson, Janet C.E. 1993. *A Syntax of Ṣanʿānī Arabic*. Wiesbaden: Harrassowitz.
_____. 1996. *Ṣbaḥtū! A Course in Ṣanʿānī Arabic*. Wiesbaden: Harrassowitz.
Wensinck, A.J. 1931. The Article of Determination in Arabic. *Mededeelingen der Koninklijke Akademie van Wetenschappen, Afdeeling Letterkunde* 71:47-64.
Wheeler, Max W., Alan Yates, and Nicolau Dols. 1999. *Catalan: A Comprehensive Grammar*. London: Routledge.
Woodhead, D.R., and Wayne Beene. 2003. *A Dictionary of Iraqi Arabic: Arabic-English*. Washington, DC: Georgetown University Press.
Wright, William. 1874. Observations on the Assyrian Verb *basu* as Compared with the Hebrew Verb היה, *hâyâ*, "he was". *Transactions of the Society of Biblical Archaeology* 3: 104-9.
_____. 1890. *Lectures on the Comparative Grammar of the Semitic Languages*. Cambridge: Cambridge University Press.
_____. [1896-98] 1967. *A Grammar of the Arabic Language, translated from the German of Caspari*. 3d ed. Revised by W. Robertson Smith and M.J. de Goeje. 2 vols. Cambridge: Cambridge University Press.
Yadin, Yigael, Jonas C. Greenfield, Ada Yardeni, and Baruch A. Levine, eds. 2002. *The Documents from the Bar Kokhba Period in the Cave of Letters: Hebrew, Aramaic, and Nabatean-Aramaic Papyri*. Jerusalem: Israel Exploration Society.
Younansardaroud, Helen. 2001. *Der neuostaramäische Dialekt von Särdä:rïd*. Wiesbaden: Harrassowitz.
Zaborski, Andrzej. 2000. Inflected Article in Proto-Arabic and Some Other West Semitic Languages. *Asian and African Studies* 9:24-35.

Language Index

Afro-Asiatic 11, 26, 28, 31, 42, 46, 50
Akkadian 7, 8, 12, 20-22, 23, 26-27, 28, 41, 45-48, 49-50, 52, 57, 61, 62, 68, 73-75, 76, 77-78, 79, 85, 89, 91, 100, 104, 105, 110, 112, 115, 116, 119-20, 122, 129, 135, 147-48, 149
   Assyrian 12, 46, 50, 73, 78, 105, 110
   Late Babylonian 12, 105, 110
   Mari Akkadian 12, 20, 21
   Middle Babylonian 12, 120
   Neo-Babylonian 12, 105, 110
   Old Akkadian 12, 21, 45, 52, 73
   Old Babylonian, *see* Akkadian
Amharic 8, 13, 18, 20, 22, 23, 25-26, 29-30, 42, 48, 60, 63, 77, 89, 124, 126, 153
Ancient North Arabian 13, 67, 69, 73, 77, 78, 79
Arabic 12, 13, 19, 21, 24-25, 28, 29, 33, 38, 39-40, 41, 43, 45-46, 47, 49, 50, 52, 53, 65, 68, 69, 73-76, 77-78, 79, 81, 83, 90, 91, 93, 105-7, 113, 115, 116-18, 119-120, 121, 125, 129, 131-32, 138, 145, 148-49, 151, 153
   Algerian Arabic 20-21, 43-44, 53, 56, 140, 142
   Anatolian Arabic 25, 135, 141-42, 151
   Baghdadi Arabic, *see* Iraqi Arabic
   Chadian Arabic 53, 55, 57, 62, 137-39
   Classical Arabic 13, 18, 19, 20-21, 24-25, 33, 35-36, 37, 38, 43, 47, 50, 53, 57, 59-60, 66-67, 75, 77-78, 105-6, 110, 115, 119, 140, 146, 148-51
   Egyptian Arabic 19, 35-36, 51, 53-55, 137, 145, 148-50, 151
   Galilean Arabic 106
   Iraqi Arabic 18, 19, 25, 35, 53, 55, 63, 106-7, 136-37, 138-39
   Jewish Arbel Arabic 60, 141
   Kuwaiti Arabic 35, 36, 53, 137, 138-39, 150
   Lebanese Arabic 35-36, 54, 58, 73, 106-7, 145
   Levantine Arabic 36, 54, 107
   Maltese 8, 14, 36, 37, 107, 115
   Middle Arabic 106, 110, 115
   Modern Standard Arabic 14, 24, 40-41, 59, 140, 149-50
   Moroccan Arabic 18, 20, 25, 35-36, 43, 52, 53, 56, 57-58, 63, 139-40
   North African Arabic 42, 54, 62, 107, 139, 141, 151
   qəltu-Arabic 40-41, 43, 135, 141
   Quranic Arabic 105
   Post-Classical Arabic 112
   Saudi Arabic 43
   Sudanese Arabic 138
   Syrian Arabic 19, 21, 25, 35, 45, 53-54, 55, 62, 67, 106, 125, 139, 145, 148-50, 151
   Syro-Palestinian Arabic, *see* Syrian Arabic
   Thamudic 13, 67
   Tunisian Arabic 20, 35-36, 43, 53, 139
   Yemeni Arabic 25, 36-37, 40, 51, 53, 55, 58-59, 62, 63, 67, 75, 78, 139, 146, 148-50, 151
Aramaic 12, 14, 31, 33, 38, 41, 44, 46, 47, 48, 55-56, 60, 61, 65, 68, 69, 73, 75, 78, 79-80, 81, 82, 83, 91, 93, 94, 100, 102-103, 105-10, 112-115, 116-20, 121, 122, 126, 134-36, 138, 144, 148, 151-52, 153

Babylonian Talmudic Aramaic, *see* Jewish Babylonian Aramaic
Bar-Kosiba Aramaic 15, 98, 102-3
Biblical Aramaic 15, 18, 31, 44, 49, 52, 55, 68, 74-75, 83, 87, 94-96, 102-3, 113
Christian Palestinian Aramaic 15,19-22, 55, 98-99, 102-4, 122-24, 125-26
Early Imperial Aramaic 14, 95, 102
Egyptian Aramaic 15, 94-95, 102-3, 113
Imperial Aramaic 15, 31, 94-95, 103
Jewish Babylonian Aramaic 15, 30, 56, 63, 100-103, 108, 130, 132, 134, 136
Jewish Palestinian Aramaic 15, 19-20, 22, 38, 56, 122-24, 131, 134-36
Late Aramaic 15
Mandaic 15-16, 30, 55, 63, 100-103, 104, 108, 130
Middle Aramaic 15, 38
Modern Aramaic, *see* Neo-Aramaic
Nabatean 15, 79, 94, 97-98, 102-3
Neo-Aramaic 8, 15-16, 31-32, 34, 45, 48, 86, 129, 131, 134-35, 144-45, 150
Neo-Mandaic, *see* Mandaic
Neo-West-Aramaic 15, 19, 21, 30, 56, 88, 104-5
North-Eastern Neo-Aramaic 16, 18, 19-20, 23, 30, 33-34, 37, 45, 48, 56, 78, 86-87, 131-32, 135, 142-43
Old Aramaic 14, 52, 68, 79, 94-95, 102-3, 109, 118, 119
Palmyrene 15, 97, 102
Qumran Aramaic 15, 55, 97-98, 102-3
Samaritan Aramaic 15, 55, 99-100, 102-4, 122-24, 125-26
Syriac 15, 19, 21-22, 23, 24-25, 27-28, 29, 30, 32, 34, 38, 41, 45, 48, 55, 59, 67, 68, 74, 76, 78, 79, 86-88, 96, 100-101, 102-4, 108, 114, 121-22, 124, 126, 131-32, 135-36
Targumic Aramaic 15, 19-20, 55, 74, 77, 96-97, 99-100, 102-104

Turoyo 8, 16, 18, 20, 22, 23, 30, 32, 45, 56, 78, 82, 87-88, 131-32, 135
Argobba 13, 24
Assyrian, *see under* Akkadian
Babylonian, *see under* Akkadian
Bengali 111
Bulgarian 69
Canaanite 12, 65, 69, 74-75, 76-77, 78, 81, 83-84, 91, 92, 108, 117-18, 120
Catalan 69, 111
Chaha 13, 21-22, 60, 63
Chinese 118
Coptic 71
Czech 114
Danish 50, 134
Deir 'Allā dialect 12, 81
Dutch 143, 144
Eblaite 12, 61
Egyptian (Ancient) 11, 26-27, 28, 46-47, 49
English 2, 4-5, 18, 24, 30, 35, 36, 39, 49, 51, 70-71, 82, 85, 133, 143-44
  Middle English 70
  Old English 2, 5, 51, 70
Ethiopic, *see* Geʻez
Ewe 118
French 2-4, 18, 24, 28, 30-31, 51, 61, 69, 71, 82, 85, 123, 126
Gafat 13, 20, 24
Geʻez 12, 13, 18, 19-20, 23, 25-26, 29, 32-33, 39, 41, 42, 43, 45-46, 48-49, 51, 52, 53, 55, 58, 60, 62, 63, 68, 74, 77-78, 88-89, 91, 106, 107-9, 110, 114-15, 116-18, 119-20, 121, 124-25, 126, 135, 147-48, 152, 153
German 5, 23, 50, 51, 71, 76, 82, 122, 126, 143, 144
  Old High German 70-71
Germanic 70-71, 129, 144-45, 148
Gothic 70-71
Greek 21, 28, 50, 70-71, 77, 140
Haitian Creole 53, 71
Hamito-Semitic, *see* Afro-Asiatic
Harari 13, 24
Hebrew 6, 8, 12, 16, 22, 31, 38, 40, 41, 43, 44, 46-48, 49, 50, 52, 55-57,

Language Index

60, 61, 65-66, 73-75, 76-77, 80, 81, 82, 83-84, 94, 96, 99, 101, 108, 109-10, 114-20, 121, 123, 127, 153
Bar-Kosiba Hebrew 93
Biblical Hebrew 16, 18, 19, 22, 24, 31, 39, 41, 44, 49, 50-51, 55, 59, 76, 84, 92, 101, 114, 115, 124, 125, 145, 149
Epigraphic Hebrew 92
Late Biblical Hebrew 16, 20, 49, 92, 110, 115
Medieval Hebrew 51
Mishnaic Hebrew 16, 20, 22, 38-39, 44, 49, 51, 93, 101, 122-24, 125, 149
Modern Hebrew 16, 22, 35, 39, 49, 51, 55, 60, 79, 93, 123, 125, 136
Post-Biblical Hebrew 16, 20, 22, 29, 31, 55
Qumran Hebrew 16, 93
Rabbinic Hebrew 51
Hindi 73, 111, 112, 115
Hungarian 18, 71, 82
Indonesian 85
Inor 85-86
Italian 69, 73, 76, 77, 82, 111, 133, 136, 144-45
Kurdish 20, 48, 78, 79, 87, 90
Ladino 96-97
Latin 4, 51, 69, 71, 73, 76, 77, 85, 111, 122, 124, 126, 133, 140
Liḥyanite, *see* Ancient North Arabian
Macedonian 69
Maltese, *see under* Arabic
Mandaic, *see under* Aramaic
Mehri, *see under* Modern South Arabian
Moabite 12, 84
Modern South Arabian 8, 12-13, 20, 22, 38, 47-48, 49, 59, 65, 68, 74, 89-90, 120, 126-27, 147
Ḥarsūsi 12, 20, 22, 38, 74, 89-90, 127
Jibbali 13, 48
Mehri 12, 38, 48, 52, 59, 82, 89-90, 147, 153
Soqoṭri 12, 48, 127

North Arabian, *see* Ancient North Arabian
Norwegian 134
Old Church Slavic 70-71
Old Icelandic 70-71, 73
Old South Arabian 8, 14, 49, 65, 69, 68, 72-75, 80-81, 83, 148-50
Hadramitic 14, 68, 76, 81
Minaic 14, 149
Qatabanic 14, 149
Sabaic (Sabean) 14, 68, 81
Persian 30-31
Phoenician 12, 16, 49, 66, 74-75, 76-77, 84, 93, 94, 103, 109-10, 116-17, 118, 119
Punic 16, 66, 93
Polish 70
Portuguese 133, 144-45, 148
Romance 56, 69-70, 107, 110, 112, 115, 122, 129, 133, 136
Romanian 69, 111, 112, 115
Russian 70, 71, 113-14
Sam'alian 12, 94, 119
Sanskrit 111
Sardinian 69, 111
Scandinavian, *see* Swedish
Selṭi 13, 21, 23
Serbo-Crotian 70
Slavic 69-71, 113-14
Spanish 23, 69, 82, 97, 110, 111, 112-13, 115, 124, 126, 133, 134, 136, 141
Swedish 82, 122, 133-34, 135, 138
Syriac, *see under* Aramaic
Thai 53
Thamudic *see* Ancient North Arabian
Tigré 13, 19-20, 22, 39-40, 42, 53, 55-56, 88-89, 109, 110
Tigrinya 13, 20-21, 24, 25, 31, 33, 39, 53, 60, 77, 88, 91, 108-9, 110, 124, 126, 148, 153
Tok Pisin 54
Turoyo, *see under* Aramaic
Ugaritic 12, 44, 46-47, 49, 61, 73-74, 81, 114
Wolane 13, 21, 23
Zway 13, 21, 23

www.ingramcontent.com/pod-product-compliance
Lightning Source LLC
Chambersburg PA
CBHW021406290426
44108CB00010B/411